CW01220777

BUILDING
COMMUNITIES

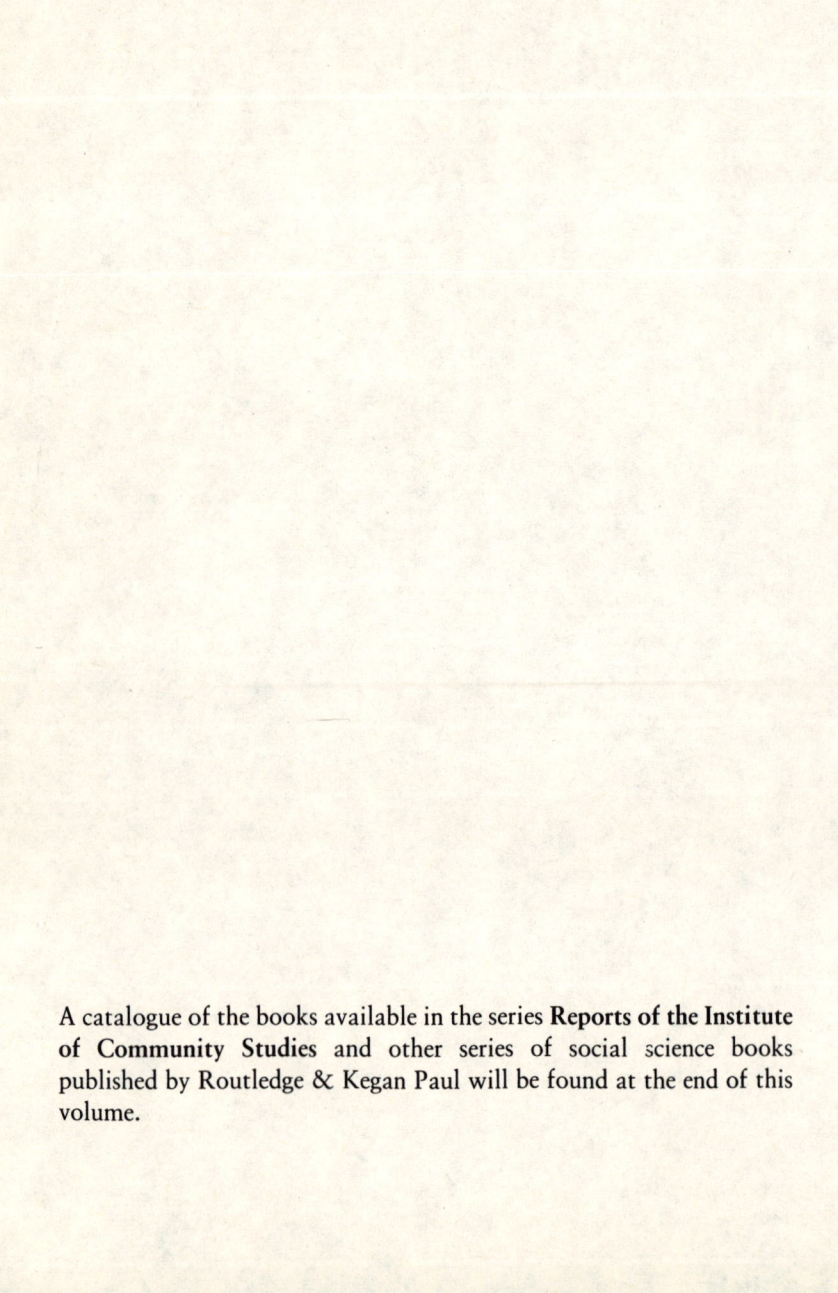

Reports of the Institute of Community Studies

A catalogue of the books available in the series **Reports of the Institute of Community Studies** and other series of social science books published by Routledge & Kegan Paul will be found at the end of this volume.

BUILDING COMMUNITIES THE CO-OPERATIVE WAY

Johnston Birchall

Foreword by
Michael Young

Routledge & Kegan Paul
LONDON

First published in 1988 by
Routledge & Kegan Paul Ltd
11 New Fetter Lane, London EC4P 4EE

Published in the USA by
Routledge & Kegan Paul Inc.
in association with Methuen Inc.
29 West 35th Street, New York, NY 10001

Typeset by Witwell Limited, Liverpool
Printed in Great Britain
by T.J. Press (Padstow) Ltd,
Padstow, Cornwall

© Johnston Birchall 1988

No part of this book may be reproduced in
any form without permission from the publisher
except for the quotation of brief passages
in criticism

Library of Congress Cataloging in Publication Date

British Library CIP Data also available
ISBN 0-7102-1143-0

To Libby and Emma

CONTENTS

FOREWORD BY MICHAEL YOUNG ... ix
ACKNOWLEDGMENTS ... xi

INTRODUCTION ... 1

1   HOUSING NEEDS AND CO-OPERATIVE SOLUTIONS ... 6

2   HUMAN NATURE AND CO-OPERATIVE VALUES ... 26

3   DEMOCRACY, THE STATE AND CO-OPERATIVE WELFARE ... 59

4   CO-OPERATIVE HOUSING IN BRITAIN: THE EARLY STAGES ... 88

5   CO-OPERATIVE HOUSING IN BRITAIN: THE LATER STAGES ... 110

6   CO-OPERATION IN PRACTICE: SIX CASE HISTORIES ... 135

7   A FRAMEWORK FOR EVALUATION ... 162

CONCLUSION   A CO-OPERATIVE VIEW OF HOUSING POLICY IN BRITAIN ... 189

NOTES ... 196

SELECT BIBLIOGRAPHY ... 211

INDEX ... 216

FOREWORD BY MICHAEL YOUNG

If Johnston Birchall had been Minister of Housing in 1945 (or still better, in 1919) perhaps Britain would have housed, and re-housed, itself. It is just possible we might have had, not Robert Owen's co-operative villages, but Birchall's co-operative urban neighbourhoods. It would have meant, even then, working to some extent against the grain; but even in Britain it might have happened, at any rate on the Swedish scale, which has been grand enough. Co-operative leadership has wrought miracles in Scandinavia. Why not here?

If that question cannot be wholly answered – to do so, every wrinkle of our social physiognomy would have to be intently observed – at least we know that the changes that have occurred, or been made to occur, have been of the opposite kind. Such damage as Hitler inflicted on British cities has (as we know) been multiplied a hundred times by the politicians, architects, planners and builders who thought they knew better than people themselves what they should want. For every bomb-site not yet filled in and built over there are a hundred obscene tower blocks. Life goes on up there in all its delight. Crane up at the lighted windows at night and behind the unneeded curtains – for up there only the angels can see in – are sky-people heating the earth-water for their cups of tea. But too many of them have double-bolted their doors. They have been walled in. They are longing for the earth. They are fleeing the city which is no longer friendly to them, or made friendly by them. The housing men have made enemies of citizens. They found a city and left it a battlefield.

The prime casualty has been the working-class community. In 1945 there were tens of thousands of them surviving, vigorously. The 'urban villages' lauded in Abercrombie's plan for London – he was the prince of planners unheeded by his children – were still intact. Fraternity hardly needed to be preached; it was practised. That marvellous vitality which was the tap-root of socialism has been pulverised by the hammer-

Foreword

blows of bureaucracy. The working-class communities have been 're-housed' in conditions physically a little better and socially a lot worse.

Can we learn from the disaster? Germany and Japan suffered greater disasters. Can Handsworth and Liverpool 8 and Easterhouse and Bethnal Green recover their spiritual *élan*? If so, housing may again be the key, and, if it happens, the housing co-ops of which Dr Birchall is such a devoted and far-sighted scholar could be a key. For all who want to enable people, to enable them to help themselves without retreating behind the other walls of the acquisitive society, this book could be the key to the key.

ACKNOWLEDGMENTS

It is only when writing acknowledgments that one realises how far back the gestation of a book really goes. The interest in housing co-ops comes from practice as a housing association manager, and some stimulating conversations with my colleagues of that time, David Mumford (chief executive of Copec Housing Trust) and Rod Hackney (community architect and recently elected President of the Royal Institute of British Architects). Then, when writing my doctoral thesis, from which much of the material for the book derives, I incurred a debt also to Harold Campbell, that great pioneer of co-operative housing, to Brian Rose (then Housing Corporation co-ops officer, and since then a colleague on the national committee of the Society for Co-operative Studies) and to so many housing co-op members and associated professionals (about 200 people were interviewed) that it is just not possible to begin to mention them individually. Recently, Simon Underwood (Solon Co-operative Housing Services) and Steve Ross (National Federation of Housing Associations) have helped me to keep up to date with a rapidly changing situation on the ground, Paul Derrick (co-operative writer and enthusiast) has helped with some tricky points of co-operative principle, Malcolm Hornsby (tutor at the Co-operative College) has provided pointers to the forgotten history of co-operative housing in Britain, and Gregory Andrusz some illuminating insights into co-operative housing in the USSR.

A special word of thanks must go to Michael Young (Director of the Institute of Community Studies), for writing a foreword. His influence began well before I arrived at the Institute. Just as I began to look around for a wider context in which to set the study of housing co-ops, he produced, almost to order, two books on consumer and worker co-operation, which did just that. Lastly, in that most difficult matter of finding a decent title, John F.C. Turner gave me permission to use his phrase 'building community' and Colin Ward suggested 'the co-

Acknowledgments

operative way'; my debt to these two most profound philosophers of housing extends of course, throughout the book.

INTRODUCTION

It is fitting that this book should be published in the Institute of Community Studies series. In the conclusion to their world-famous study of *Family and Kinship in East London*, published in 1957, the founders of the Institute, Michael Young and Peter Willmott, argued strongly that very few people wanted to leave their inner-city community. They advocated the rehabilitation of those terraced houses which could be improved, and the phased renewal of others, so that improvements in housing conditions would not be achieved at the expense of existing communities, and all the richness of their kinship and mutual aid networks.[1] It took another twenty years for the housing and planning professionals to heed their warning, and by then for many of those communities it was too late; some had been dispersed to the new towns, others to remote council estates, and the ones who remained or drifted back were put into housing which was not that much better in the long-run than the terraces they had left. If you walk out to the road which runs behind the Institute of Community Studies, you will see at one end an empty tower block boarded up because the windows had started to drop out. Walk along to the other end, and you are in the realm of the cheap and nasty walk-up council flat, surrounded by open space which no one knows what to do with. In between are the few remaining streets of the old terraces, mostly improved now and looking very snug. The problem is that they can only be afforded by the incoming middle classes, attracted by the prospect of capital gains and a shorter journey to the City. Further down the Mile End Road, though, there is a new housing co-op, whose members hope to 'recreate the old Young and Willmott type community'.[2] History moves in circles, as well as in straight lines.

What is this housing co-op then, which can rebuild communities? It is a form of tenure, new to Britain but old and well established in other countries (particularly in Scandinavia), which applies the principle of

Introduction

consumer control to housing, not as owner-occupation does, through individual ownership, but through collective ownership of dwellings by the dwellers. For those who want to know about them, there are very few leads to follow; there are only two books on the British housing co-op movement, and both were written before the major expansion of the last decade.[3] Yet with all-party support, and possible new roles both in the conversion of council housing estates to tenant control and in the provision of new forms of rented housing, this movement is poised to become very significant indeed. Everyone who cares about housing policy, the inner cities or community architecture, whether politicians, architects, housing managers, academics or simply interested observers, will want to know something about co-ops. No, I will put it stronger than that; they will have to know something about co-ops. This book will probably tell them more than they want to know, but they will be forgiven for picking up those chapters thought to be most relevant to them. Here, then, is a brief outline of the book.

Firstly, in Chapter 1 we discuss housing needs and the variety of possible solutions which can be applied to them; we see the co-operative option as applied in the case of one hypothetical but I hope not untypical woman, Mrs Mason. This leads into a discussion of what we mean by housing, and presents a viewpoint which is radically different from that of most professional providers of housing. Finally, we attempt to define the various types of housing co-op. Chapter 2 begins with probably the most fundamental question one can ask, whether human nature is naturally co-operative or self-seeking. On the answer to this question depends one's assessment of which types of co-op (if any) are viable forms of social organisation in the long-term. Secondly, we examine the competing claims of that universal trilogy of human values, liberty, equality and fraternity, asking if they are compatible in theory, and if in practice members can live in a housing co-op without compromising their liberty for the sake of equality, their fraternity for the sake of liberty, and so on. Four competing world-views are outlined, by which intellectuals try to sum up and make systematic the everyday views of those who are engaged in the housing process. There is a plethora of labels to choose from, but for the sake of clarity, and because one is selecting deliberately from a wide range of theory (not all of which can be done justice to), we might label them simply: individualists, pluralists, collectivists and communitarians.

Individualists argue that human nature is inherently competitive, and that co-operative organisations cannot, and ought not to, survive. Their

Introduction

argument for liberty devalues the sense of community which co-ops generate, and leads to a very individualistic ethic of self-interest. *Pluralists* argue that human nature can evolve into different forms, and that the aim should be to produce better people. Their argument for liberty stresses all-round self-development rather than crude self-seeking, but they recognise that individuals can only develop creatively when there is a sense of social identity, and this has to be fostered by small-scale community organisations. *Collectivists* see human nature evolving in response to the dominant mode of economic production, and pin their faith on a new kind of person who can only emerge within a post-revolutionary socialist society. Their argument for a more equal society looks entirely to a future to be secured by the 'masses' and plays down the contribution of co-ops, except as transitional or prefigurative forms of socialism. Finally, *communitarians* argue that human nature is inherently co-operative, and that given a chance, people can run co-ops successfully. Their argument for fraternity stresses the need to nurture the seeds of a new society based on small-scale, decentralised and self-regulating associations, which are real communities. In this way, a whole range of arguments is developed, for and against the co-operative movement in general, and housing co-ops in particular.

Chapter 3 continues along similar lines, but tracing the outcomes of these four world-views in arguments about the nature of democracy, the role of the state, and the way in which social welfare in general, and housing in particular, should be provided. The individualists are not too concerned with democracy, are suspicious of the state, and want to leave it to the market to provide for social welfare. Yet for the sake of social order, they will concede that some subsidy has to be given to house the poor, but prefer that it be channelled through private trusts and non-profit housing associations. There is shelter here for British housing co-ops under the wings of a more paternalistic 'voluntary housing movement', but there is not much comfort. The pluralists stress direct democracy in small local organisations, as a buffer against the growing remoteness of the state. They are more keen to promote state social welfare, providing it is delivered by local voluntary organisations, whether or not these are democratic; again there is a role for co-ops here, but alongside their 'big brother', the housing association movement. The collectivists postpone democracy to the post-revolutionary utopia, and see the state as a weapon held by the bourgeoisie in the interest of capital, but which can be turned against them if captured by a genuinely working-class movement. They see

Introduction

social welfare as caught up in the insoluble contradictions of capitalism, and so are almost totally negative about voluntary welfare-delivering agencies, including housing co-ops. Finally, the communitarians show how co-ops form a vital element in an integrated world-view, which posits a co-operative social and economic system in which direct democracy, social justice and economic productivity can be combined without the need for a centralised bureaucratic state.

In Chapter 4, the subject is approached from a totally different direction, that of history. A simple theory is suggested about what makes a particular co-operative form develop, based on five variables: pressing human needs which cannot be solved by individual self-help, an appropriate structure for co-operation, individual and organisational promoters, a favourable legal and financial environment, and climate of opinion. First we trace the growth of housing co-operatives in Britain in the late nineteenth century, out of their roots in mutualist working-class associations such as the terminating building society, the building club and more generally, the consumer co-operative society. Then the first housing co-op (Tenant Co-operators Ltd), and the first wave of co-op development (the tenant co-partnerships) are revealed as a part of our social history which was submerged when municipal housing took over after the First World War. The almost total lack of development in Britain post-war is contrasted with the much larger and more influential movement in Norway and Sweden, How is it, when in the last century the co-operative method had been exported from the British consumer co-op movement all over the world, and an embryonic housing co-op movement had been in existence, that by the latter half of this century we had to relearn from the Scandinavians how to set up housing co-ops? Finally, the history of the second wave of co-op development is charted; the co-ownerships of the 1960s and 1970s.

Then in Chapter 5, we continue with the third and most important wave, the development of common ownership and tenant management co-ops from 1975, along with some other more minor forms such as short-life, shared ownership and privately-funded co-ops. The preconditions for their promotion are identified, their organisational structure and origins described, their growth is charted with statistics on each type, and then the formation of secondary co-ops and a national federation are described. Finally, current difficulties and prospects for the future are identified, in the light of some major new housing policy initiatives; the Glasgow community ownership co-ops scheme, support for tenant management co-ops in the new Housing and Planning Act

Introduction

1986, and the Housing Corporation's promotion of 'assured tenancies' and a new form of mutual housing society.

In Chapter 6, we bring the discussion down to a different level, that of the individual housing co-op. Six co-ops are introduced, and their stories told, so that the reader can to some extent enter into the experience of co-op members, and appreciate just what they have achieved.

In Chapter 7, we ask how successful these and other co-ops are in practice. Several key variables are suggested by the sociologist P.I. Sorokin: *Adequacy* refers to the ability of a co-op to meet tangible goals, such as effective management and maintenance, the provision of new or improved houses designed with the members' help, the drafting and enforcing of rules for social behaviour, the use of financial surpluses to enhance the use-value of the houses, the protection and improvement of the local environment, and so on. *Intensity* refers to the ability of the co-op to foster a sense of community, to put on social activities, to look after the elderly and young children and to encourage informal mutual aid. *Purity* refers to the ability of the co-op to live up to co-operative principles. There are five principles. The first, open and voluntary membership, defines who can join co-ops, and under what conditions. The second, the democratic principle of one member one vote, begs questions of how democratic co-ops are in practice; does the spectre of oligarchy lurk behind the curtain of participatory democracy? Then there is the principle of distribution of economic results which sets out the fundamental right of co-operators to distribute surpluses; to allocate to reserves, to spend on communal improvements, or to make a return to members of a 'patronage refund'. The education principle is identified as the key to member commitment and participation, and to dweller control over the housing management and development processes. Finally, the principle of co-operation between co-ops shows how federation between housing co-ops and links with worker, consumer co-ops and credit unions should strengthen the movement, and lead towards the ultimate goal of a 'co-operative commonwealth'.

ONE
HOUSING NEEDS AND CO-OPERATIVE SOLUTIONS

Coming into Birmingham New Street on the inter-city express, the traveller, if not completely preoccupied with finding a ticket and gathering luggage together, might look out beyond the waste-lands of disused railway sidings and the Saltley gas-holders, to the miles of grey slated terraces, which seem to flow like waves over the gently undulating hills, broken only by the occasional church spire. It is far from an awe-inspiring sight, especially on a drizzly day in November, when the wet roofs seem to merge with a grey sky, and the chimneys remain bleakly empty of all but the uninviting fumes of the gas fires which now burn in the homely grate. But if the traveller is an architect or a housing manager, who has been working there for several years rehabilitating the old houses the sight might well be awesome, because those waves of grey roof-lines are a reminder of just how much work has still to be done in saving the thousands of decently built but old and worn-out houses which make up so much of the English landscape. From the train, it would be impossible to pick out Mrs Mason's roof with the slipped slates and sagging gutters, which let in that drizzle in a steady downdrip which turns the wallpaper of her front bedroom yellow, and gives the whole house a musty smell of never-quite-dried-out damp. Her elderly mother lies under mountains of blankets in her bed in the front parlour, while the cat dozes in the only really warm spot, in front of a spluttering gas fire. Faded photographs on a mantelpiece, the same colour as a stain of rising damp which lifts the wallpaper under the bay window, are the only reminder of her husband, killed on D-Day two months after Mrs Mason was married.

There is a knock at the door. Mrs M takes her apron from round her rather portly frame, runs her hands with more anxiety than deliberation

Housing needs and co-operative solutions

through her hair, and answers it, taking care to leave the chain on guard. Standing in the drizzle is a very young man, with an attaché case under arm, and an air of self-importance. He shows her a card which explains that he works for the housing department, and, unguarding the door along with her expression, she steers him into the back living room. Before he can state his business, she has begun to pour forth about the rats in the back yards, the 'tinkers' who have lit fires in the empty houses, the state of the pavements, and reaching crescendo, vents a final gust on the landlord, who has not done any repairs since she moved in, in 1944. The man asks for the landlord's name, which stops Mrs M in full flow, as she realises she does not know; the 'agent' has reported two recent changes in the ownership of the whole block. The council man sees his chance to divert attention from her complaints, and explains that one property developer after another has seen his chance, and then off-loaded the whole (in the parlance of this dubious profession) 'portfolio' on to someone with less pressing cash-flow problems. Mrs M lets this go sailing over her head, and then settles into a catalogue of complaints about the house. The young man grins, and with just a hint of malice, holds up an official looking piece of paper; it is the closing order on her 'property', and an offer of rehousing, at the council's discretion, within the next three months; the whole street is earmarked for demolition.

Two months and one rehousing later, Mrs M is standing in a lift, catching her breath at the smell, and trying not to look at the obscenities on the walls. She steps out, round the dog-dirt on the landing, and scurries along to number 501, where she hurriedly lets herself in, turns two locks, bolts and chains the door, and shouts 'Mother?' The old lady is sitting at a window, looking down on to a wind-swept expanse of grass, a monotony broken only by a row of decapitated saplings, and two clumps of spiky shrubs which have impaled a number of passing chip papers. Her bad temper shows in the slumped cast of her bony shoulders. 'I've not slept a wink for those kids, thundering up and down the landing on their bicycles. They come right past the door.' Mrs M goes into the tiny kitchen to brew a cup of tea, and remembering the council's rule-book which states that condensation is caused by tenants' carelessness in cooking, washing clothes, and breathing heavily, opens the window to let the steam escape. Her clothes are already going mouldy in the built-in wardrobe.

Housing needs and co-operative solutions

The bin-chute was blocked up the first time she tried to put the rubbish in it, and so plastic bags bulge on the kitchen floor. She has spoken once in the ten days they have been here, to a neighbour who disappeared back indoors with his milk, her greeting left suspended on the cold air. Today she has been to the supermarket on the bus. The Saturday before, she had to get two buses, into town and then out again to see her sister, who lives a few hundred yards from Mrs M's old home. She will go there again this Saturday, if she can afford it, and again will go past her old, boarded-up house to look for the cat, which has disappeared. She hopes that this time, she will not cry quite so bitterly at the loss of her old home and all the familiar things that went with it, and that she will find the way back to the flat without losing her way.

Alternatively... there is a knock at the door. Mrs M takes her apron from round her rather portly frame, runs her hands with more anxiety than deliberation through her hair, and answers it, taking care to leave the chain on guard. Standing in the drizzle is a very young woman, carrying a briefcase. She has a business-like air, and introduces herself as a housing officer for the Saltley Church Housing Trust, which is about to buy up the entire row of houses. Mrs M shows her into the back room, but instead of launching into a tirade of complaints, contents herself with a plaintive 'Well I hope you do better than the last landlord with the repairs; you can hardly do worse!' She shows her the rent book, and the young woman explains that the Trust is a housing association which specialises in buying older houses all over the West Midlands, and has a programme of improvement work funded by the Housing Corporation and the local council. After Mrs M's house is done up, she will have to pay a higher rent, but it will be a 'fair' one, fixed by the rent officer. Mrs M can hardly believe her luck, and offers the young woman a cup of tea. When she says that tenants can move out to another house while the work is being done, and then move back, she gets out the tin of chocolate biscuits. Later, when the rather bossy young woman has gone, Mrs M sits in the cold of the November evening, trying to imagine what it will be like; to have a new roof, an unchipped bath, a drain that does not overflow, a new floor in the back bedroom, where she had had to get her brother-in-law to put down some hardboard to stop the bed going through, new windows that can be opened and shut, and joy above measure, central heating.

Three years later, after the Trust has finally fitted the house into its improvement programme, Mrs M is helping her mother up the stairs. The Trust's architect had had the old outdoor toilet demolished, which

Housing needs and co-operative solutions

had served her mother well since she lost the use of her legs, and several times a day, she has to lift and push the old woman up to the white-tiled bathroom. In fact, the whole house is a sea of whiteness; brilliant white emulsioned woodchip on all the walls, kitchen fittings, radiators, hardboard doors, and on all interior and exterior paint-work. She remembers coming to see the work while in progress, taking the bus from that hideous flat they had put them in as a – what did they call it? – a decant. She had joked with the workmen about it looking like a hospital, and had asked them if they would leave the cupboard in the back living-room; it had been made by her husband Jack, just before he went off to get himself killed, and she had sort of grown used to it. After about ten minutes, when she had fed the goldfish in the pond in the back garden, and was just going up the stairs to see the new bathroom, the same young woman had rushed in, accompanied by a builder, and had told her off for trespassing. She was bustled outside, and told that while the house was 'on site' under no circumstances could she go inside. The questions she had been meaning to ask, about Jack's cupboard, and could they keep the outside toilet, and would they mind not dumping rubbish in the pond, all died on her lips, and she had gone sadly back to the 'decant', wishing she had never allowed them to bully her into moving out.

It had been a great day when, after being decanted for six months, (they said there had been delays with the builder) she had dressed her mother and set off in the van for home. The euphoria had worn off quickly, when she found that the electricity had been turned off, and that because of a mix up with the builder, it would be put on again only when the relevant form reached head office. After three days and several phone calls to the housing association, she had finally succeeded in getting the meter man to call and put back the main fuse. Weeks later she still cannot settle. All the old familiar things have vanished; Jack's cupboard, the old front door with its beautiful carved knocker, the leaded stained-glass window on the landing. As for the magnificent wooden fireplace from the front room, her neighbour Mr Woolley swears he saw one of the architects going off with it in the back of his car. The fish have died, the pond and garden are a mess of mud and rubble, and the privet hedge has been rooted up and replaced with a tacky little fence that will not keep a whippet out, never mind Mr Woolley's alsatian dog. No, she cannot settle, and does not know why. She does not want to seem ungrateful, but it does not somehow feel as if it is her home any more; all the little things that made it so have gone, and her furniture and carpets look cheap and old-fashioned against the gleaming paint-work. She finds it hard to recall quite as vividly those brief few months of married life which had started here so long ago. It is as if her husband has finally left her, with all her memories slipping away. When the young woman had come to do an inspection, Mrs M had found herself complaining about a window that stuck, and about the central heating which did not seem to work. The girl had relit a light which worked the gas, and told her to read the instruction book, and she had felt stupid, which made her even more bad-tempered. She settles her mother by the new gas fire, and sits down to have a rest. And in all this brilliant whiteness, Mrs M finds herself shedding just one or two self-pitying, and she is sure quite unjustified, tears.

Alternatively ... there is a knock at the door. Mrs M takes her apron from round her rather portly frame, runs her hands with more anxiety than deliberation through her hair, and answers it, taking care to leave the chain on guard. Standing in the drizzle is a very young man, with a canvas bag slung over his shoulder, and a bicycle which he has parted under the front window. He explains that he is from the Saltley Community Housing Association, which is about to buy up the whole block. He wants to discuss the possibility of improving her house after it has been bought, and to list some immediate repairs which might be needed. Mrs Mason is so taken aback that she suggests he put his bike in the hall where it will be safer, and steers him into the back living room. He explains that the housing association works from offices on the main road, next door to the law centre, and that the Housing Corporation has given them the job of buying houses just within Saltley, so as to improve them, and let them at a fair rent. Mrs M says she knows the office, because some of her friends on Adderton Road are 'Saltley' tenants, their houses have been done up very nicely, and yes, the rents do seem very reasonable considering all the work that has been done. The young man, who asks her to call him Bob, jots down the fact that she lives with her mother and that the roof leaks badly at the front. He explains that in order to get on with the work quickly, the association will send an architect round as soon as the houses are bought, and will then keep in touch at regular intervals to ask Mrs M about the kind of improvement she wants.

Two months later, with the sale completed, Bob calls back with a new rent book, and asks if she prefers to pay her rent weekly at the office, or have the rent collector call. She decided on the former, since it is near where she shops, and she quite fancies meeting some of her

Housing needs and co-operative solutions

friends who are Saltley tenants to show them that she is one too. He asks if she wants a full improvement, which entails moving out to an empty house nearby, or just a part improvement, which means a new roof, windows, doors and so on, which can be done with the tenant still in the house. He strongly advises the former, because unless people are disabled or very elderly it is the best deal available. When she hears that she can have a decant house in the next street, and that the work will take about 10 weeks, she agrees; the prospect of having the roof stripped off while her mother is still in the front living room is even more harrowing than that of moving her bodily to another house. Bob also offers the possibility of a permanent move locally, saving the effort of moving twice, and Mrs M considers this, but emphatically opts for getting her own house back in the end.

Over the next few months, Bob calls back twice. The first time he jots down on a long questionnaire all the things Mrs M wants to keep in the house, such as the cupboard, the front door, the stained-glass window and the fireplaces. He notes the need to fence off the gold-fish pond from the building work, that garden fencing should only be provided where there is a gap in the privet hedge, and most important, that the elderly mother needs a downstairs toilet. Finally, he measures the kitchen cooker and washer to see that they will fit in with the architect's drawing for the new kitchen units. The next time he comes round at about 7 o'clock at night, looking tired out, but with an architect in tow, who shows her some outline plans for the house. They are not too hard to follow, because the plans are in colour, with furniture drawn in, and she is able to point out where she wants her plug sockets. The architect listens attentively. He has learned never to under-estimate tenants, since the day when he had woken up Mr Grimshaw who was on the night-shift; Mr G had taken him in, made a pot of tea, and proceeded to draw a plan of how he wanted the house improving which involved reversing the kitchen and living-room so as to put the latter next to the park rather than the busy main road. The plan had been so good that the architect had torn up his own ideas and adopted it for all the empty houses on the street. Then just before she moves out for the building work, Mrs M is asked to go to the office and choose her wallpapers, kitchen worktop colours and vinyl tiles, from pattern books which are laid out in the interview room.

The housing association has to battle to get the Housing Corporation to agree to the downstairs toilet, but covers the costs of this and other extras by putting together several houses in one contract, and thus getting a low tender. While the house is on site, Mrs M cannot resist going past to see how it is going, and when one day she sees Bob and the architect there, they invite her in to look round. Inside it is like a skeleton with all the flesh removed, old timber floor joists and wiring hanging like worn-out bones and sinews, but with new plasterwork and stud partitioning going up to patch and strengthen the old frame, and new windows like fresh eyes from which to see the familiar old street. While she is upstairs, she checks that the bedroom doorway will leave space for her big double bed and wardrobe. The architect makes a note to have the eventual doorway moved slightly over from where it is on the plan. It will cost no more, and in any case he agrees it gives a better layout for bedroom furniture. On the move back, the new house seems strange but also in some ways the same. The builder has left the front door and living-room cupboard, but given them a new coat of paint, and the garden is virtually untouched. She looks eagerly to see how her choice of wallpaper and kitchen worktops will blend in with the new carpet she has bought, and which was laid yesterday before the move in. The builder has had the electric and gas put on already, and she only has to have it transferred into her name. That afternoon, a housing assistant calls to show her how to use the central heating, and how to light the pilot light if it goes out. Some of the windows are a bit sticky, and one of the worktops seems loose, but Bob has asked her to report any faults at the office. She cannot wait to see her friends and compare notes about the various improvements they have had done. The only worry she has now, is about who her new neighbours will be, who will occupy the empty houses in the street.

One final alternative ... there is a knock at the door. Mrs M takes her apron from round her rather portly frame, runs her hands with more anxiety than deliberation through her hair, and answers it, taking care to leave the chain on guard. Standing in the drizzle is a middle-aged man who she recognises immediately. He is Jim Holyoake from the local residents' association, and he says that some of the private tenants in the area are thinking about forming a housing co-op, to buy out the landlords with a view to doing up the houses and keeping them in proper order. Mrs M asks him in, and after saying a brief hello to the old lady in the front room, he settles himself by the back room fire and explains what the idea is about. It seems that without waiting for the council or a housing association to get round to doing something about the dreadful state of all the Bradford Estates properties, of which there are about 75 locally, the tenants can get together, form a co-operative housing association, buy the houses and improve them with Housing Corporation or council money. They would then let them to themselves at a reasonable rent, and do all their own allocations, which means they could choose their neigbours, use some of the rent money to do environmental improvements, pressurise the council into doing the pavements, and so on. All this is too much for Mrs M. She cannot see how a tenant can be a landlord, paying rents one minute and spending them the next, nor how the council would actually provide them with the money to buy their own homes. Mr G patiently explains that while individual members of the co-op would still be tenants, they would own and control the houses collectively as the landlord. The next question from Mrs M is the usual one, of how a group of ordinary people could deal with all the difficult jobs which only the 'educated' could understand; Mr G is ready with the answer, that they would hire their own architect, solicitor and co-op worker, who would do all the negotiating, oversee the building work and so on. All that the tenants have to do is to organise themselves.

Over the next two years, Mrs M becomes very busy. She had not thought that she had any skills to offer, but has been elected as minute secretary to the committee and general meeting, which meet alternate fortnights. She has dusted down her old type-writer, has relearned to type and is secretly studying shorthand. Her social life is as busy; she bakes for the regular buffets which follow some of the general meetings at the local church hall, and is on the Co-op's social committee. The back living-room had been used for a while as a temporary office, by the young woman who had been seconded as development worker from the West Midlands Secondary Co-op which had taken the fledgling Saltley Housing Co-op under its wing. Since the Co-op office has opened above the law centre, things have been quieter, but the architect who is overseeing the first phase of the building work has taken to dropping in for a cup of tea and a quick use of the phone. Now that she is not so busy, Mrs M gets a friend to pop in to look after mother, while she goes to Age Concern meetings; a new branch has just been opened, and is run mainly by Co-op members and people from the local church.

Good housing remains the priority though, and the wait for the building work to begin has been a long and sometimes frustrating one, with delay after delay experienced in a bewildering 'snakes and ladders' game, in which the Co-op had climbed one ladder at each stage of the bureaucratic funding system, only to slip down a snake when trying to buy houses at a higher cost than allowed, or trying to get approvals for schemes which turned out to be over cost-limits. For instance, she had been depressed when, after all the work she had put into making the Co-op a success, the Corporation had objected to the downstairs toilets she and a neighbour felt they needed; at a stormy meeting the members had insisted on fighting the issue, and by designating the two houses as 'old persons' dwellings', had got their way, and had also added some electric 'help' signs which were to be put above the front door.

Having been consulted by the Co-op's development sub-committee, Mrs M knows that her house will be improved soon, and that she will move round the corner to an empty house while the work is being done. At a meeting held for members from her terrace, she has seen and approved the plans for the work, which include not only the house improvements, but a new car park formed from part of the back gardens, and some landscaping and a small playground on the bombsite at the end of the terrace. It is not just good housing that she is looking forward to, but the slow rebirth of a community which had been shattered by the threat of demolition, the boarding up of houses, the moving of residents to remote housing estates, and the subsequent decline of a once-proud working-class community into a no-man's land of vandalism, crime and fear. For instance, the next-door house had been boarded up and empty for years, and Mrs M had been sick with worry that the 'tinkers' would squat in it, use the floor-boards for firewood and then set themselves and her own house alight, as they had further down the terrace. But soon the house is to be let to some old friends of hers, Mr and Mrs Marshall, who had accepted rehousing by the council when the street had been earmarked for demoliton, but who had never settled in five years in a sixth-floor flat on the Bleaklow housing estate. True, much of this work could have been done by one of the local housing associations, without taking up the time and energy of people like Mrs M. But the achievements of the Co-op are not only measurable in improvements to 'bricks and mortar'. They are evidenced in more subtle ways, in the self-confidence with which Mrs M chats to visitors, the strength of her voice when she makes a point at meetings, the challenging way she meets the eye of the local council official. But more subtle still is a change in the way she in her own mind's eye looks no longer backwards into the past, but forwards, towards a future which is, for the first time ever, partly under her and her neighbours' control.

Housing needs and co-operative solutions

ENDS, MEANS AND THE HOUSING PROBLEM

At first sight, housing is far from being a complex concept. As a noun, examinees of the Institute of Housing will testify that there is no subject more boring than 'housing'. As a form of building, trainee surveyors will testify that there is no subject more straight-forward; since the invention of the machine-cut brick and the flushing lavatory during the industrial revolution, very little has been added by our own technology beyond the polythene damp-proof course. It is the sheer boredom of the subject that has propelled architectural students to those absurd flights of fancy, which, combined with successive attempts to adapt a simple but labour-intensive technology to the assembly line, have provided us with most of our housing 'problems'. In fact, the housing problem is a simple one: the need for land, materials and a few elementary skills, and for the resources to renovate and renew what has been built. In a socialist utopia it would be solved so easily that the main effort would be expended in beautifying what has been built with carvings and wall frescos:

> It was a longish building with its gable ends turned away from the road, and long traceried windows coming rather low down set in the wall that faced us. It was very handsomely built of red brick with a lead roof; and high up above the windows there ran a frieze of figure subjects in baked clay, very well executed, and designed with a force and directness which I had never noticed in modern work before.[1]

Of course, for William Morris's fantasy to come true, there would have to be access to these raw materials, and time to practise such skills, and one would have first to have a society in which these are not constantly being experienced as scarce commodities. When some people are compelled by the logic of the market to live in houses that will always be too big for them, and others to be unable to afford space just when they need it most when raising a young family, when many single people whose needs are most modest cannot find homes at all, and when the state has to intervene to redistribute some capital away from luxury spending back to basic housing provision for homeless families, the housing problem becomes exceedingly complex. Housing co-operators do not unravel this kind of complexity, but are caught up in it. They are victims or beneficiaries of the housing 'system', just as surely as are high-rise council tenants and first-time buyers of Barratt boxes. it is not on the basic issue of how land, housing, building materials and labour are financed, that discussion of the housing co-op alternative is most useful.

However, housing is not just a noun, but is also a verb.[2] Assuming they have access to land, materials and skills, people *do* it. They house themselves or other people, or both at once, and it is on this issue, of who houses whom, and for what purposes, that co-ops are most fruitful. Just because some architects and other housing professionals have in the past found the subject of housing, as noun, quite boring, and then have begun to play with their minds so as to produce 'machines for living in', 'total environments' and other suchlike abstractions which win awards and then have to be demolished because no real human beings can stand to live in them, the issue of housing as a verb *must* be raised. Housing is a process, subject to the never-ending cycles of wind and frost, damp and decay, which parallel remorselessly the human cycle of birth, growth, death and dissolution; houses have constantly to be rejuvenated. The process can occur slowly, by replacement of slipped slates and unblocking of gutters and the regular painting of windows, or it can be speeded up after years of neglect, by total improvement. When the houses are finally demolished, if the builders have built well the materials and foundations can be used again, so that like the human genetic stock, nothing that dies is entirely lost, but is at least partially recycled.

Nor is housing an end in itself. Its value lies in being a means to other things; physical and emotional security, good health, access to work, to open space, to transport routes, to friends, neighbours and kin. It provides space in which to pursue hobbies and skills, some of which are turned back to maintaining and recreating the home itself. It provides a place for family life to begin, grow and break out, and in the endless cycle of dependency growing to independence, it becomes doubly valued; a castle to flee to, or to be imprisoned in. In a market economy, individually owned property stores up wealth, to be leaked as consumer spending when people trade down to a smaller home, or transported as capital across the generations when, also trading down to a smaller home, people die. In a council housing tenure, tenanted property stores up very little, except sometimes a comparatively low rent, but it does usually carry with it the right to pass the tenancy on to one's children, though more often than not long after those same children have been through their period of worst housing need and are settled somewhere else. Housing can be set within a real community, in which people are recognised as having a place, and consequently whose self-identity, role and status are bound up directly with the house and its setting. It can be set in a transitional area, whose gardens grow only a rapacious border of 'For Sale' signs, which serve as metaphors for the rootlessness and transitional status of a young urban middle class. It can be set on a hill-side overlooking the city, in a monstrous sprawl of barrack-block concrete whose ugliness affects even the most alienated housing manager, and from which there is no escape save through the TV screen, the bottle or the glue pot. Housing is a means of access to the fulfilment of other vital needs; it gives and it withholds. It has a direct effect on human well-being in general. And when it is what housing *does* to people which is at issue, then housing co-ops can and ought to be found right at the centre of controversy. Or to put it another way, co-ops challenge traditional notions of how housing should be *done*, of who should do it, and to whom, and with what consequences. Given that housing is a means to a diversity of ends, and that the way in which it is done affects not only the quality but also the very nature of those ends, the way in which it is done must become a policy issue in its own right.

Mrs Mason's housing problem is a simple one of the need for repairs, made complicated by the neglect consequent on an absentee type of ownership which sees a home as merely a long-term investment in land. Given as a necessary first step, that the state makes money available to buy out such ownership, though, the solution to the problem can take a number of forms, some of which create more problems than they solve. For example, the first solution takes a hammer to crack a nut, and in the process leaves the kernel of people's housing experience smashed to pieces. The slum clearance drives of the 1950s cleared away much housing that could not be saved; back to backs, tiny cottages that were too small, and all the jerry-built inner city slums which had disgraced Victorian building standards, just as some of the owner-occupied estates do today. Yet the bulldozer drove on, into the well-built and substantial-sized terraces which had been built for the upper working-class railway workers who had been Mrs Mason's forebears. Such housing, even when neglected, stands the test of time far better than anything being built in the 1980s. yet more out of habit than conviction, but perhaps also with a sneaking sense of distaste for their own lower-middle to working-class origins, the new professions of environmental health and housing management disdained anything that stood in the way of 'progress'. Backed up by councillors who were easily persuaded that they were building Jerusalem on England's green and pleasant fields, they razed the inner city, and deposited its people in the slums of the future, far enough beyond the suburbs to be completely without amenities, and high enough in the air to be without any real chance of building a new sense of community.

Of course we have learned by our mistakes. Mrs Mason could have been offered a maisonette in a nearby part of the inner city, or even better, a phased renewal scheme which would have set her and her mother in a new house only a few blocks away. But whatever the outcome, it is clear that the choice would not have been hers, but would still have depended on a mixture of bureaucratic officialdom and professional hubris.

The second option seems better, that a housing association, smaller and so less bureaucratic, of charitable status and so more human, should go in where the council has failed, should buy up houses discreetly, and one by one modernise them for suitably deserving occupants. The trouble is that while in the early days of erratic funding and uncertain reward such associations probably *were* less bureaucratic and more charitable, in order to carry out the housing renewal tasks assigned them, they quickly (after the 1974 Housing Act) grew more like the big-brother they were meant to replace. With their management committees staffed by local councillors and the sort of people who become local councillors, and their offices by housing profesionals who were becoming accustomed to crossing between the housing association and local authority career ladders, they soon learned the language in which housing is always a noun, and the people who live in houses merely adjectives. But what about the community housing association, the locally based, small-scale organisation which can avoid all the pitfalls, and even introduce a measure of local control by residents and tenants into the equation? There *is* a big difference between an association based within a recognisable community, and a city-wide concern, even if the former is tempted to extend its boundaries in order to keep its professional development staff employed, and if the latter is tempted to split down into semi-autonomous area offices, in order to keep bureaucracy and hierarchy within manageable limits. The difference was brought home to me one day while talking to a young housing officer from a Birmingham-wide association, which was doing very similar work to my own more locally-based work in Saltley. He had all the trappings of a radical approach to housing; the denim suit, the silently superior air, the secretaryship of the local Labour Party. He asked me what I did with my 'residuals'. I could not answer, not having the faintest idea of what they were. He explained, not very patiently, that he meant the tenants who were inherited along with some of the houses which we bought from private landlords. I replied that we called them 'the clients'.

When housing is a noun, the tenants are residual. They live and die in their homes, but for housing managers they adorn, wear out and sometimes disfigure the 'dwelling unit', the 'four-person-two-bedroom flat', or in Scotland the '5 apartment'. For some professionals there is real pain when, after 'handing over' a new property in perfect condition, they see the tenants settling down to turn it into a home. They would never dream of altering the plans to suit a particular family, having in mind that the unit will have to be let to a stream of applicants over its lifetime. Often this is not the case; one family will certainly see out a stream of housing managers. Nor do they understand that attention to the needs of one family may alter architects' perceptions of what is required, may mature their judgment, steady the occasional late-night flight of fancy at the drawing-board. Nor that one family may be very much like another, and that a home drawn to one person's liking will probably suit someone else more than one drawn to an inhuman standard.

But if community housing association staff and architects can move towards treating housing as a verb, why then put Mrs Mason through the fourth scenario, the housing co-operative? The problem is that community-based housing associations, and their municipal equivalent, decentralised area and estate offices, are still staffed by the *landlord*. That is, she and the housing officer Bob are locked into a permanently unequal duet of roles which are only experienced as satisfactory because the officer chooses to act in a humane way. There is no structural safeguard other than mutual goodwill and the law of landlord and tenant, and the various and varyingly effective methods which such associations have of involving tenants in the actual making of policy. If the landlord wishes to offer Mrs Mason alternative accommodation, either for decanting or for permanent occupation, even under the protection afforded by landlord-tenant law a court would nearly always grant possession to him. But more insidiously, if the mutual respect ever broke down or simply wore thin under the stresses of a complex improvement process, or if a less sympathetic housing official were to replace the current officer, Mrs M would experience the full weight of that unequal power relationship which lurks just under the surface.

That is the negative argument for housing co-ops. The positive one would take into account all the benefits which can be gained from allowing and encouraging people to be their own landlord, benefits which can be expressed in terms of housing as a noun, but which run into considerations of all the other things that the process of housing gives access to, and then spill over into the less tangible, because less materialistic, benefits of personal and group development, the sense of community, of achievement, of autonomy, and so on. It is an argument which moves inexorably from consideration of how to maximise the use-value of housing, to that of how to maximise human potential. It is an argument which requires further elaboration at the level of competing social philosophies, and this is what it will receive in Chapters 2 and 3.

WHAT IS A HOUSING CO-OP?

Before we begin this rather large task, though, we have to attempt to define a housing co-op. I say 'attempt' because the only way to do this properly is through a detailed study of all the different types of organisation calling themselves co-ops (and some which do not call themselves co-ops, but might be anyway) in the light of co-operative principles. This will be done in Chapter 7, but we cannot wait until then to get some grasp, however rudimentary, of the essence of the subject. One simple definition is that they are a voluntary association by means of which dwellers can collectively own their own housing, and control the process of housing. This is cumbersome, but it captures the dual nature of housing as noun and verb; a product in itself and a process by which the product is created and maintained. There are three elements here: ownership, control and process. We might call them variables, because they certainly vary in a bewildering mixture of organisational forms. Take ownership; figure 1 shows a triadic relationship between common, shared and co-ownership. The following discussion may appear unnecessarily technical, but, as we shall see in Chapter 7, and as Alex Laidlaw agrees: 'The question of capital investment and each member's equity is probably the most difficult and controversial in the development of housing co-ops.'[3]

In the common-ownership co-op, the entire equity is held collectively. Though individuals have to buy a nominal share in order to become members, this is a more a membership fee than a stake in the property, and it is usually either forfeited if the member leaves, or is repaid at par value. Members may invest capital only in loan stock, which will attract limited interest but will not rise with the value of the property, and cannot be traded for the right to occupy. The main British form, known variously as a fair rent, par value or non-equity co-op, might better be described as a common-ownership, since it only requires a shareholding of £1 per member. So might most Canadian co-ops, since the $500 down payment the latter require is still regarded as nominal, though in this case when it is withdrawn the share is repaid in 'constant dollars' to allow for inflation. It is possible to raise a limited amount of capital without infringing the common ownership and par value principle; the Stockholm Housing Co-operative Association (SKB) requires only a small membership fee of about £5 and an annual fee of about £8, but in order to be eligible for housing, members have to take out loan stock of about £1000, and then save £50 a year with the co-op until they reach a savings limit of £600.[4] They then pay a deposit of between £300 and £1400 on entering the dwelling, but this is not so much a share in the equity as a safeguard against bad upkeep of the dwelling.

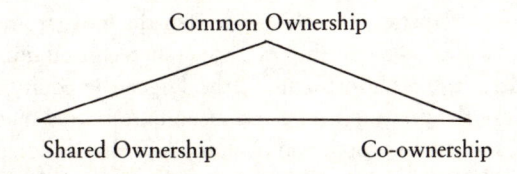

Figure 1 Types of ownership

Co-ownership means individual ownership of shares in the collective property. The first breach in the common-ownership principle in the direction of co-ownership comes when members have to take up a substantial share before being offered a dwelling. In early American co-ops, which had no government support and therefore had to raise some capital through the members, a down payment in share-capital of $500 per room was common, along with the optional take-up of preference or loan stock.[5] In Sweden, loans of 99 per cent of development costs are available, and so the first members to occupy only have to make up the 1 per cent, while in Norway, a recent decline in subsidies has meant a rise in members' capital, of up to 35 per cent of the total development costs, averaging £17,500 per dwelling.[6] Generally the larger the individual stake, the greater the likelihood of some kind of remuneration for the capital invested; in the Co-partnership Housing Societies which were formed in England just before the First World War, a minimum of £50 equity was required of tenant-members, rewarded with 5 per cent interest. Co-ownership housing co-ops which were developed in the 1960s in Britain dropped an initial requirement that incoming members make a down payment, but paid a premium on leaving, based on a complicated formula which was meant to avoid speculation, while rewarding members for their contribution towards paying off the collective mortgage.

It is theoretically possible for a co-op member to own the equivalent in shares of the market value of his or her own dwelling. This was the avowed intention of the first housing co-op formed in Britain in the last century, the Tenant Co-operators Ltd; the idea was to ask only that tenant members buy a £1 share, and that gradually surpluses would be made on the rents, which would accrue to each tenant's share account until the exact value of the house was reached. Note that at this stage, while outside shareholders would have been bought out, the co-op would still be in existence, as the shares would still be held individually in a collective enterprise. Does this mean that the move from common-ownership towards co-ownership raises merely technical questions and points of definition? Unfortunately, the larger the equity share, the greater may be the pressure for its sale at an unrestricted market value. In Norway, the rise in proportion of individual shareholding since the Second World War has been accompanied by irresistible pressure for sale in a market which increasingly resembles owner-occupation. Alternatively, if equity shares are kept at an artificially low value, and members cannot benefit from the large increase in the value of the property, either black-market sales may take place or the co-op may be wound up and individuals allowed to convert their shares to individual title to their own dwelling. Partly for these reasons, many co-operators believe that the common-ownership end of the continuum is more truly co-operative.

Shared ownership means that the individual and the collective equity are split up. Unlike co-ownership, there is no tension between the individual and the collective interest; they are simply separated. Part-way down the continuum from common to shared ownership is the Glenkerry Co-op in East London, which has bought a long-term lease on a tower block from the local authority (which remains the freeholder), and has a unique structure which allows the sale of 50 per cent of the market value of each flat to the occupying member. The only control is that the figure is set by an independent district valuer, which means that prices stay low in relation to the local property market. Shared ownership co-ops go further, in offering a variable proportion of the dwelling as individual ownership, and allowing owners to buy further proportions as they are able. Eventually the co-op will cease to exist, having been bought out completely, or, if the dwellings are flats, may become the ultimate in shared ownership, the condominium, in which individuals own their apartments outright, but have a share in a resident-owned company which owns the freehold and the common areas, and which provides services at cost to the members. We will leave until Chapter 7 the question of whether a condominium can still be considered a co-operative.

If collective ownership were the only definition of a co-op, then tenant management co-ops would be excluded. These are formed by tenants of housing associations or local councils, who wish to run their own estates by an agency agreement negotiated with the landlord. In England they usually provide all management services, while in Scotland they have so far drawn back from any involvement with rent collection, because of a reluctance to deal with arrears. They even allocate empty property from their own waiting lists, though often stipulating that applicants be already on the local authority list. If they are to be included in the definition of co-ops, then this brings the control variable into prominence; co-ops are associations by which dwellers control their own housing, even if they do not own it. There may be little difference between a common ownership co-op and a tenant management co-op in their day-to-day operation, and in the benefits they bring to members. The control exercised by the managers may in some cases be greater than that exercised by the owners, because of restrictions placed on the latter by funding agencies; in Britain, for example, management co-ops tend to be able to convert an empty house or flat to a co-op office and meeting place, whereas ownership co-ops in receipt of Housing Association Grant funding may have to let all the dwellings. More generally, a lively, effective management co-op will in practice provide more collective control over the environment than will a badly-run ownership co-op.

This brings us to the third variable, the housing process. There are three main stages which have to be gone through by anyone who provides housing where there was none before: we might summarise them as planning, development and management. At the planning stage, a group comes together to form the nucleus of a co-op, either on their own initiative or on that of a sponsoring body. In Britain, the former tends to be the case, and members then seek out a secondary co-op to do development work for them, while in Scandinavia, people join a secondary co-op first, and are then allocated a place in a new primary co-op. They then have to formulate a plan, which includes purchase of land (if a new-build co-op) or (if a rehabilitation-type co-op) of unimproved housing. Architects, quantity surveyors and sometimes structural engineers have to be engaged to draw up a preliminary design and costings, though in some cases (such as house-building co-ops in Ireland and Canada), 'off the peg' type house designs can be simply laid out on a site plan, without the involvement of experts.[7] Planning permissions are then sought, and the financing of the scheme is agreed with whatever agencies lend or grant money to co-ops; each country has its own quite distinctive and invariably complex system, the principles of which will be discussed more fully in Chapter 5. At this point full plans are drawn up, and the future of the scheme is (at least in theory) assured. The development stage probably begins when the scheme is put out to tender, or in the case of a self-build co-op, when work actually starts on site. Eventually the completed scheme is occupied by the co-op members (or in the case of improvement work where members were already in occupation, handed back), and the third stage begins, of long-term management. When the dwellings have eventually reached the end of their useful life, the whole process can begin again, with either demolition and renewal, or full improvement work.

Now, in theory, a co-operative can begin and end at any point in this process. The main distinction is between house-building co-ops, which do not enter the management stage, and full or continuing co-ops, which do. The house building co-op is simply a group of people who come together to provide housing for owner-occupation, at a cheaper cost than they could incur if they went ahead on their own. It may be used simply to buy land for parcelling out as individual plots, or it may develop the site, hire a builder, and go all the way to completion of the development stage. Alternatively, the development may be done by the members themselves; the small but interesting growth in 'self-build housing associations' in Britain is, as the name implies, of this latter type. The house-building co-op is the predominant form in Ireland, where they provide for about 5 per cent of new house starts,[8] and in rural Canada, where in Nova Scotia for instance, they provide about 15 per cent of all new housing.[9] Although such co-ops are genuine co-ops while they exist, and no doubt contribute to the building up of community spirit among the owners of the housing produced, they tend by their very nature to be temporary; not surprisingly, this seems to be the main problem identified by their promoters.[10]

True housing co-ops are continuing associations which manage the housing collectively. They will usually have done their own planning and development (though occasionally promoters take 'off the peg' schemes and convert them to co-ops at the management stage), but they will still be what Alex Laidlaw calls 'All the way co-operative housing'. We have a working definition then, with which to proceed in the next two chapters to the more interesting subject of world-views within which the case for co-ops has to be argued; sadly, the house-building co-op, even in its most exciting variant, the self-build association, will have to be the subject of another book.

TWO
HUMAN NATURE AND CO-OPERATIVE VALUES

What is it that makes people interpret housing problems and solutions in such radically different ways? We could say that it is simply a matter of occupational cultures; that staff trained in a bureaucratic, centralised local authority housing department will define their task, and the meaning they give it, quite differently from staff brought up in a community housing association, and completely differently from secondary housing co-operative workers. But this begs the question. The working environment is produced and reproduced by people who may have selected this particular environment, or been selected for it, because it fits in with their own values. The mystery is, why do people come to hold such different values, and what motivates them to define the world in the way they do? The question may be abstract, but it is not idle. Values are everywhere, defining the way we interpret the world; they create reality for us. Reality, to one particular housing association manager I know, is that there are two types of tenants, the good and the bad. The good are 'the salt of the earth', and they are entitled to a polite, if patronising service. The bad have to be weeded out, refused repairs on the grounds that they must have wilfully damaged their property, and if they get behind with the rent, subjected with grim glee to immediate distraint procedures, whereby bailiffs break in and take away their colour television. Reality to this association's welfare officer is that it is the welfare of the houses which matters, and that annual inspections must be done to show up those tenants who through slovenliness, poverty or ill-health have fallen below the correct standard of cleanliness and decor.

It is not enough to say that 'experience counts', that contact with people in need will create the right kind of sympathetic response; experience is filtered through a tinted and smoky prism of values; people simply do not *see* the same world. Of course, experience can change our values; they are in a dialectical relationship. For instance, when our housing manager visited a housing co-op, his view of reality was shaken to its very foundations; in his world such things do not, cannot, exist. He had to recreate the meaning of his experience, to reassert reality, but had only two ways of doing so; either the co-op members were an extraordinary elite, or his view of tenants had been mistaken all along. In fact, he opted for the former method, preserving a sense of his own professional importance, and its corollary, the inferiority of his tenants, and thereby keeping his assumptive-world more or less intact.

World-views are very resilient; people have invested much of the meaning of their lives in them. To unthink our values is to run the risk of seeing much of what has gone before in our lives as having been mistaken, and so worthless. World-views are also quite consistent; people tend to take on a whole cluster of mutually compatible values, which support each other and provide a more or less complete set of propositions with which to interpret and manage the everyday world.[1] This means that in order to understand what moves people to define housing problems in the way they do, we are not faced with a kaleidoscopic picture, but with a few major viewpoints. Furthermore, social philosophers have more than sketched out such viewpoints; they have provided us with a comprehensive guide to them. Unfortunately, there are any number of '-isms', labels with which to describe such world-views, and at the risk of introducing yet more, I would suggest four major ones, focusing not on the '-isms' but on the '-ists', the people who hold them. Thus there are individualists, pluralists, collectivists and co-operators. As I hope will become clear, these labels summarise four ideal-types, around which many people can identify themselves. And as ideal-types, they are not meant to be exhaustive of every possible combination of values, but to be distillations of the purest form of positions which many people, to a greater or lesser extent, hold.

A CO-OPERATIVE VIEW OF HUMAN NATURE

(a) Individualists

Probably the most fundamental question we can start with, concerns human nature. When people say that housing co-operatives 'just will not work', they are making a statement about human nature, that people are inherently individualistic and competitive, unable, even if willing, to co-operate. They are following Adam Smith in seeing the individual as inherently self-interested, 'much more deeply interested in whatever immediately concerns himself than in what concerns any other man'.[2] But how, then, does society manage to hang together? Why are we not totally immersed in a Hobbesian war of 'all against all'? For the individualists, Adam Smith provides two answers. Firstly, people have an innate sense of justice, which nature has given them in order to subsist in society with their fellows. The use of the word justice is misleading; it is no more than the individual's sociability, based on 'an original desire to please and an original aversion to offend his brethren'. Is this enough, though, to keep in check a downright pursuit of selfish interests, leading to a breakdown in social order? To strengthen his argument, Smith provides a second answer, bringing in the famous 'invisible hand' image, that in a free market, individual self-seeking is spontaneously converted into social benefits; despite the impersonal nature of market exchanges, by supplying what someone else demands, a person is 'led by an invisible hand to promote an end which was no part of his intention'.[3] Such a view is very resilient. It allows Herbert Spencer to be pessimistic about human nature, declaring that 'Man is shapen in iniquity and conceived in sin',[4] yet optimistic about the ability of egoists to co-operate. It allows Milton Friedman to see self-interest not as myopic selfishness, but merely as a recognition that individuals have their own interests and goals.[5] Not only does the market channel self-interested actions into public good, but it checks those abuses which egoism gives rise to, through the discipline of the price mechanism.[6] People are therefore allowed to be what they are, without needing to feel guilty of inhumanity to others.

The competitive individualists who inhabit this world-view are co-operators only in furthering their own ends within a market. They cannot and should not be expected to compromise their interests to the extent which is necessary in, say, housing co-ops, and will look to a free market in owner-occupied and privately rented housing as the natural expression of a nature which can really only be relied on to be altruistic within the family, and at least until they have had their own demands met, egoistic towards everyone else.[7] They would expect that in practice, given the limitations of human nature, co-ops would conform gradually to owner-occupation, eventually losing their distinctively co-operative purposes. It is no accident that when a Conservative government sponsored housing co-ops for the first time in the 1960s, it was on the co-ownership model, and that the main aim was to enable young people to build up sufficient equity to move on to owner-occupation. It is also no accident that, as we shall see in Chapter 4, another Conservative government amended the law to allow the winding up and sale of those same co-ownerships to their members. One in eight council houses in Britain has recently gone the same way. However, the argument rests also on there being a real choice in a free market. Heavy tax relief subsidies to owner-occupiers, discounts to council tenants, steep rises in council house rents, and the cutting of funds for public and voluntary-sector house-building, have so increased the relative cost of choosing not to be selfish and individualistic, that the outcome can be said to be manipulated; few people have any real choice not to be the kind of person which the competitive individualist says we are. If the market can be fixed, the prophecy can be made self-fulfilling.

(b) Pluralists

Only the most hardened competitive individualist can rest content with a definition of human nature in which a person consists solely of his or her worth in the market. Surely all-round self-development is the real goal, and economic markets only one means of reaching it. Von Humboldt, a different kind of individualist, says: 'the end of man ... is the highest and most harmonious development of his powers to a complete and consistent whole', and that the object 'towards which every human being must ceaselessly direct his efforts, and on which especially those who design to influence their fellow men must ever keep their eyes, is the individuality of power and development.'[8]

This is a powerful statement of the worth of the individual, for which liberal pluralists are rightly renowned. But is it still too individualistic to see the significance of co-operative association? The most famous liberal of all, J.S. Mill, does not at first correct this impression. In his essay *On Liberty*, he sees human nature as fallible, but perfectible through the growth of reason, for which open discussion and diversity of opinion are necessary. This could mean that the liberal individual is formed merely out of the debating club, and that co-operation is not necessary to the development of character. He gives two quite weak arguments which seem to confirm this view. Firstly, the collation of opinion and the synthesis of half-truths into whole ones are themselves a social development; this hardly leads to a strong justification of co-operative forms, though it does suggest a co-operative style of education. Secondly, though, it is the combination of discussion and *experience* which provide this growth in knowledge, and for this there need to be 'different experiments of living', the worth of which 'should be proved practically, when anyone thinks fit to try them'.[9] What sort of experiments does he mean?

Turning to his *Principles of Political Economy*, we find a different side of Mill, still the individualist, but also the committed co-operator. At the time when he was writing, no one had thought 'fit to try' housing co-ops; the latest update of his *Principles* was published in 1871, 15 years before the Tenant Co-operators Ltd began the first housing co-operative 'experiment in living'. He does, however, deal at length with producer and consumer co-ops, for which he has the greatest admiration, and of the ideas concerning collective property which were available to him, he says 'It is for experience to determine how far or how soon any one or more of the possible systems of community of property will be fitted to substitute itself for ... private ownership.'[10] The test of any new form of property is whether it produces a higher form of human nature, and he has a strong faith in the 'civilising and improving influences of association', by which he means co-operatives.[11] In fact, after reviewing the progress of the co-operative movement in France and Britain, he says:

> It is hardly possible to take any but a hopeful view of the prospects of mankind, when, in two leading countries of the world, the obscure depths of society contain simple working men whose integrity, good sense, self-command and honourable confidence in one another, have enabled them to carry these noble experiments to the triumphant issue which the facts recorded in the proceedings pages attest.[12]

Mill writes at such length about the effects on human nature of the co-operative method, that the editor of the latest edition of his *Principles* has (to our great annoyance) cut out the 'facts recorded in the previous pages' altogether!

Mill was concerned mainly with the economic spheres of production and consumption, and with the relationships between capitalist and wage-labourer, and he is echoed in recent liberal thinking by a more psychological approach which emphasises the need for creative work for which one can take responsibility, in which one can be involved, and from which one can derive personal status. Modern liberals also emphasise, though, the role of community in defining individual status and function, and in combating the de-personalising influence of mass urban life, and this points more specifically towards the significance of housing co-ops.[13] However, there may be prices to be paid for co-operation, in the adapting of individual plans of life to common goals, and of individual self-expression to group norms of behaviour. If the individual is a tree, 'which requires to grow and develop itself on all sides, according to the tendency of the inward forces which make it a living thing',[14] how far is it cramped by the other trees in the forest? It will be interesting to see if liberal pluralists do see individual liberty as being compatible with co-operative living.

(c) Collectivists

The central texts of Marxism contain few references to human nature; it is a concept which the dialectical materialist method rejects as idealistic, because it fails to recognise that the individual is largely a product of a particular social formation, which is itself largely determined by the economic forces dominant at a particular stage of human evolution. For example, Engels, writing about the historical development of capitalist society, contrasts the type of person produced by the old tribal societies, with those of 'civilisation'. On the Iroquois people he says:

> the kind of men and women that are produced by such a society is indicated by the admiration felt by all white men who came into contact with uncorrupted Indians, admiration of the personal dignity, straightforwardness, strength of character and bravery of these barbarians.[15]

He sees civilised society as 'a degradation, a fall from the simple moral grandeur of the ancient gentile society', and, like Mill, has little sympathy with the kind of human nature which market individualists take for granted: 'The lowest interest – base greed, brutal sensuality, sordid avarice, selfish plunder of common possessions – usher in the new, civilised society, class society.'[16] He sees the achievements of capitalist society as having been accomplished by 'playing on the most sordid instincts and passions of man, and by developing them at the expense of all his other faculties'.[17]

All this seems promising for the development of an alternative view of human nature to that of the market's 'shabby individual', greedily in pursuit of 'wealth, more wealth and wealth again'; like the pluralists, he believes that character is wider and human potential deeper than the individualists allow, and that different types of society produce different qualities of person. But instead of analysing those features of tribal society which had nurtured a better human nature, such as small-scale common ownership, direct democracy and decentralisation, and then trying to apply them in a new form to a future socialist society, Engels is sure that tribal man is doomed to extinction, that there is no going back, and that only through totally different methods (the massive socialisation of the means of production) can man recover that lost innocence. Such a lack of consideration of the relationship between the features of a future socialist society and the quality of human beings it might produce leads indirectly to Lenin's shallow assumption that the 'training and disciplining' of millions of workers by the huge centralised apparatus of state socialism, would lead to the emergence of the new personality, and to true communism. Co-operative socialists (whom Engels labels 'utopian' because of their concern to spell out the kind of relationship between society and human nature which they would like to see develop) have argued persistently that political changes from the 'top-down' are not enough to produce the end sought, and that Engels, the 'scientific socialist', is the real utopian.

However, when one turns to the early Marx, and especially to his treatment of alienation in the *Economic and Philosophical Manuscripts*, one discovers a much more fruitful treatment of human nature, albeit from a standpoint which, in failing to follow the rules of the materialist method, embarrasses some Marxists, but which is potentially fertile ground for those socialists interested in the co-operative form.[18] For Marx, human nature exists not as a separate essence, but as relationships between people; subjectivity is a function of inter-human or social relations. Alienation refers to the way in which under capitalist social relations, people become thing-like and things take on personality, because of a process in which the people become dominated (in Coletti's words) by: 'all the forces and powers they themselves have created, which tower above them as entities alienated or estranged from them'.[19]

There are three forms of alienation: from the product of one's labour, from the act of production and from other people. Of course, the argument is about production, and the way in which capital becomes an independent entity which grows in its power to enslave and to impoverish, the more people work to try to free themselves from its grip. Coupled with a critique of large-scale industrial production methods in general, as well as in capitalist societies, this can be turned into a powerful argument for worker co-ops, but it has at first sight little relevance to the neglected realm of consumption. And this is another problem with the collectivist approach; it takes notice of consumption issues such as housing only in relation to the means of their production, and ignores questions of ownership, management and consumer control. Applied to the realm of distribution and consumption, though, to the way housing is delivered and used, the concept of alienation could become fruitful. Are people not alienated also from their means of consumption? Does not the massive public housing estate both literally and metaphorically 'tower' above people, as an entity alienated from them? Are not its consumers also alienated: from the consumption good, from the act of consumption and from other consumers?

One way to apply Marx's argument would be to emphasise the fact that the tenant as producer of the home and local environment may *feel* as alienated from it as from the product of wage labour, though the enemy be a distant public bureaucracy or an absentee private landlord, rather than a capitalist entrepreneur. Marx and Engels disagree; the relation of tenants to landlords is not one of the selling of one's labour power, but of the appropriation of wages by the landlord after they have been earned:

> No matter how much the landlord may overreach the tenant, it is still only a transfer of already existing, previously produced value. ... It is therefore a complete misrepresentation of the relation between landlord and tenant to attempt to make it equivalent to the relation between worker and capitalist.[20]

Housing co-ops are not, then, going to change human nature by changing the relationship between landlord and tenant; the fault, and the fight, lie elsewhere.

Is Marx any more positive about those types of co-op which operate in the sphere of production and distribution? Apart from occasional positive references, Marx generally refuses to connect co-operative enterprise with the overcoming of alienation. Why should this be? Erich Fromm lists three reasons: neglect of the need for a moral transformation of human nature as well as a change in economic relations, a grotesque misjudgment of the chances for the realisation of socialism through revolutionary means, and the simplistic assumption that the socialisation of the means of production are sufficient (as well as necessary) means for the transformation to socialist society. Marx lacks psychological insight into the deep-seated passions and strivings which, rooted in man's very conditions of existence, need to be channelled in creative rather than destructive directions. He neglects the cultural factors which act back on the economic base, and idealises a working class which is deeply compromised psychologically and morally by irrational needs and satisfactions which originate in pre-revolutionary society. The result is that 'both the criticism of capitalism and the socialist aim in human terms become more and more overgrown by economic considerations',[21] and that an underlying assumption is made of man's natural goodness, which will assert itself as soon as the economic shackles are released. What experiments in public ownership of the means of production (and in council housing, of a vital means of consumption) have demonstrated is that alienation is not just a matter of ownership, but is also one of scale, and of degree of democratic control by ordinary people, in their overlapping roles as workers, consumers and citizens. What matters is the actual conditions of production, consumption and citizenship, the actual relations pertaining between people in power and those who need access to good work, a good home and a living sense of community. In these respects, the collectivists are not radical enough. They are still situated in a middle-class nineteenth-century tradition over-optimistic about human nature, over-emphatic on political and legal changes to the neglect of socio-cultural and psychological factors, and assuming a centralist orientation. As we shall see, to the extent that Marxists transcend these limitations, they revitalise Marxism and at the same time expand the concept of alienation so that co-operative solutions become increasingly attractive.

(d) Communitarians

Robert Owen, generally regarded as the first co-operative theorist,[22] has much to say about human nature. He criticises market competition for promoting feelings of insecurity, of being deprived of the means of existence, which leads to the need to secure individual interests over against others, and hence to egoism: 'This feeling has created a universal selfishness of the most ignorant nature, for it almost ensures the evils which it means to prevent.'[23] During the early years of the last century, Owen put forward proposals on a grand scale for co-operative villages which would supply their members' wants through mutual co-

Human nature and co-operative values

operation, and in so doing would eradicate selfishness through want of an adequate motive to produce it. Behind this utopian vision is a simplistic view that individual character is determined by social forces; change the social context and the individual will be changed: in his words, a 'second creation of humanity' would be affected: 'by creating entirely new surroundings in which to place all through life, and by which a new human nature would appear to arise from the new surroundings.'[24] This is strong justification indeed, for co-operative housing, especially if it were combined with producer co-ops and perhaps subsistence farming. Unfortunately, like Marx, Owen has an over-simplified, rationalistic view of human nature. His environmental determinism led in practice to over-optimism about the speed at which people could be changed into co-operators, in a series of more or less disastrous experimental communities, which foundered partly because of an open membership policy and lack of co-operative education; at New Harmony, for example, he insisted on taking all comers, the result being the eventual re-assertion of 'selfishness' and the conversion of the community to individual family smallholdings.[25]

Just as the consumer co-operative movement developed Owen's belief in co-operation in the more successful, if much more mundane, direction of the co-op store, later communitarian theorists developed more realistic views of human nature. Proudhon, for example, begins from almost an individualistic free market pessimism, that individuals are egoistic, that they have certain inherent social instincts such as the desire to own property, and that an ineradicable tendency towards evil exists, which rules out optimistic beliefs in automatic improvement. But he has no faith in the market's 'invisible hand', having experienced (as a peasant farmer and self-employed printer) its in-built inequality of opportunity, and having acknowledged the liberal pluralist goal of the development of the all-round individual which capitalism frustrates. He goes even further, balancing the methodological individualism of the liberal, with Owen's grasp of the sociological context of personal growth; the result is a strong conviction that in society a collective reason can under certain conditions produce social justice. This is a much stronger concept of justice than Adam Smith's sociability, and is akin to Rousseau's general will; a recognition by individuals that there can be a transcendent interest which is not just the sum of shifting individual interests.

But how does he reconcile the opposition between the individual ego and the collective interest? The answer is that he does not attempt to overcome opposites, but recognises irreducable antinomies which simply have to be accepted as part of the human condition; human nature is made up of opposing forces, which have to be accommodated to each other.[26] The task then becomes one of creating a social order in which individual evil inclinations are held in check by social institutions which both recognise the limitations of human nature and foster the collective sense of justice. For this, he seeks a third way, between individualistic capitalism and collectivist state socialism, for: 'Political economy leans towards consecrating egoism; socialism leans towards putting the community before everything else.'[27] Only by combining the strengths of both world-views can we reach a more adequate knowledge of human nature and potential: 'Since each in turn is denying something, socialism humanity's past experience and political economy humanity's reason, both are inadequate statements about the truth of human life.'[28] By this reconciliation of antinomies, Proudhon hopes to conserve all that is good in society, and progress towards something better. The outcome is a prescription which is highly pertinent to co-ops; that a 'polytechnic education', in which the individual gains an appreciation of other people's interests, will foster a collective spirit which will balance the opposites; this he calls 'mutualism'.[29] Such an education would be gained within a co-operative economy of worker-owned enterprises, but the argument could apply with equal force to the consumption side, in housing co-ops.

Does this mean that there is no need for a revolution which will secure for the workers the full fruits of their labour? On the one hand, Proudhon scorns Marx's 'mystical' belief in revolution, and insists on the need for tolerance, polemic and above all, for irony. He mistrusts revolution from above, which is despotism, and against Marx's almost apocalyptic vision of the post-revolutionary utopia, believes that a permanent antinomy between the forces of good and evil allows only for a tendency towards progress. On the other hand, though, a permanent revolution based concretely on the masses, making use of their own spontaneous energy, and growing organically, is required. It is: 'a spontaneous transformation that takes place throughout the body politic ... a new organism replacing one that is outworn.'[30] It is in this sense, that housing co-ops could be seen at least in theory, as part of a revolutionary movement.

Proudhon's influence in France led to relatively successful experiments in worker co-operation, and to the outstandingly successful (if short-lived) worker self-management of the Paris Commune. However, the experience of the Christian Socialists who were employing similar arguments in Britain led to the formation of worker co-ops very few of which survived adverse trading conditions and, significantly, internal dissensions. What evidence is there, then, that under the specified conditions this collective interest will emerge? Kropotkin's contribution is to put the belief in co-operation on a firm scientific basis, in his analysis of mutual aid as a principle of evolution; he shifts the 'survival of the fittest' from the individual to the co-operating group, amassing evidence to show that it is the most co-operative species rather than the most ruthless or powerful which survive best.[31] Since mutual aid is built into the 'masses' as a spontaneous ability to co-operate, and is 'a feeling infinitely wider than love or personal sympathy',[32] a consciousness of human solidarity, of the dependence of the individual's happiness on that of all, it *can* be relied on. The mutual aid feeling: 'has been nurtured by thousands of years of human social life and hundreds of thousands of years of pre-human life in societies.'[33] Proudhon's antinomy between the individual and the group is fused here into a socio-biological principle which takes the discussion right back to basics, to human survival and the organic interconnection between individuals.

In Kropotkin, Proudhon's ambivalence towards revolution is continued, and eventually resolved into a belief in organic evolutionary change, which grows within the old society and like a seed which forces its way to the surface, bursts out violently. Prefigurative actions are needed to show the way, and to provide the building blocks of the new society. Housing co-ops might be seen as a modest part of such prefigurative action, and if society is seen in a quasi-biological sense as 'an aggregation of organisms trying to find out the best ways of combining the wants of the individual with those of co-operation for the welfare of the species',[34] then housing co-ops could be seen as cellular structures of the new order.

Martin Buber takes up this idea, and in similar language postulates 'a renewal of society through a renewal of its cell tissue'.[35] In considering human nature, he throws back at Marx the accusation the latter had made of Proudhon, that he is utopian; since the post-revolutionary Marxist utopia relies on a radical change in human nature, and since, he says, the Marxists are prepared to use people as tools in order to get there, the gap between ends and means has to be filled with a redemptionist, apocalyptic vision which is essentially non-rational:

Human nature and co-operative values

'Uniformity as a means is to change miraculously into multiplicity as an end; compulsion into freedom'.[36] The alternative is to see perfection as 'something towards which an active path leads from the present', and which taps powers 'latent in the depths of reality'.[37] We must base our strategy on the identifying and promoting of hidden tendencies which are latent in the present, so as to prepare the way for a revolution which will simply set free and extend a reality which has already 'grown to its true possibilities'. Genuine socialism emerges, which is built up of local communes, trade associations and federations. Inasmuch as the basic cell of this new reality is a geographically distinct community, it would seem that some kind of housing co-op is a key aspect. Landauer makes this clear, in detailing what is necessary if a real social revolution is to take place; revolutionaries must be prepared to 'clear the ground' by making common property available, and by federating these commonalities, in a spirit of community which dwells in the individuals so as to counteract egoism and point beyond material interests: 'Nothing can prevent the united consumers from working for themselves, and with the aid of mutual credit, from building factories, workshops, houses for themselves, from acquiring land; nothing – if only they have a will and begin.'[38] However, there is a danger here in over-stating the case; the more important one claims housing co-ops to be, the more stringent has to be one's evaluation of the actual co-ops which exist. Just how stringent is illustrated by Erich Fromm's taking up of the argument from where Buber leaves off. He argues the need for simultaneous changes in the sphere of industry, political organisation, spiritual and philosophical orientation, character structure and cultural activities, if a sane society is to be created in which human nature reaches its true potential.[39] Not surprisingly, given such a huge task, he emphasises that radical change depends not on its tempo but on its tangibility. Like Kropotkin, he has faith in the 'masses', but in their innate striving for mental health, for a productive orientation and for the will to overcome the alienation which Marx identified. A sane society would have ten features:

i. It would treat individuals as ends in themselves.
ii. It would give destructive qualities no chance to be used for greater material gain or prestige.
iii. Acting according to principles would be encouraged.
iv. Public and private relations would not be artificially separated.

Human nature and co-operative values

v. It would operate within manageable, observable dimensions.
vi. It would foster active and responsible participation.
vii It would further human solidarity, permit and stimulate people to relate to each other lovingly.
viii. It would further the productive activity of all in work.
ix. It would stimulate the use of reason.
x. It would enable the expression of inner needs in collective art and rituals.

Housing co-ops have the potential to promote all these aspects of the sane society. Whether or not they do so is a question to which we shall return.

CO-OPERATIVE ENDS AND MEANS

In advocating and practising particular means of solving the housing problem, people carry with them not only assumptions about human nature, but also about the ends which it is right to seek. The most basic ends are encapsulated in the trilogy 'liberty, equality and fraternity'; other ends such as democracy or efficiency, and arguments concerning human need, seem to be justified in the main from viewpoints which people take on this more fundamental trilogy. It is in the light of these three ideals that we assess the ultimate quality of our attempts to provide for human welfare.[40]

(a) Individualists

Free-market individualists regard individual freedom as the supreme good. It is the freedom to seek to maximise one's own benefit, to gratify one's own desires in the market, but it is not freedom from obstacles such as want, homelessness, ignorance and so on.[41] As Hayek says: 'it is true that to be free may mean freedom to starve, to make costly mistakes, or to run mortal risks.'[42] The only claims people have on each other are negative ones, to leave each other alone, not to interfere in each other's purposes. The only rights people can claim are the right to own property, to citizenship, free movement, choice of employment and freedom from imprisonment without trial. There are no natural rights to a home, to warmth, to a sense of community, to paid work within one's own area, to live near one's relatives and so on. Because freedom is defined by its opposite, coercion, and since for coercion to occur there have to be identifiable people forcing us through monopoly power to serve their ends, much of what might normally pass for coercion is ruled out. Provided there are other employers, other landlords, the loss of a job or a home is not coercion, and therefore not a loss of freedom.[43] This partly explains why Conservative governments in Britain have successively (but not very successfully) tried to revive the private rented sector in housing, and to increase access to home ownership; freedom to choose is paramount, even if people do not have the resources with which to make the choice. However, an appeal is made to faith in a free market, which (through supply-demand equilibria and Pareto-optimal outcomes) is expected to maximise everyone's utility, to produce more wealth than would any other kind of economy; the homeless and the badly housed, by waiting for market forces to lift them up, will be better off in the end, or at least their children will.

It follows that claims for a more equal distribution of housing are invalid. Not only does liberty take priority over equality, but one really has to choose between them; all attempts to equalise are by definition threats to the liberty to hold one's own property. Moreover, by interfering with market forces, such attempts are held to lower the total amount of wealth generated, and so make everyone ultimately worse off. For this reason, Adam Smith talks of present-day peasants being better off in absolute terms than in previous times their king would have been, and Hayek commends the rich for trying out 'new styles of living not accessible to the poor'.[44] Yet he admits candidly that the market 'does not guarantee the results to everyone'.[45] Co-operators, who are usually among the more disadvantaged in the housing market, would claim that they can increase the welfare of those who are excluded from the market's beneficence, thereby increasing equality of opportunity and of condition, more effectively than could market forces.

What of the third value in the trilogy, fraternity? We have noted Adam Smith's faith in the ability of markets to create spontaneous order; the only addition to this needed in the market-individualist view is a minimal state which can impose contract law on those too envious and impatient to play by the rules of the market.[46] Co-operation becomes merely 'the exchange of services under agreement',[47] and social life merely 'the aggregate result of the desires of indivuals who are severally seeking satisfactions ... following the lines of least resistance.'[48] There *is* spontaneous co-operation, but it is undertaken for

Human nature and co-operative values

entirely private ends, and then only when it is necessary to achieve something which requires joint action, and under terms of strict market exchange. Spencer distinguishes four types of co-operation:

i.   like efforts for like ends, simultaneously enjoyed,
ii. like efforts for like ends, not simultaneously enjoyed,
iii. unlike efforts for like ends, and lastly
iv. unlike efforts for unlike ends.[49]

The first type is illustrated by primitive 'hunter-gatherer' societies, where the rewards from communal effort are shared out immediately and equally, in the hunting band and in the provision of communal forms of shelter such as a cave or long-house. The second is exampled by settled agrarian societies where more complex forms of mutual aid build up, such as the collective harvesting of individually worked plots of land, and the building of houses for allocation to individual families. Because rewards are delayed, it needs an implied contract, a felt obligation enshrined in custom, or in the case of a modern self-build co-op, a detailed contract specifying a minimum of hours to be worked on other people's houses. The third type is exemplified by the medieval guild, in which a greater division of labour emerges but people still work towards common ends; the housing co-op makes its entry at this point, because members may volunteer to do different tasks, but working towards the common goal of decent housing. Lastly market exchange, whose cohesion depends on strict rendering of equivalences, is regarded by Spencer as the summit co-operation. It requires, as Hayek spells out, a refusal to meet the needs of needy neighbours, a denial of all fraternity, so as to create the impersonal signals of the market economy. This turning from common ends to serve the needs of 'thousands of unknown others' in the market, is of course a direct denial of the relevance and legitimacy of co-operatives. If, as Spencer charges, co-ops are atavistic, looking back to an earlier form of society, then co-operators would agree that they are (in Paul Goodman's memorable phrase) 'neolithic conservatives', trying to conserve what is best in past societies, without worrying about being regarded as old-fashioned.

(b) Pluralists

For liberal pluralists, liberty is still the supreme good, but is not just self-interest, but self-respect and respect for the liberty of others: 'all men are equally worthy of consideration' in certain fundamental respects.[50] Since human nature is developmental, needing space within which to grow and flourish, it follows that we have no right to harm the self-development of others. Individual spontaneity must be subject to external control 'in respect of those actions of each which concern the interest of other people'.[51] Rights are tempered with duties, not to deprive others of their liberty, or to impede their efforts to obtain it. This argument opens up distinct possibilities for housing co-ops; if the free market can be criticised as doing harm to some sections of society, such as in its denial of access to housing for the poor, then a weak but firm argument may emerge on grounds of liberty, for people to band together to solve their own housing problems outside the conventional housing market.

Modern liberals have in fact moved far from a pure laissez faire housing policy, declaring that: 'Restrictions have to be placed on liberty in the interest of liberty itself.'[52] It is only a short step to the positive definition of liberty as liberation from the social conditions which thwart self-development, and consequently to some very strong arguments for co-operative welfare-producing organisations; it is no accident that many of the early consumer co-operators were also staunch liberals, and that the most famous liberal of all was a strong supporter of co-operation; Mill says of the relation of co-operation and freedom: 'we may, through the co-operative principle, see our way to a change in society, which would combine the freedom and independence of the individual, with the moral, intellectual and economical advantages of aggregate production.'[53]

What then of equality? The logic of the value of freedom for self-development is that equality of opportunity should be promoted. Equality of condition is more problematic though, because although it is not incompatible with liberty, and is to some extent a precondition for it, the pursuit of such basic equality *is* incompatible with liberty.[54] Yet since equality of opportunity generates new inequalities, some redistribution, even of a forced kind, is necessary. The outcome of such theoretical considerations is a policy of taxing away inherited incomes, but sanctioning earned incomes, of allowing capitalism as the supply of one of the factors of production, but limiting its remuneration, and transferring wealth via social welfare to the poor. The aim is to spread the ownership of property and capital rather than to abolish them. In the economic sphere this means encouraging employee stakes and profit-sharing in private firms,[55] and in housing policy, the encouragement of owner-occupation, and also of housing co-ops and tenant self-management where individual ownership is not possible; weak theoretical grounds for co-ops result in prescriptions for policy which include them (in all their forms, common-, shared- and co-ownership), alongside a wider diffusion of private property.

It is the liberal valuation of fraternity or community which offers the strongest grounds for co-operative forms. When he begins from liberty, Mill seems at first rather unpromising; he sees communal solidarity as ancillary to, and dependent on, self-development; the individual is bound to society only insofar as *self*-improvement makes society (as an aggregate of individuals) more worth belonging to.[56] But when he begins from co-operation, he turns the argument around, and makes association the condition for self-development: 'if public spirit, generous sentiments, or true justice and equality are desired, association, not isolation of interests, is the school in which these excellences are nurtured.'[57] Modern liberal pluralists have sometimes overlooked this sociological aspect of Mill's argument; Berger and Neuhaus charge them with having a blind spot, seeing individuals in relation to public order with no mediating structures in between. They wish to promote 'people-sized institutions', based on the neighbourhood, the family, church and voluntary association.[58] A plurality of associations is needed in order to provide a choice of individual identities and, paradoxically, to promote *common* purposes, because social solidarity builds up through these mediating institutions to the wider society. Nisbet criticises Mill (perhaps, in the light of our rediscovery of his views on co-operation, unfairly) for treating the individual as the 'primary and solid fact', with relationships being purely derivative; the person is *not* autonomous, self-sufficing and stable, but in need of status, membership and a sense of community. In fact, Nisbet points out, with the benefits of modern insight into psychology, we now know that the isolated individual is pathological, and alienation from others is a state dangerous to mental stability. In this light, modern urban society is seen as failing to provide the prerequisites for individual growth; it promotes insecurity and disintegration, because of a 'widening gulf between the individual and those relationships within which goals and purposes take on meaning'.[59] *Both* the values of freedom and fraternity are at risk, and in the urban community 'hang by a slender thread'.

The solution is to promote those intervening institutions which provide individuals with a sense of belonging to a moral community. But to have the required psychological influence, the primary social group needs to regain two vital elements: real functions, and authority, which together generate social solidarity. Nisbet's argument is a key one for housing co-ops, since collective user-control of housing does restore both functions and authority to the neighbourhood level. In fact, Nisbet's definition of community could also be one of a housing co-op;

> Community is the product of people working together on problems, of autonomous and collective fulfilment of internal objectives, and of the experience of living under codes of authority which have been set in large degree by the persons involved.[60]

Yet the modern pluralist argument turns out, when applied, to be both wider and weaker than this; it includes the family, church and voluntary associations in general, and less democratic forms of housing provision, such as housing associations, seem to be promoted without mention of housing co-ops. In fact, the liberal pluralist treatment of liberty, equality and fraternity contains several potentially fruitful arguments for co-ops, which, strangely, only Mill himself has made explicit.

(c) Collectivists

There are two distinct ways in which Marxists treat values. One is the criticism of 'bourgeois values' as products largely of a capitalist economic system. The other is an implicit, but never fully discussed, set of values which it is felt would accompany a post-revolutionary society. Firstly, Marx and Engels are scathing about the kinds of freedoms allowed by market individualists. Such freedoms, when looked at in a positive sense as freedom to live a truly individuated life, allow only those with property to become individuals, and since the majority are progressively having what property they own taken away from them (by the process of increasing accumulation and centralisation of 'monopoly capital', and consequent forced proletarianisation of part of the middle classes) the sum total of even these liberties is being reduced. As Engels points out ironically, freedom of property turns into freedom *from* property for all but the large capitalist.[61] The result will be the annihilation of bourgeois freedoms by a wage-earning class who: 'have nothing of their own to secure and fortify; their mission is to destroy all previous securities for, and insurances of, individual property'.[62] Engels, writing at a time when only the elite of the working classes in Britain could afford to own their own homes (and then not through the market, but only through mutual aid in building societies), could not foresee the growth of home ownership during the present century. The progressive centralisation of capital in the production sphere has been accompanied by a diffusion of capital in the sphere of consumption. For the collectivist, such a diffusion has been irrelevant to the primary sphere of production, and has introduced a dangerous false consciousness and weakening of class identification. Thus, the ideal form of housing provision is seen as the large, uniform council estate, on which both the features of propertylessness and class identity can be preserved. If in the process, this form of property relation is found to be alienating, just as that of capital is in the productive sphere, then this is not considered a fault of the collectivist strategy; any kind of freedom for the individual or the local community is regarded as illusory, while the main source of alienation in the productive sphere still remains to be overcome.

What kind of freedom would emerge if this were to happen? The end of exploitation would also be the end of alienation, and would enable positive liberty to emerge on a firm foundation of equal access to it: 'we shall have an association in which the free development of each is the condition for the free development of all'.[63] However, while their concept of freedom is clear enough, Marx and Engels are ambiguous about what they mean by association. They do not consider the vital questions of scale and type of common ownership of socialised property. They are scathing about the 'petit-bourgeois' socialism of Proudhon, which they, like Spencer, see as atavistic, an attempt to return to pre-capitalist forms which have already virtually been destroyed by monopoly capital. They wish: 'to centralise all instruments of production in the hands of the State, i.e. of the proletariat organised as the ruling class; and to increase the total of productive forces as rapidly as possible.'[64] There are at least four assumptions here; that only a revolutionary change in the entire economic system will enable freedom from wage-slavery, that socialised property necessarily means centralised state-ownership (at least until the state withers away), that only this 'vast association of the whole nation' will ensure such productive forces as will overcome scarcity, and that it is impossible to go back to decentralised, small-scale forms of common ownership and control.

It is interesting to note what happens when Marx and Engels' prescription is actually tried. Lenin at first follows it faithfully, and in the midst of the Russian revolution spells out the implications: 'The whole of society will have become a single office and a single factory, with equality of labour and pay.'[65] He thinks that it will become possible to speak of freedom only when the state begins to wither away; meanwhile in the transitional post-revolutionary socialist society, even though control by the 'people' would be universal, the workers would have to be disciplined by the state as hired employees. State capital would replace private capital, but would still be the 'rule of the dead over the living'. Not surprisingly, there is at first no place for co-ops in his strategy. However, he soon realises that he has made a mistake, that his New Economic Policy has gone too far, because it has 'lost sight of the co-operatives'; now he argues that even if prior to the revolution they had been 'collective capitalist institutions', under social ownership of the means of production 'co-operation ... nearly always coincides fully with socialism'. All that remains, then, is to 'organise the population in co-operative societies'.[66] But here there is a snag; one of the essential principles of co-operation is that it is *voluntary* association, and cannot just be organised by decree from above. It has to be nurtured in a spirit of freedom.

In 1924, Lenin established two types of housing co-op in the Soviet Union, for house-leasing and house-building. Tenant committees had already proved far more efficient than the local authorities (the Soviets) in managing public housing, and by the end of 1926, two-thirds of the public stock had been transferred to the house-leasing co-ops; by 1936 they were managing 84 per cent of municipal housing.[67] Yet they were opposed by many in the Communist party, and in 1937 were abolished by Stalin, along with the entire co-operative sector. Of course, it could be argued that it is unfair to draw on the practice of the Soviet Union to illustrate a truth about state socialist attitudes in general. Let us turn to a more local example; in 1983, the Militant-led Labour party in Liverpool came to power, and immediately ceased all funding of housing co-ops, taking six new-build co-ops back into municipal ownership. Those who view the world through 'collectivist' eyes are still deeply uneasy about the personal and associative freedoms which the co-operative method demands.

What then of equality? Marx brilliantly and remorselessly exposes the in-built tendency towards inequality in capitalist society, but what sort of equality would be promoted in a socialist society? It would not be that crude absolute equality of condition which market individualists claim as the collectivist argument. Marx's famous dictum 'From each according to his abilities, to each according to his needs'[68]

Human nature and co-operative values

recognises that needs vary with individuals. But he sees the problem as essentially a material rather than a moral one, since in the communist utopia production will have reached a point where all needs can be taken care of, and there is no scarcity. Rather than grappling with the difficulties inherent in notions of distributive justice, he prefers to stress production, since: 'Any distribution whatever of the means of consumption is only a consequence of the distribution of the conditions of production themselves.'[69] We are back with the refusal to consider problems of distribution, from the consumer's point of view. Once the means of production are socially owned, Marx believes that problems of distribution will solve themselves: 'with the abolition of class distinctions, all social and political inequality arising from them would disappear of itself'.[70]

This shelving of the problem of inequality until the socialist utopia is attained raises more questions than it solves. It leads to the refusal of some contemporary Marxists to recognise the relevance of differences in quality between public and co-operative housing provision, because on the one hand, the current housing system merely redistributes surplus-value produced under conditions of capitalist production and so is a secondary issue, and on the other, that in the socialist utopia all housing needs will be met automatically by the vast increase of productive forces, regardless of the form which the distribution of housing takes.[71] When applied to the problem of providing housing now, under a capitalist system, it leads to a crude egalitarianism, which dictates that all housing needs must be solved in the same way, en masse, and in strict order depending on how long people have been waiting for it; in Liverpool this has meant that co-operators, who have waited for thirty years or more to be rehoused from slum tenements, and who have struggled to provide their own solution, have been labelled elitist queue-jumpers.

What then of fraternity? Marx and Engels' analysis is pre-eminently one of the conflict between classes, rather than of social order. The idea of fraternity or community is seen as a bourgeois one, whose purpose is to mystify rather than to enlighten.[72] They see the history of all hitherto existing society as one of class struggles; the current struggle between bourgeoisie and proletariat is described as a 'more or less veiled civil war'.[73] Consequently, it is futile to seek for something which can only truly exist in a post-revolutionary, classless society. It is no use then for co-operative socialists to argue that the break-up of council estates into tenant-managed co-ops, and the setting up of housing co-ops in inner-

Human nature and co-operative values

city areas will create a better sense of community; the whole of society is entangled in an 'insoluble contradiction with itself', it has split into irreconcilable antagonisms which the state is powerless to dispel, contradictions which will only be overcome with the overcoming of the capitalist system of production.[74] Such a neglect of the value of existing communities has its outcome again in Liverpool; co-op members are accused by Militant housing officials of being reactionary for defending their close-knit communities against rehousing in council estates all over the city, and of being discriminatory for daring to want to choose their own neighbours.

Marx does not see the value of the sense of mutuality fostered by the locally-based consumer co-ops of his day:[75] 'as far as the present co-operative societies are concerned, they are of value only in so far as they are the independent creations of the workers, and not protégés either of the government or of the bourgeois.' Even worse, if co-ops do succeed in fostering a localised sense of community, and if this crosses class boundaries, they become a retrograde step from a class to a sectarian movement. Marx is worried that co-ops can *prevent* class conflict by diverting the working classes into activities which have a re-integrative effect; the measure of their apostasy from the class struggle is that ruling-class reformists (such as J.S. Mill) have at times 'become the full-mouthed apostles of co-opertive production'.[76] Yet he goes on to say that *after* the class struggle has done its work, co-ops can be seen in a positive light, but only, one suspects, as national-level institutions:

> If co-operative production is not to remain a sham and a snare; if it is to supersede the Capitalist system; if united co-operative societies are to regulate national production upon a common plan, thus taking it under their own control, and putting an end to the constant anarchy and periodical convulsions which are the fatality of Capitalist production – what else, gentlemen, would it be but Communism?[77]

Engels makes a similar point against the Lassalleans, that after the struggle with capital is over, 'co-operative production in industry and agriculture and on a national scale' will result.[78] It is not surprising, then, that Lenin should eventually turn to the co-operative method in reorganising the Soviet economy. And yet when he came to putting Marx and Engels' promises into practice in Soviet Russia, he failed to realise that (as the 'communitarians' were never tired of pointing out) the elements of a spontaneous fraternal order had always been to hand, in the urban co-operative societies and the village communes. In his naivety about the relationship between social structure and social order, he cleared away all those structures which stood between the individual and the national state co-operative, and then expected to organise spontaneous participation. He wished to tap the masses' sense of solidarity and community, and thought that it could be achieved 'without violence and without subordination', through state-sponsored co-operatives. History has not been on his side.

(d) *Communitarians*

Is it possible to combine liberty, equality and fraternity so as to maximise them all, or are there inevitable trade-offs to be made between them? More pessimistically, are they in permanent contradiction? Engels describes a situation in which all three were in some kind of equilibrium:

> All the members of an Iroquois gens were personally free, and they were bound to defend each other's freedom; they were equal in privileges and in personal rights, the sachems and chiefs claiming no superiority; and they were a brotherhood bound together by the ties of kin. Liberty, equality, and fraternity, though never formulated, were cardinal principles of the gens.[79]

Significantly, this judgment comes only in a footnote to his historical analysis of the growth of capitalist society. The task that communitarian socialists attempt is to bring such a footnote into the main text, to bring it to bear on problems of social structure in a modern post-industrial society; to try to discover forms of organisation which will once again promote all these values.[80] Their task is made harder by both the vastly increased division of labour and technological sophistication of a modern society, and by growth in individuality, which puts new demands on the notion of liberty.[81] Not surprisingly, given the difficulty of the task, their results fall roughly into two types: the liberal stress of Proudhon on freedom, and the communist stress of Kropotkin on community. Housing co-ops can be found which represent both these types.

What makes Proudhon distinctive among communitarian socialists is, despite a vigorous advocacy of co-operative forms, his admission of a lasting tension between individual liberty and association; the latter should only be entered into as required for needs of production, consumption and security.[82] His antinomic method allows him to argue both for a liberal and a socialist view of liberty. He defines liberty in the liberal way, as 'man's right to make use of his faculties, and to do so as he pleases',[83] without abusing others' right to equal liberty, and he also espouses the liberal pluralist view, that only in a multiplicity of associations can individual freedom be guaranteed. Yet he insists on two elements of a socialist understanding of liberty, the right to 'free use of land and materials', and the need to organise society as a whole so that abuses of liberty become increasingly impossible.[84] The comprehensiveness of his argument stems also from a practical appreciation of what it takes in reality to make the liberal ideal of the rounded, independent person; a training in both manual and mental work, access to the tools by which good work can be done, and through communion with others, access to a common heritage, shared well-being and identity of purpose. He is against both capitalist wage-slavery and communism, terming his 'third form of society' a 'synthesis of the community and of property, LIBERTY'.[85]

The same blend of liberal and socialist values issues in a precise attitude towards property. On the one hand, small-scale, dispersed property is necessary to guarantee liberty, but on the other, since all accumulated capital is collective property, created by previous generations, 'no-one may be its exclusive owner'.[86] On the one hand property is abused by capitalism, which obscures its positive organic function, while on the other, given a moral basis, and 'surrounded by protective, or more accurately, emancipating institutions' property is a guarantee of liberty. For Proudhon, the argument leads straight to a worker co-op economy, but there are strong grounds here also, for housing co-ops. The collective, functional property which they promote, has value in two senses; in a positive sense for the personal liberty of their members, providing the conditions for all-round personal growth through involvement in both the production and consumption of housing, and in a negative sense, for the liberty of citizens in general, providing a bulwark against the power of both the state and large-scale capital.

But will there not sometimes be tension between the individual and the association? GDH Cole points out that free institutions do not necessarily mean personal liberty, and individual participation in them should be seen as a voluntary surrender of powers. Consequently, co-operatives should be developed along functional lines, so that the individual is not totally reliant on any one group; housing co-ops might serve the domestic needs, worker co-ops the productive needs of the individual, as part of 'a number of relative and limited loyalties, of varying importance and intensity, but not essentially differing in kind'.[87] This notion of functional property is interesting; Tawney traces a historical development from a medieval economy in which property carried both rights and duties, to a free market economy in which the ownership of property was detached from all moral responsibility, and argues for the reinstatement of a functional against an acquisitive society. Although he does not recommend co-ops in particular, the principle of function, of property carrying with it both rights and duties, is particularly pertinent to housing co-ops; as we shall see further in Chapter 7, like other types of co-op, they follow the co-operative principles of fixed and limited interest on capital, the restriction of membership to users, the one person one vote principle and so on, which are key elements of any strategy for replacing absentee share capital with ownership and control by consumers and producers.[88] But is not public housing, run by democratic local authorities, as good as co-operative housing, in restoring rights and duties to property? Tawney is equivocal. Nor does Cole answer the question directly, as he is mainly concerned with producer co-operation, but his argument is equally serviceable in the sphere of consumption. He advocates the separation of the state from production in industry, because in order to safeguard liberty, there has to be a third way between bondage to the state or to capital; *self*-government in industry is a guarantee of political liberty.[89] On this argument, housing co-ops would always be superior to housing provision by local authorities, because they underpin local democracy with a tangible constituency of independent associations, which cannot be reduced to the 'municipal tutelage' of the local state.

Is Proudhon's worry about the liberty of the individual an exaggeration? Other co-operative thinkers have had no qualms about the safeguarding of liberty in co-operative association. Robert Owen thought that in his all-inclusive and largely self-sufficient co-operative communes there would be full liberty to express one's thoughts on all subjects; a rationally planned society would foster rational discourse and therefore 'mental liberty'; like Marx he under-estimated the non-rational forces latent in human character.[90] Kropotkin also attempts to justify the multi-functional commune against the separation of housing from worker and consumer co-ops, while giving more weight to the affective side, in his concept of mutual aid. Because he begins with the co-operating group which ensures the survival of the individual, he sees individuality as arising *out of* the mutal confidence of group members, which allows individual initiative to thrive, but in a non-egoistic way. He has no patience with the 'petty, unintelligent narrow-mindedness which, with a large class of writers, goes for "individualism" and "self-assertion", and considers the market individualist as the human equivalent of the bird of prey which waits for the off-fall from a more mutually supportive species; such individual freedom is not worth preserving.[91] But supposing that true individuality *can* only be fostered in mutualist institutions,[92] what protection is there from the danger of what Kropotkin himself called group egoism?[93] Here Martin Buber comes to Kropotkin's aid, with one major suppporing argument, that a commune movement (meaning specifically the Israeli Kibbutz) can be 'deeply involved in the process of differentiation and yet ... intent on preserving the principle of integration'; different forms can develop within a federation, which express different human types, and so can offer a choice of life-styles to the individual, along a continuum from individualistic to communistic.[94] This is a most important argument, which offers hope that, provided the movement is well enough developed, and providing it can hold together in federation despite widely differing life-styles (a problem with the Kibbutz example) individual freedom *could* be guaranteed within a framework of the all-round 'commune' type co-operative.

What is the significance of this discussion for housing co-ops? Firstly, although there are some commune-type co-ops, usually in large houses, and sometimes sharing common work and income as well as common living-space, most housing co-ops are of the restricted type favoured by Proudhon and Cole. Because they only involve that part of the individual concerned with the home environment, they may be expected not to pose much of a threat to personal freedom. And yet the home is for most co-op members a very important part of their lives, affecting health, family relationships, opportunities for work, recreation, social and kinship ties. When liberty is experienced, it comes in the form of opportunities for self-development, through co-operative education, access to the tools and skills which add use-value to the home, control of one's environment, the sense of shared purpose and of common property and so on. But when it is infringed, members may find it hard to uproot and begin life again somewhere else. This would be easier if the co-op sector were large and diverse; members could simply transfer to a co-op which suited their particular life-style. In countries such as Britain though, where co-ops are few and far between and it is hard to find alternative accommodation via owner-occupation or public housing, it is imperative that the rights of individual members are upheld; this is a question to which we shall return when looking at some actual examples of co-operative practice.

Communitarian arguments concerning equality are less easy to apply to housing co-ops. Because in Britain all the housing tenures are locked into various kinds of state subsidy, and because, in an extremely inegalitarian society, state subsidies will continue to be needed by co-ops, the communitarian arguments seem less relevant than those of collectivists who see a strong role for the state in redistributing wealth. Communitarians have been as keen as state socialists to promote equality as an end, but have (for reasons we will explore in the next chapter) rejected the idea of strong state intervention. They therefore have to posit some kind of co-operative economy, in which wealth will be generated by associations of workers and consumers, and distributed according to the co-operative principle of distribution according to work and consumption rather than capital. With the latter firmly put in its place (capital serving labour and the consumer, rather than, as at present, the other way round), rough equality between citizens would be guaranteed. Yet without a strong state to redistribute wealth, the goal has to be only *rough* equality of condition, ensured by a general availability of property as the tools of production. Like the liberal pluralists, Proudhon sees that the economic nature of co-ops means that, to some extent, there would be an equalising upwards rather than a levelling down. He is against complete equality, preferring a mean which allows some reward for effort, but within limits.

The communitarian view applies best to those kinds of co-ops which do not require state aid. Worker, consumer and agricultural co-ops, friendly societies, building societies, credit unions and so on, have always tried to be independent, and through the internal generation of capital reserves gradually to raise the standard of living of the disadvantaged. But housing is a peculiarly capital-intensive, long-lasting product, requiring a great deal of investment. Although some housing co-ops can be set up with private funding (an option we shall explore in the last chapter), and still offer real savings in housing costs to their members, those which set out to house the people most in need have to be locked into a state funding system which makes available subsidies either directly or via subsidised interest rates. Nevertheless, because housing co-ops also create surpluses (if to a lesser extent than do other more directly productive types of co-op) and then distribute them to members either equally or in proportion to labour or consumption, they also generate equality. In Canada and the USA, equality has been pursued within co-ops even more effectively, since it is common for higher-income members to agree to pay a higher rent, so that poorer members can have their rent reduced. During the Second World War, wives of men in New York co-ops who were drafted had their rent halved, and made up by an internal co-op subsidy. Moreover, co-operators, following Proudhon, have set definite limits to the kind of inequalities allowed; most 'secondary' co-ops (a type of co-op formed by the 'primary' co-ops as a development agency) operate an equal wage structure for their workers, sometimes topped up with special payments to meet family responsibilities.

However, other communitarians are more radical. Robert Owen aims at 'perfect equality' of a more exact kind in his proposal for co-operative villages. The mechanism for the maintenance of this would be (as in the Iroquois gens which so impressed Engels) constant redistribution within the co-operative according to need. Kropotkin follows this line, but goes further, taking the lesson from tribal societies (particularly the Eskimo) that in order to re-establish equality (and thus in the long run to safeguard fraternity) even personal property should be redistributed regularly. Few housing co-ops are this radical, though some of the commune types have a wage-pooling system, in which each contributes according to ability, and takes according to need. In Britain, most co-ops are set up under the Housing Corporation's 'fair rent' system, and are committed to housing those in greatest need, according to the size of accommodation needed. This also upholds the principle of equality of condition. Lastly, because they are to a limited extent wealth-generating, for instance through the efforts of members to do their own management and maintenance, co-ops can afford to assist each other with cash grants and loans. In this, they are fulfilling Proudhon's visions of a society of free associations, which voluntarily redistribute wealth not just within each co-op but within the movement as a whole.

Collectivist or state socialists often argue that on grounds of equality local state housing provision is to be preferred, since it allows rent pooling between older and newer housing estates, which equalises out the cost of similar housing. This is a powerful argument, except that its logic would point towards a pooling also between local councils, since some have the advantage of cheap land and a housing stock built when the cost of borrowing money was cheaper. There is no reason why a co-op cannot also pool rents; the SKB co-op in Stockholm does so between all of its 4,700 flats, but at the expense of the usual co-op emphasis on small scale. There is no reason in theory, though, why small co-ops could not operate a voluntary cross-subsidy, or why the state should not operate a quasi-rent-pooling device such as the British 'fair rent' system, in which co-op members pay a similar rent regardless of the actual building cost.

It is when we come to consider the third value of the trilogy, fraternity, that the case for housing co-ops really begins to strengthen. Because communitarian socialists are suspicious of the state, wanting either to abolish it outright, or at least to minimise its power, they above all other theorists pose the problem of social order in an acute and relentless way. Paradoxically, their radicalism seems at first sight to be rather conservative. Robert Owen is the first in a long line of anti-state socialists, to express a fundamental scepticism about political revolutions: 'it is absolutely necessary to support the old systems and institutions under which we now live, until another system and another arrangement of society shall be proved by practice to be essentially superior.'[95] He predicts that the breaking down of social order would result in a state of turmoil from which some of the democrats of the revolution would emerge as a new 'aristocracy'. Yet he is too sanguine about the prospects for avoiding class struggle by appeal to universal reason; though they would appreciate his faith, co-operators might question whether the overwhelming moral influence of the co-operative movement is sufficient to bring about radical social change.[96]

Proudhon's analysis is much tougher. He steers a course between the twin evils as he sees them of capital and the state. Market relations are seen as ruinous to social relations; in the competitive individualists's world: 'friend could legitimately, logically and scientifically ruin friend, or son abandon father and mother, or worker betray his employer'.[97] He boldly states what many suspect, that the market individualist's argument for liberty is a sophistry invented to abet the exploitation of the greatest number by the smallest. On the other hand, the state's social contract is a solidarity 'of a burdensome and often harazardous kind'; against Rousseau he argues that the abstractification of the real 'collective force' of the citizens sacrifices them to the state. Liberty and authority are like heat and cold, contrary principles which need to be contrasted with each other in order to have any meaning: 'One does not come without the other; one cannot suppress one or the other, or resolve the two into a single expression.'[98] So he needs to find a mechanism by which to create a working equilibrium between the two principles, a mechanism which will produce an unforced solidarity between people, which once discovered can be set to work spontaneously, without recourse to the coercion either of a competitive market or an authoritarian state. This is a tall order indeed. But Proudhon does discover such a mechanism. Like the market individualists, he sees social order as generated in the economic rather than the political sphere. The task is to solve economic problems so that individual and collective interests are at one, without, however, being reduced to each other.[99] Firstly, like Durkheim he sees social solidarity as rooted in those natural relations created by the division of labour, but (unimpeded by Durkheim's functionalist method)[100] he goes much further; only by changing the whole basis of the price mechanism through worker-owned enterprise, coupled with mutual guarantees between co-ops based on real productive potential, can liberty and order prosper together. Competition is replaced by co-operation on the basis of equal conditions of production.

There is more justification here for worker co-ops than for housing co-ops, though we can see how Proudhon's antinomy of authority and liberty might be brought into equilibrium in the latter by the mechanisms of equal right to participate in the means of consumption, and how the division of labour within a housing co-op might promote social solidarity. Kropotkin is of even greater significance in providing reasons for thinking that housing co-ops might produce a spontaneous social order, without recourse to either punishment of minorities or centralised authority. He has no need for antinomies, since he begins from a base-line of sociability in animals, and progresses in his analysis up the evolutionary scale to human beings, in whom association becomes more conscious and more extensive. Sociability, 'the need of the animal of associating with its like – the love of society for society's sake, combined with the "joy of life"' produce in every social group a sense of mutual recognition which results in mutual sympathy, 'a certain collective sense of justice growing to become a habit'.[101] Compassion is a natural outcome of social life, which produces a simple ethic expressed in the golden rule; do to others only what you would have them do to you under similar circumstances.[102] Through habitually living together in close proximity, housing co-op members can come to sympathise with each other, to treat each other as they would wish to be treated themselves. Is it a corollary of this, though, that fraternity is limited to the group, outside of which people are treated as at best strangers, at worst enemies? Kropotkin is optimistic that there can be a gradual extension of the size of the 'in-group', through the principle of federation; significantly, in almost every country where housing co-ops have been formed, steps have soon been taken towards forming a National Federation, and towards links with other co-operative sectors.

Can we assume with Kropotkin, that social order can safely be left to the 'constructive genius of the masses in their mutual aid institutions', that the progressive extension of co-operative forms into more and more areas of economic and social life will enable the state to 'wither away'? Unfortunately, while co-operative movements have waxed and waned over the last two centuries, at the same time there has been a much more powerful contrary development; the state has been intervening more and more, producing 'loose aggregates of individuals connected by no particular bonds, bound to appeal to the Government each time that they feel a common need.'[103] There is an obvious contrast here between housing co-ops, as mutual institutions, and council housing estates, creations of the state. Like the medieval guild, we can expect the co-op to be 'an association for mutual support in all circumstances and in all accidents of life'. (We shall see just how supportive they are when we look at some examples in Chapter 6.) Yet if, as Kropotkin admits, 'under the present social system, all bonds of union among the inhabitants of the same street or neighbourhood have been dissolved',[104] housing co-ops are bound to be affected by the alienation prevalent in the wider society. How far, really, are they able to create durable social bonds, to bind together people subjected elsewhere to all the pressures of competitive individualism and impersonal citizenship?

If they do turn out to be successful communities, then for Martin Buber they assume the utmost importance in a radical evolutionary strategy. They are the 'cell-tissue' of a new society, growing within the old: 'a living and life-giving collaboration, an essentially autonomous consociation of human beings, shaping and re-shaping itself from within'.[105] They preserve the community forms which remain within a society threatened with atomism between the twin forces of state and capital, and they fill them with a new spirit. Yet they have to steer between the twin internal dangers, of collective egoism, the sense of the organisation as having a life of its own to which the individual is subordinate, and share-capital individualism, the sense of the organisation as existing only for the benefit of individuals. To the extent that they are successful, housing co-ops will create a real, tangible socialism: 'The heart and soul of the Co-operative Movement is to be found in the trend of a society towards structural renewal, the reacquisition, in new tectonic forms, of the internal social relationship.'[106] Even more specifically, Buber claims that communitarian socialism in general (we might add, housing co-ops in particular) meets a 'need of man to feel his own house as a room in some greater, all-embracing structure in which he is at home, to feel that the other inhabitants of it with whom he lives and works are all acknowledging and confirming his individual existence'.[107]

But in his view it only meets these needs in the form of a commune. The partial community of the housing co-op alone is not enough; worker and consumer co-operation has to be built into it, in one multi-purpose association. To some extent this happens, whenever members extend the co-op's services through providing laundries, allotments, nurseries, play schools and so on. On the other hand, co-operators may wish to aim less high, to take less risks, and so preserve individual freedoms in the way Proudhon suggested they could, by fostering separate worker and consumer co-ops. Either way, it is clear that they represent for the communitarians an important and radical social formation, which it is worth promoting. Whether housing co-ops can actually bear the weight of such grand, some might say grandiose theory, remains to be seen, and we shall be presenting some case studies which help us to understand both their strengths and limitations. If they do prove disappointing to the communitarians, then at least they may live up to the more modest hopes of the liberal pluralists.

THREE
DEMOCRACY, THE STATE AND CO-OPERATIVE WELFARE

The average housing manager, planner or even co-op development worker does not go about his or her task with a conscious outlook on human nature, and a desire to maximise a particular constellation of liberty, equality and fraternity. These are buried deep in our world-views, and emerge in various attitudes to more tangible issues such as the value of democracy, the legitimacy and authority of the state, and the means by which social welfare should be produced and distributed. It is through the heat generated by these deeply held attitudes that housing policies, along with public policies in general, are forged.

(a) *Individualists*

As advocates of a social order based on market contracts, and of a state whose main purpose is to provide conditions under which contractual exchange can safely be undertaken, the competitive individualists are unsympathetic to Rousseau's idea of a hypothetical *social* contract between citizens and the state; they want to see it before they will agree to sign! Democracy is accepted not as an ultimate value, but simply as one way of legislating among others. Consequently, the degree of extension of the right to vote is a matter of expediency, and if there is majority rule, it must be limited by principles the minority also accepts.[1] In Hayek's evolutionary view, the results of majoritarian democracy are usually bad; it is always minorities which have the best ideas, and by the time an idea becomes the majority view, it is no longer the best idea. There is no appreciation here then of the collectivist argument that council housing is provided by a representative democracy, or of the communitarian argument that co-ops are direct democracies. There is justification, though, for the type of housing development organisation the present Conservative government in

Britain supports: large housing associations and private development trusts, which may have some token tenant representation, but which are heavily geared towards innovation at the expense of dweller control.

Such indifference towards the claims of democracy is accompanied by abhorrence of the state, which is criticised on several grounds. Firstly, it tends towards a centralisation of power which, despite greater and greater inefficiency, goes on growing unchecked. In the sphere of housing, even the most bitter opponents of the market individualist world-view have to admit that they have a point. Consider the sheer size which some local authority housing departments have reached in Britain, such as the Greater London Council which at one time had a stock of a quarter of a million dwellings, and Glasgow, which with a stock of around 180,000 is now the largest municipal landlord in Europe. Seven councils have more than 50,000 dwellings to look after, and another 52 have between 20,000 and 50,000. It has proved almost impossible to run such huge operations efficiently; as Tony McBrearty, housing chairman of the GLC just before its abolition, admitted: 'The GLC was a lousy landlord. Its stock was badly maintained and badly managed.'[2] Centralised management and maintenance have been shockingly wasteful of resources, until their cost has in some London boroughs begun to exceed the rental income altogether, even as the service has continued to deteriorate.[3]

Secondly, the individualists claim that the state is a danger to personal liberty. Again they have a point. In relation to council housing, personal liberty has been infringed in several ways. Housing managers could have seen their relationship with tenants as a purely contractual one, like that in the private rented sector, and this would in fact have been preferable to the relationship that they have traditionally fostered, that of the philanthropist and supplicant. Hence what Colin Ward calls 'municipal serfdom', the petty and overbearing wording of many tenancy conditions, which assumed that tenants would, if not expressly forbidden, keep coals in the bath and pigeons in the loft. Hence the fact that until recently council tenants in Britain had no security of tenure, and threat of eviction could be used against anyone considered a nuisance by the housing managers.[4] Hence also the discriminatory allocation policies which have sent people defined as 'problem families' to certain estates which have then been stigmatised and denied a repair service, so that the definition of the problem becomes in time, self-fulfilling. Hence the institutionalised racism which has time and again been shown up in reports on allocation policies, even in areas like the London borough of Tower Hamlets, where ethnic minorities are in desperate need.[5] The market individualists have been quick to exploit the discontent which this has caused; Alex Henney, for example, turns the argument about liberty on its head, and claims that only half of council tenants would choose to be so, if they had a free choice.[6]

Thirdly, state action has unintended consequences, which lead to more action to alleviate the original action, in an upward spiral of state spending and legislation. The favourite example, cited by Spencer and in almost exactly the same language by Friedman a hundred years later,[7] is that of slum clearance; well-meaning attempts to demolish slums have resulted in the displacement of the population to nearby areas which then become slums through overcrowding. This is not quite true of the post-war slum clearance in Britain, which was accompanied by offers of rehousing. However, as the bulldozers drove inexorably on, clearance began to mean that people who lived in quite decent terraced houses which in many cases they owned, have been forcibly rehoused in peripheral housing estates. Then when these new estates were in many instances found to have serious faults in design and construction, the spiral continued with a rapid decline into worse slums than they had replaced, with increased state spending to alleviate the new problem.

Fourthly, they argue that by providing housing outside a free market, council housing suppresses price signals, which are the normal way in which costs are controlled and consumers express preferences. Once this vital link between supply and demand is lost, all welfare services become inherently wasteful on the supply side, and restrict consumer choice on the demand side; as Henney puts it, since one in six council tenants are dissatisfied with their housing, 'seldom has so great an expenditure yielded so little satisfaction'.[8] Conservative government policy in Britain has therefore been to promote the sale of council houses, either to the tenants or to property companies, and to convert subsidised rents to more 'realistic' levels which reflect consumer demand, so that the rigours of the market-place are in one way or another restored.

Fifthly, they argue that state aid changes people's character for the worse, making them dependent and sapping their personal and group initiative; the demoralisation of many council tenants, their lack of pride and involvement in their home environment, their reliance on the landlord to do every repair, are seen as the result of an inherently dependent relationship. Co-operators would agree in one respect, that the talents, skills and energy of council tenants are wasted when they have no way of combining them with self-management and the rewards which accrue from it. Sixthly, since the state is seen as only acting legitimately in its functions of defence, law and order and the promotion of those public works which cannot be privatised, support is given sparingly and grudgingly to state-funded welfare; hence the small and in Britain diminishing funds allocated to the Housing Corporation for spending on housing association and co-operative schemes. The state's main function is seen as to act as an umpire within the market, enforcing the rules of free competition, but not guaranteeing everyone a home to live in.

Because of the bad record of state-provided housing, the arguments are more convincing in this area than they might be had state subsidies gone to a more effective form such as co-operatives. In fact, all over the industrialised world, council housing has become so unpopular that it is being decentralised, sold off or handed over to tenant management co-ops. In the United States, the House of Representatives recently passed a bill that encourages tenant management corporations and sale to individual tenants at massive 75 per cent discounts. In Scandinavia, the development has been along different lines, with separate municipal housing companies managing all but 154,000 of the 2.2m dwellings in social ownership. But still, in Sweden the 13 largest of these have over 21,000 dwellings in stock, and they are being decentralised, or transferred to either ownership or management co-ops.[9] Within all of these government policies, whether promoted by market individualist or social democratic governments, tenant management and ownership co-ops have received increasing support.

We know now what kind of welfare the individualists do not want to promote, but how, without state provision of housing, do they propose to house those who cannot afford to buy or rent in the private market-place? Two types of justificatory argument are used here, one from first principles and one from utility: firstly, the market has its justification in natural rights which protect the liberty of the individual; go outside the market and you lose your liberty. Secondly, the market is in any case the most efficient way of producing wealth; some might remain homeless, but the sum total of welfare is greater than it would have been under any other system. Put together, these arguments mean that the right of the individual to keep his or her property are 'essential prerequisites for individual welfare'.[10] When the state taxes people's wealth in order to provide, say, subsidised housing, if it is not very careful, it will actually reduce both their liberty and their welfare. For instance, welfare spending necessitates taxes on capital, which forces businesses to move to countries where there are less taxes, and so leads to loss of jobs, and a *decline* in the sum of welfare produced. To counter this, the state may take powers to plan and regulate the market, but these are invariably clumsy and inefficient, since the complexity of the market defeats such planning. As Hayek says, 'We have never designed our economic system. We were not intelligent enough for that.'[11]

If the market provides for a maximum of human welfare, we might ask why there should be state welfare spending at all, in countries ruled by market individualist type governments; in order to ensure the uninterrupted production of wealth, its distribution via the outcomes of free market transactions *has* to remain unimpeded. Moreover, since everyone has the chance to maximise his or her personal welfare, poverty can be blamed on the poor, as the result of a failure to deal in the market effectively.[12] However, social expenditures can be justified to some extent; providing a minimal income for the poor is an expedient way of ensuring one of the state's legitimate functions: law and order. It coerces the citizen who is taxed, so as to avoid greater coercion by those disaffected citizens who are too poor to see the justice of the market individualist's argument! However, the state's providing a subsidy outside the market is one thing, but the actual provision of housing is another; it should be provided by almost any means other than directly by the state. Where housing co-ops receive state subsidy, then, as in the 'fair rent' type co-ops in Britain, it is justified as part of a pragmatic expenditure on the poor, which ensures social order while not increasing the size of state bureaucracy.

(b) Pluralists

The liberal pluralist view of democracy provides once again weak but firm grounds for the promotion of co-ops. J.S. Mill's writing on the subject is mainly concerned with national-level democracy, but parts of his theory could equally well describe small-scale direct democracies such as co-ops. When he talks of 'government', let us have in mind the small as well as the large scale. He describes government as a combination of two elements: the political *structure* or machinery which is capable of being planned on the basis of principle, and the *process* by which the machinery is worked in real situations, which

Democracy, the state and co-operative welfare

depends on the 'opinions, tastes and habits of the people'.[13] For a government to work, three conditions are needed:

1 that people are willing to accept this particular form of government,
2 that they are willing to keep it going, and
3 that they will do what is required of them to fulfil its purpose.

It follows that good government depends on the qualities of the citizens, and on their will to participate in it, and that the machinery must be designed so that it can be worked by people at the stage of political virtue which they have actually reached.[14] It is no use putting people in housing co-ops if they are not prepared to participate.

On the other hand, structure can act back on the process, so that a good form of government can improve the people: 'We may consider then, as one criterion of the goodness of a government, the degree in which it tends to increase the sum of good qualities in the governed, collectively and individually.'[15] In fact, the type of authority exercised over people, and the distribution of power, are seen as (excepting religion) the most formative influences on human character; and so putting people in housing co-ops may actually make them into better people. But unlike the great utopian co-operator, Robert Owen (who allowed just anyone to join his communities, in the expectation that they would become good co-operators just by being there, and then watched them fail), Mill realises that people cannot change fundamentally overnight, or even within one generation. This means that housing co-ops, as political systems, are to be judged by the extent to which they are appropriate to the level of development which their members and potential members have reached. If they are appropriate, they will encourage the members to participate, and in the process become better people. But if they are not appropriate, because through adherence to old habits, defects of character or ignorance, the members are not prepared to participate actively, then the co-ops will degenerate into oligarchies or factional forms of government. In such cases paternalistic but responsible housing associations or local authority housing departments may be preferable. Yet Mill is adamant that there is no substitute for democracy, and that it should be available to all the people. Only by being fully participating citizens can people exercise their freedom of choice and thereby grow in character.

Unfortunately though (from our point of view), Mill fails to apply his argument to small-scale direct democracies. Because his focus is on national-level governments, and because he denies that direct democracy is possible in large-scale modern society, he settles for representative-type government as the goal to be achieved, and then devotes all his arguments to making this work, through proportional representation, separation of powers, and so on. Because he is sceptical of there being a sufficiently large educated public, he puts his faith in local councils as the main school for democracy, along with, of all things, jury service! Nevertheless, as Pateman points out, despite the unsatisfactory nature of his proposals, dominated as these are by fear of the potential power of the working classes, his argument for participatory democracy still stands.[16] Take, for example, this statement: 'Every one is degraded, whether aware of it or not, when other people, without consulting him, take upon themselves unlimited power to regulate his destiny.'[17] Such a statement could well be a description of the way in which the local government housing and planning system in Britain has, despite being under the nominal control of a representative democracy, so often worked against ordinary people at the most local level.[18] Not surprisingly, liberal pluralists working at this level have applied Mill's argument to good effect. For instance, while Mill himself was sceptical about extending democracy down to parish councils, universal education and the increasing remoteness of so-called local government have led to the use of his own arguments to advocate the extension of the parish council to urban neighbourhoods.[19] It is only a short step from here to the argument that housing co-ops, among other neighbourhood-based organisations, can foster participation in such councils, as well as contributing to the general political education of citizens.

However, there seems no natural stopping place within such arguments between liberal pluralist and more radical communitarian socialist views of democracy, except on the grounds of practicality. These may be grounds enough, though. For instance, Dahl and Tufte remind us that even though Mill dismissed direct participatory democracy, it is still alive in co-op type organisations.[20] But they too have reservations, pointing to the limitations of direct participation in such fundamentals as the range of an unamplified voice, the need to limit the time spent in debate and so on. Even if Rousseau's special conditions were met, such as rough equality, frugality and self-sufficiency in the small city-state, they see the elements of a political tragedy in such a state's vulnerability to larger, more ruthless neighbours.[21] Yet the view that small-scale democracies are necessary to the larger citizenship becomes even more persuasive, against the background of an increasingly alienated mass politics in the modern liberal democracy:

> very small units seem to us necessary to provide a place where ordinary people can acquire the sense and the reality of moral responsibility and political effectiveness in a universe where remote galaxies of leaders spin on in courses mysterious and unfathomable to the ordinary citizen.[22]

The problem as they see it, though, is that the smaller the unit, the more insignificant the activity, and so participation runs up against a lack of motivation in the citizen. However, housing co-ops ought to surmount this obstacle, since unlike tenants' or residents' associations, they combine small size with the exercise of some vital collective functions.

Arguments for political participation at the local level are also strengthened by the pluralists' fear of centralised state power, which has sponsored arguments ranging from Mill's elaborate scheme for proportional representation, through the modern pluralist emphasis on the balancing effects of interest groups, to Dahl's reformulation of the liberal goal as 'polyarchal' democracy.[23] Polyarchy demands that eight conditions be approximated to:

1 that every member votes,
2 that identical weights be given to each vote,
3 that the greatest number wins,
4 that any preferred alternative course can be inserted for consideration,
5 that all voters possess identical information about the alternatives available,
6 that the alternative with the greatest number of votes wins,
7 that the orders of elected officials are actually carried out, and
8 that elections are the controlling factor.

These hard conditions may be attained, if anywhere, in small co-ops. However, what even this reformulated liberal position fails to demonstrate is how even the most perfect democracy on a small scale can materially affect the problems of large-scale representative government. In answering this question one is drawn eventually along a continuum towards communitarian socialist arguments.

For example, MacPherson criticises liberal 'developmental democracy' for attempting to foster self-development while refusing to remedy deep-seated inequalities, and criticises its pluralist reformulation for avoiding the class nature of government in such an unequal society.[24] His goal of participatory democracy is something to move towards, not just a moral underpinning of representative government, and it entails a strategy of incremental (but radical) change based on neighbourhood and community associations coupled with worker control of industry. A pyramidal system of democratic councils would be built up from these building blocks, eventually to provide a tangible base for self-development by remedying inequalities and *replacing* party government. Similarly Pateman, while stressing Mill's educational role for participatory voluntary associations, sees these as promoting social and political action which goes beyond liberal requirements, towards the communitarian society envisaged by G.D.H. Cole.[25] While some firm arguments for housing co-ops can be found in the pluralist world-view, it seems to be the communitarians who bring out their full implications.

What does all this imply for economic and social welfare? Mill criticises the market individualists' world-view by pointing out that progress in creating wealth may be at the sacrifice of virtue, that there is more to life than merely the acquiring of material goods. Yet he believes in competition and a modified market economy; he hopes that through worker co-ops the antagonism of classes might be overcome, without too much sacrifice of productive efficiency,[26] and this hope is reflected in modern liberal policies towards worker participation in industry and the encouragement of small businesses, including co-ops.[27] Yet liberals are prepared to live with the contradictions inherent in what T.H. Marshall calls the 'hyphenated society' of democratic-welfare-capitalism in which the two antagonistic value-systems of welfare and the market are kept in an 'uneasy equilibrium of opposites' by the democratic political process.[28] There is a need for production which can only be met by a free market, a need for rights to welfare which can only be met by a welfare 'consciousness' which stands completely outside the market, and a need for consensus between these two antinomic but interdependent value systems, which can only be met by political bargaining in a pluralist democracy.

The role of co-op type associations in this view of social welfare is theoretically quite substantial, and it is worth looking in more detail at how such a view has developed in Britain over the last fifty years. We begin with William Beveridge, the liberal architect of the British welfare state, who wanted to combine the 'old spirit of social advance by brotherly co-operation', which he found in the friendly society, consumer co-op, mutual savings banks, housing societies, trade unions and so on, with the universality and comprehensiveness of state social welfare. The advantages of the former include their ability to meet felt needs, their diversity and vigour of growth, and their ability (through members' knowledge of each other) to generate fraternity. In sketching out the lines of a future welfare state, he was certain that 'the spirit of mutual aid among all classes ... must continue in one form or another, if the Britain of the future is to be worthy of the past.'[29] Yet when it came to implementing a comprehensive social insurance scheme and national health service just after the Second World War, the incoming Labour government found it impractical to base their organisation on the existing network of co-operative type friendly societies, and opted instead for state bureaucracies. Since then, in the development of social policy, there has been tension between two contrasting goals; that of efficiency in service-delivery, which has resulted in larger and more bureaucratic welfare services and the enhancement of the power and prestige of professionals, and that of attempting to decentralise welfare services so as to provide some tangible basis for a sense of community, to provide consumers with a right to consultation and so on. Size has generally triumphed over democracy, though not without having to concede some ground: the introduction of community health councils with the reorganisation of the National Health Service in 1974, the emphasis in the Seebohm Report on community-based social services which should foster mutual aid, the rights to consultation offered in the Skeffington Report on local planning, the advocacy of community councils by the Royal Commission on Local Government, and of course, the increasing advocacy of co-operative housing.[30]

As a fellow-liberal, following in Beveridge's footsteps, T.H. Marshall began to struggle with these contradictions, changing his view even as the lessons of large-scale, bureaucratised delivery of housing, health and education were being learned. At first, he described Beveridge's idea of the welfare state in idealistic terms as an extending of co-operative mutual aid to the national level, so that it created a sense of common citizenship, which permeates the life of a whole society. Thus, he described the National Health Service almost as if it were a co-operative, as 'a system of mutual aid operated by the citizens, through parliament.'[31] Yet later he began to detect a decline in the welfare consciousness of citizens from the mutualist feeling of the post-war 'austerity society' to the more individualistic feeling of the later 'affluent society', a decline which he felt signalled danger to the rights to welfare, which rely on 'a conception of a community dedicated to providing for the vital needs of its members by systems of mutual aid'.[32] He noted that state social insurance no longer carried the message of this welfare consciousness, and that market values were encroaching more and more on that consensus which had produced, and was needed to sustain, a comprehensive welfare system. What then was the solution to this dilemma? He suggested that: 'We need to develop a new model so adjusted to the conditions of the time that it may once more become a central part of a social system accepted by all.'[33] This new model of welfare would include general arguments concerning citizenship, promulgated by welfare professionals, but it would also involve the promotion of co-ops and self-help groups, and the preservation of the 'remnants' of a sense of local community.[34]

While Marshall provided only hints as to what this new model of welfare would entail, others have recently developed it more substantially. Gladstone, for example, has coined the phrase 'radical welfare pluralism', to describe a new outlook based on Beveridge's appreciation of mutualist welfare, adapted to the conditions of a state-dominated welfare system, but intended to break out of the stalemate of arguments between state collectivism and market individualism.[35] The role of the state would be restricted to the equalising of resources, and the sponsoring and regulation of voluntary action, except where there is a natural monopoly such as in acute hospital provision. He sees housing associations as a paradigm of how rapid growth can be achieved in voluntary provision, when combined with state promotion and regulation. The result would be a long-term, gradualist evolution of decentralised, destandardised and deprofessionalised services. Similarly, Hadley and Hatch argue for 'pluralist, decentralised and participative patterns of service' and criticise state bureaucracy and professionally dominated services, the lack of consumer participation, the inability of a centralising state to foster fraternity, and so on.[36] They trace the growing crisis of the welfare state, caught between a no-growth economy and an increasingly alienated citizenry, and list the elements of the alternative: participatory democracy, decentralisation, the nurturing of change from 'below', accountability to users, and the reduction of the role of the state to monitoring and developing this plurality of voluntary services, within a framework of social security.

There is, however, an ambiguity which none of these writers have resolved. Just what sort of voluntary association is it that is to be promoted? After all, there are large differences between such associations in size, degree of efficiency, ability to innovate, type of management structure, level of accountability to, and participation by, consumers and workers. Hadley and Hatch talk of local, open management, with employee participation, consumers' right to information and to form user groups. But like Gladstone and Beveridge, they see housing *associations* in general, rather than co-ops in particular, as the way forward. Beveridge had in fact made the same mistake, including housing associations under his category of 'mutual aid', when in fact they were models of philanthropy. He admitted that there were few housing 'co-partnerships' (an old form of co-op), without drawing the obvious conclusion that most associations were paternalistic and highly undemocratic forms. Even now, after having experienced huge growth and an increasingly key role in government housing policy, most British housing associations are (unlike their counterparts in say, Denmark), totally undemocratic, being managed by a voluntary, un-elected management committee, without consumer representation. Liberal pluralists provide some firm arguments for reliance on localised voluntary associations in social welfare delivery, in which there would be some element of consumer participation. What they do not quite provide is an argument for the specifically *co-operative* form.

(c) Collectivists

The collectivists' approach to democracy is coloured by Marx and Engels' famous declaration: 'The executive of the modern state is but a committee for managing the common affairs of the whole bourgeoisie.'[37] Two points have to be noted. Firstly, the capitalist state manages the affairs of the *whole* bourgeoisie, and so has 'relative autonomy' from the short-term interests and preferences of actual capitalists. This gives rise to functional views of the state, which attempt to show how it has the particular function of reproducing the conditions in which capitalist accumulation can take place, by ensuring the reproduction of capital and labour power, and of the social relations on which these depend.[38] Secondly, it is the *modern* state which has these features; as Engels reminds us, it has developed historically with capitalism, and is still developing.[39] This means that while state power is assuming more and more the character of the national power of capital over labour, it is also subject to inroads by the

Democracy, the state and co-operative welfare

proletariat, which means that it can to some extent be turned against the bourgeoisie.[40] Engels says:

> the modern representative state is an instrument of exploitation of wage labour by capital. By way of exception however, periods occur in which the warring classes balance each other so nearly that the state power, as ostensible mediator, acquires, for the moment, a certain degree of independence of both.[41]

But the exception only proves the rule, that this state is a capitalist state, and so, although the proletariat can use the democratic freedoms it allows, the ultimate aim must be to smash it. The 'battle of democracy' only begins to be won when the proletariat is raised to the position of ruling class. There are at least two implications of this. Firstly, democratic processes are not valuable in themselves; if 'universal suffrage is the gauge of the maturity of the working class',[42] it cannot be anything more, because it is immediately transcended by the supreme political act, revolution. Secondly, working-class strategies which rely on state aid are doomed to be merely reformist; the aim is to transcend, not to harness the democratic state. The most Engels can allow for the Lassallean plan for state-aided co-operatives is that they are one 'subordinate transitional measure', among many others.[43] If this were the last word, it would mean an almost completely negative Marxist view of housing co-ops, but as we shall see, with the advent of the more reformist strategy of 'Euro-communism', Marxists may be rethinking this position. If they are to advance through the maturing of the working class and a creative use of the ballot box, then it follows that many of the political liberal justifications for small-scale democracies, as educators to larger political consciousness, could be utilised, if for a more radical end.

But even for Marxist revolutionaries is there not a role for co-ops among other democratic working-class organisations, firstly in prefiguring the socialist society, so as to provide an insight into what might be possible, and secondly, in helping along the transition to socialism when it comes? This depends on what sort of socialist society is envisaged, and the problem is that Marx and Engels refused in their writings to be specific. They were afraid of speculating about the way in which a socialist society would organise itself once the capitalist state was captured, claiming that as scientists they were only discovering laws which had to be observed as they unfolded. Nevertheless they were stung into a sketchy prescription by the persistent criticism of anarchists (or what we have called 'communitarians'), who insisted on a guarantee that during both the pre-revolutionary struggle and the revolutionary transition, democratic processes would be safeguarded; as we shall see further below (when we come to the communitarian point of view), they were worried that in the throes of revolution a worse tyranny, of the revolutionary party, might simply replace that of the capitalist. Engels' impatient reply was that: 'with the introduction of the socialist order of society, the state will dissolve of itself and disappear.'[44] But how can he be so certain? Instead of hard evidence from revolutionary practice, Engels offers a definitional conjuring trick which runs like this: since the state is an instrument of class rule, and since the revolutionary proletariat abolish class rule, then they also abolish the state 'as state'.[45] More substantial is his supporting argument from history, that since the state grew out of a need by a minority oppressor class to ensure social order, then this main function of the state will become unnecessary. But this does not really deal with the possibility that a new minority, the leaders of the revolution, for instance, might create a new kind of state in order to perpetuate their own power. In his view, after the revolutionary overthrow of the state, all that is left of it is 'the administration of things and ... the conduct of processes of production'.[46]

After the experience of the Paris Commune in 1848, Marx felt confident (speaking not from some personal utopian vision but out of analysis of the 'laws' which the Commune's practice revealed), that in such a revolution the 'armed people' would replace the old practice of having a professional standing army, that representatives would be chosen by universal suffrage and would be revocable on short-term tenure, that the commune would be both executive and legislature, and that public service would be done at workman's wages. There is no doubt that this is a powerful prescription for democracy: 'Instead of deciding once in three or six years which member of the ruling class was to misrepresent the people in Parliament, universal suffrage was to serve the people, constituted in communes.'[47] Such a view *could* lead straight to advocacy of co-ops. Rudolf Bahro, for example, links this idea of the Commune immediately replacing the state with a positive interpretation (more positive than the one Buber gave when we quoted it in the last chapter) of Marx's remark about united co-operative societies regulating national production on a common plan, and he sees the 'edifice of social life' as being built upon the communes.[48] Does this mean that housing co-ops (as multi-functional communes) might form part of the socialist plan, to take effect immediately after the revolution? Unfortunately, one has to bear in mind that Bahro, writing at this time from East Germany, was finding it necessary to find arguments from within the Marxist canon, against the tyranny of the Soviet state.[49] If Marx *had* been so clearly favourable towards small-scale co-ops or communes, it would be difficult to explain his sharp and continued antagonism towards anarchists such as Proudhon.

The point at which Marx differs, and it is a decisive one, *is* on the question of scale. He says that the Commune had been 'mistaken for an exaggerated form of the ancient struggle against over-centralisation', but that its true significance is as essentially a working-class government; it is its revolutionary power which impresses Marx, not its potential as a federative body, produced out of small co-operative units.[50] Yet there is still potential here. Engels describes his idea of the post-revolutionary society like this: 'Society, which will reorganise production on the basis of a free and equal association of the producers, will put the whole machinery of state where it will then belong: into the museum of antiquities.' He then gives tacit approval to the hope expressed by one of his sources, Morgan, that the next, higher plane of society 'will be a revival, in a higher form, of the liberty, equality and fraternity of the ancient gentes'. Now this takes us full circle to the argument of the last chapter; the 'gentes' are the Iroquois tribal communities which, as we have seen, ought to imply a decentralised society, organised in communes and worker co-ops, based on direct democracy, and with a federal structure.[51] Yet, as Lenin points out, it is the necessity of systematically imbuing the masses with the need for a violent revolution, undertaken by the organised working class, which lies at the root of Marx and Engels' theory, and he reminds us of Engels' saying: 'A revolution is certainly the most authoritarian thing there is.'[52] What follows for Lenin is the need for a vanguard party to lead the proletariat, and then for the dictatorship of the proletariat to lead the whole people towards a centralised socialism which, because of the ambiguities in Marx, Lenin can claim to be what the latter originally envisaged: 'Marx was a centralist. There is no departure whatever from centralism in his observations.'[53] And yet this is coupled with an equally strong assertion that communism alone is capable of providing really complete democracy, so complete in fact, that even democracy will wither away, and there will be no important decisions to make. Faced with such complacency, the claims of co-operators that co-ops are a training ground for socialism can make no headway.

Democracy, the state and co-operative welfare

How, then, do the collectivists view social welfare in general, and housing in particular? The present capitalist mode of production is condemned for not providing for people's real needs. Even though it is the working class which creates productive wealth, the concentration of capital, the inherently unfair competition between capital and labour, the introduction of machine-intensive production and so on, conspire to cheat this class of all but the means to bare subsistence. Even then, subsistence is not guaranteed to all; the fabled equilibrium of supply and demand, which is supposed to make the market the most efficient mode of production and distribution, is seen as disguising the inherent disorder of fluctuations in price, which drive the workers now above, now below the level of subsistence. Marx brilliantly reverses the market individualists' economic laws, pointing out that: 'With just as much right, one could regard the fluctuations as the law, and the determination by the cost of production as chance.'[54] The result is a deepening and insoluble contradiction, that while the relentless competition of the capitalist market creates a colossal productive potential, competition also takes place between the workers for fewer and less skilled jobs, so that they cannot afford to consume what they have made. Epidemics of over-production coincide with continuing poverty, or as Engels puts it, we have: 'a society suffocating from its own superfluity, while the great majority of its members is scarcely, or even not at all, protected from extreme want.'[55]

Suppose, then, that the working class provides for its own welfare, in democratically controlled enterprises? Engels describes 'co-operative societies for retail trade and production' as having 'given practical proof that the merchant and the manufacturer are socially quite unnecessary'.[56] Yet in this theory of history there is no room for them; the historic role of capitalism is to *supersede* the guild system, to develop the productive forces to the point where the separation of capital from labour is total, where the workers are progressively immiserated, but the means of production (both capital and labour) are centralised. The next step is the inevitable and simple one, of a revolutionary appropriation of capital by political means, and the introduction of a planned economy, in which salaried employees of the state take over the functions of the bourgeoisie in directing production. But at this point, the prophecy becomes frankly utopian: 'with the take-over by society of the productive forces, the social character of the means of production and of the products will be utilised by the producers with a perfect understanding of its nature.'[57] The result is a 'practically unlimited' development of the productive forces, which will guarantee to meet the needs of all. Now we can understand why Lenin asserted that in the second, communist stage of the revolution, even democracy would wither away; if there is no scarcity, and production has been reduced to a few easy administrative routines which anyone can perform, no decisions need to be made which require the people's assent. In the light of such a blinding vision of a communist 'land of cockayne', it is no wonder that the significance of the co-operative society can hardly be seen. Yet it is a *blinding* vision, that is one which avoids hard questions about the ecological limits of economic development, about the inherent inefficiency of centralised production, about the impossibility (in the absence of market-price signals) of knowing what the consumers want, about the imperfections in human nature which might render the definition of need still problematic, and so lead to intra-class conflict, the rise of a bureaucratic power-elite, and so on.[58] Consideration of such problems can lead to fruitful discussion of socialist markets, in which co-ops would provide decentralised forms of common ownership, while consumers would be able to influence the course of production and the price of products through the exercise of effective demand, thus avoiding centralised bureaucratic planning and administration.[59]

However, this does not clarify the role of housing co-ops in particular. For this we need to consider Marxist analyses of *social* welfare under capitalism, and their conception of how housing and other social needs would be met under socialism. Recently, Marxist writers have developed a very complex view of social welfare, which reflects the complexity of their view of the nature of the state. Firstly, welfare functions in a capitalist society to reproduce working-class people as 'labour power' and to ensure the profitability of capital. Some social expenditures actually bring a return to capital, by providing industrial infrastructures and subsidising this reproduction of labour power. But others, particularly social control measures, are a direct charge on the profitability of capital. Because of the crisis of underconsumption and a growing pool of surplus labour, the problem of social order grows, and so spending increases, giving rise to a 'fiscal crisis'.[60] This means that struggles in the sphere of production against private capital can be supplemented by struggles in the sphere of consumption, against the state, thus deepening this crisis.

But what of those non-state institutions, such as co-ops, which also attempt to provide for social welfare? The simple answer is that they are irrelevant, because, in the interest of capital, the state is taking over welfare functions formerly carried out by the working class itself. In Gough's view, it is 'gradually usurping the role of kinship and community in the past, and of charitable and voluntary bodies in the more recent past'.[61] What few occupational, charitable or voluntary forms of welfare provision are left are financially dependent on and regulated by the state. The argument carries some conviction: given that housing co-ops must, if they are to house the most needy, become locked into a system of state funding and supervision, from the point of view of independent working-class action they must be seen to be compromised. Similarly, Ginsburg points out that the continual restructuring of the state apparatus in response to both the centralising of capital and working class power, has: 'paradoxically forced the gradual removal of the potential for democratic control which to some extent existed in previous structures'.[62] Even though, as he admits, there is widespread working-class ambivalence towards state welfare, disillusionment and suspicion created by negative individual and collective experiences, yet there is no alternative to state service delivery, because bureaucratism and administrative remoteness are essential devices for rationing welfare benefits according to criteria of 'deservingness', and for containing pressure for change. There is no rationale here for overcoming such remoteness by the autonomous administration of welfare goods, such as housing, by working-class people themselves. The points of departure for creating critical and progressive strategies simply do not lie in this direction.

What kinds of working-class organisation are required, then, in order to intensify the struggle over state welfare? In the catalogues provided by Marxist writers, co-ops are rarely mentioned. Gough lists social service trade unions, welfare professionals, and clients' movements such as claimants' unions, women's aid, squatting and self-help groups. Self-help is generally seen as a market individualist concept, and it is significant that Gough includes these groups not because they attempt to meet their members' needs through mutual aid, but because they 'have called for the extension of some or other aspect of the welfare state'.[63] Another list includes tenants' associations, Labour local authorities, trade unions and trades councils as the main agencies of working-class action; tenants' associations are not seen as potential agencies for a 'tenants' takeover' of council estates, but as one form in which mass pressure can be exerted for more public spending.[64] On housing in particular, another writer lists struggles over a Conservative housing finance act, squatting and rent strikes as significant, with a national tenants' organisation as the ideal instrument of struggle; local, autonomous housing co-ops simply do not fit into a strategy aimed at a centralised state.[65] Moreover, a sense of localised community allows the working class to be fragmented by sectional loyalties which weaken their mass base, and divert them into pressing for small-scale reforms for which they have to compete against each other.[66]

Sometimes, Marxist writers seem tantalisingly near to seeing the advantages of co-ops, but then fail to make the connection. Cockburn describes squatting in terms which could also apply directly to housing co-ops: 'Squatting is not only a practical solution to individual housing need, it is a statement about property and ownership. As such it is a political movement.'[67] It involves people living more communally, 'in a more co-operative and mutually supportive style than families are normally accustomed to do'.[68] What, then, of the significance of the more mundane but even more fundamental statement co-operative common ownership makes about property and ownership, and the mutual support co-op members can give? Firstly, any attraction co-ops might have is overshadowed by a suspicion that they, like recent moves towards tenant participation on local authority housing estates, are a means of incorporating radical groups, and of co-opting their leaders. Because participation is such a 'two-edged sword', Repo insists (in an argument curiously reminiscent of Mill on the need for education before universal suffrage) that the Marxist evaluation of it depends on gauging the degree of political maturity among working-class people which, if it is not there, means that demands for 'community control' do more harm than good.[69] Secondly, Cockburn has provided a convincing account of how participatory democracy can be harnessed by the corporate management of the local state, so as to provide information on the working class, and to safeguard and legitimate policy decisions. Particularly at risk are organisations which take on functions on behalf of the local state, because they can easily be diverted from their political role, and become incorporated into the state. Cockburn makes a crucial distinction: 'Now – in making use of state services one does not necessarily become part of the system – in sharing in their administration one may well do so.'[70] Because housing co-ops are service organisations, providing something for their members which the state might otherwise be forced to provide, they can be seen as doing the state's job for it. In particular, when tenant management co-ops take on run-down council estates, there is the suspicion that the local state is being let off the hook, that management and maintenance problems are being off-loaded, and public expenditure avoided.

What kind of housing do they want? There is a built-in assumption that council housing is the best form possible; it provides rent-pooling, a rational and cost-effective allocation of housing to those in need, as Cowley says 'despite the inefficiency and authoritarianism characteristic of state bureaucracy'.[71] The faults of council housing tend to be blamed on public spending cuts rather than on the effects of professional hubris among planners and architects, inappropriate building methods, lack of consumer participation and so on.[72] Above all, council housing is seen as the result of, and as a continuing base for, working-class struggle.

There are two kinds of difficulty with these arguments. Firstly, they specify a form of political organisation which in its stringency rules out much of the activities which actual working-class people are engaged in. Secondly, they neglect the almost intractable difficulty of creating a socialist consciousness among working-class people, sufficient for the latter to live up to the Marxists' expectations. To illustrate the first of these difficulties, it may be worth looking at the way in which one Marxist, Castells, has had to revise his theory of urban social movements. Originally he was convinced that he could see a new form of social conflict taking place, linked to the collective organisation of daily life: 'the rise and progressive generalisation of urban protest movements, that is to say of contradictory systems of social practices, which call into question the established order, on the basis of contradictions specific to and inherent in the urban situation.'[73]

Stuart Lowe has traced three phases in Castells' thinking. In the first phase, these urban social movements are defined stringently as: 'organisations in the urban system with a clear issue-base and capable of creating a shift in the balance of class forces'.[74] They are qualitatively higher and more politically advanced forms than urban movements in general, because they are linked to the dominant level of class struggle (between capital and labour at the point of production), and led by a Marxist vanguard which seeks out a correct political line of action. However, in phase two, inter-class movements become acceptable, an autonomous role is given to consumption struggles, and reliance on a vanguard is not necessary. He sees new contradictions developing in the urban system, which do not correspond to the traditional class relationships, but to the position in the *consumption* process. A strategy of democratic socialism, and a popular front which includes middle-class professionals are advocated in response to this analysis. As Lowe

Democracy, the state and co-operative welfare

emphasises: 'Urban-based protest movements that he had previously written off as reformist ... have gained a new status in the strategy of building the popular front.'[75] The emphasis changes, to allow cultural struggls for community, for individualism, and autonomy from political parties, with direct democracy complementing representative democracy. Clearly housing co-ops and other co-operative forms could become part of such a strategy. In phase three, Castells goes further, calling for the defence of cultural identity and the creation of autonomous local cultures. This reintroduction of the idea of community represents a complete break with the Marxist class perspective. The goal of social movements is now the development of autonomous urban meaning over against the state, and their core elements are the ability to provide firstly, need-based collective consumption, secondly, a sense of cultural identity and thirdly, local self-government and the decentralisation of service provision. It is clear that in theory at least, a vigorous housing co-op movement *could* fulfil all three of his core elements. But what has prompted such a drastic revision of the Marxist theory? It is the difficulty of finding examples of the pure class-based type of urban social movement, and then the difficulty of working out just how a socialist consciousness can be created out of the alienated, rootless individuals who such a movement is predicated on. There are hints, scattered among Marxist writings, which could also be developed in the same direction. For example, Cockburn points out that there is an ideological struggle going on within the institutions of family and community, which because we need to live in them, cannot be deferred until after the revolution; at this level, socialist reality has to be created in the present:

> We want a possibility of genuine growth and learning through association that is fairly continuous over time. We want a base from which to link ourselves into many different collective groups, especially class groups, without being splintered between them all. We want supportive, practical working relationships, not pre-determined by sex, or by age, or constrained by the physical space available to us.[76]

Yet this need for moral community is curiously limited; women's food co-ops are recommended, because in relation to patriarchy we need to define socialism now. But what about more structured types of co-op, and those other alienating relationships which should be overcome; landlord and tenant, professional and client, even capitalist and wage-

Democracy, the state and co-operative welfare

earner? Some recent thinking does go further in this direction. One study group, for example, lists not one correct line, but three lines which need to be pursued simultaneously: to make the best of opportunities for working-class advantages (a reformist strategy), to wage war outside the state (a Marxist strategy) and to take opportunities to: 'carve out a little corner in which we have freedom to organise things in our own way, a non-capitalist way'.[77] This third option explicitly includes co-operative housing, and it would be engaged in to encourage socialists, and be an example to others. The task is to create as present reality, non-hierarchical forms of organisation, in which people can relate as collectivities rather than as isolated individuals, can dissolve the distinction between professionals and clients, and can define real needs from the point of view of the users. These essentially co-operative organisations would prefigure socialism, would be a glimpse into the future. However, the group regard all three strategies as necessary, depending on the circumstances of each area of struggle. Co-op type organisations would need to be complemented by wider action, because of the tendency for such groups to remain parochial, and to be co-opted by the state. But there is no doubt that they would be a legitimate and necessary part of a socialist strategy.

However, there is still something lacking in these kinds of argument, from the point of view of committed co-operators; there is no use of co-operative principles to define more closely the structure of such prefigurative organisations, and no drawing on the deeper arguments of the communitarian socialists. And there is a timidity about inferring from co-ops the kinds of association which would develop within a truly socialist society. The fear of being labelled 'utopian' is as inhibiting as it is was to Marx, with the same result that the prescriptions remain (considering that highly developed principles and practices of a world-wide co-operative movement are to hand) surprisingly vague. Furthermore, when Marxists do offer more rounded prescriptions for the future society, they tend to overlook the similarities between their structures and that of existing co-ops. For example, Cowley specifies for a socialist society, a complete rupture with any of the forms of ownership which exist today on the basis of private finance. Of course, housing co-ops are as indebted to private finance capital as are council housing and owner-occupation; Marxists are very clear in pointing out the ways in which profit is made out of public housing. Yet he describes a utopia in which: 'people, through the collective arrangements of their community and neighbourhood life, will have a real say in the type and quality of housing constructed and control its repair and upkeep.' And again: 'the social ownership of housing will involve an entirely different organisation of society to that which exists today. It will be based on common ownership, co-operation and the equality of freely developing individuals.'[78]

Surely, in its best practice co-operative housing prefigures such a society.

(d) Communitarian socialists

With the communitarian socialists, direct democracy really comes into its own. Robert Owen had laid down the main elements: self-governing communities small enough to practise direct member participation in decision-making, with larger structures created by federation at various levels, appropriate to those interests which needed to be more generalised. He had also by way of contrast developed a critique of representative democracy which had been born out of bitter experience, believing that 'manhood suffrage is a popular bauble, that will do neither good nor harm in its practical results.'[79] Proudhon applies these elements to the more complex setting of industrial societies in which a division of labour compels more interdependent economic co-operation and more sophisticated forms of exchange, by developing a mutualist economic theory, and a more subtle theory of federation. Mutualism, in the context of democracy, means more than just a liberal attempt to build political rights on to a substructure of economic inequality; it means providing a material base of rough equality, on to which people can build political participation: 'Giving political rights to the people was not in itself a bad idea; what was wrong was that first of all they should have been given property.'[80] It also means the subsuming of politics itself under economics, so that the citizen can make a real social contract with a voluntary association, a 'positive and effective compact' which has been discussed, voted on, and is revocable. The theory of federation then builds on the same values, in a set of structures which is transparent to the individual co-op member, that is, which allows the retention of more sovereignty than one gives up, at each stage of structural growth. Housing co-ops are formed on this pattern, and conform to Proudhon's advice to 'Form groups of a modest size, individually sovereign, and unite them by a federal pact.'[81]

What, then, is the role of the state? Like Marx and Engels, Proudhon identifies an oppressive economic system as the cause of a centralised state; the latter alienates the 'collective force' of the citizens on behalf of the property-owning minority. Also like the Marxists, he sees the ending of the class domination of this minority as a necessary condition for the abolition of the state, but realises that it is not a *sufficient* condition; associations must be built up which can form the building blocks of a new form of society; otherwise, as Proudhon says of the authoritarian communism of the Blancists, 'We would simply have exchanged our present chains for others.'[82] At the back of his argument lies the insistence on the safeguarding of individual liberty: 'The limitation of the role of the state is a question of life and death for liberty, whether collective or individual.'[83] All this provides both strong arguments for co-ops and difficulties in the way of their promotion; on the one hand, state aid is necessary for the starting of co-ops, but on the other hand it brings grave dangers of lack of autonomy and the interference of an essentially oppressive agency. Proudhon envisages a reduction in state power, the 'dividing of everything that can be divided', the taking back by the periphery, of powers the centre has usurped. This would 'reduce the role of the centre to that of general initiation, of providing guarantees and supervising'.[84] This is exactly what the state has done in relation to co-operative housing in many countries, providing start-up grants for development agencies, guaranteeing mortgages and supervising the movement in a general way. Where it has subsidised the cost, it has done so (in Scandinavia and Canada, but not in Britain) in an unobtrusive way, by subsidising interest rates on loans. John Turner has outlined (from long experience of the self-help housing movements of the third world) a theoretical model on which state aid *could* be acceptable. Participation is regarded as a function of the making and implementing of decisions, which on a matrix provides four possibilities. Firstly, sponsors decide and sponsors provide; this is the position which private, council, and housing association tenants are in. Secondly, sponsors decide and users provide; this happens when a local council forces a landlord to improve his property. Thirdly, users decide and sponsors provide; this happens whenever housing co-ops or house-building co-ops extract subsidies, cheap land or basic services from local or central government. Lastly, users decide and users provide; unsubsidised co-ops come in at this level.[85] The point is that if the role of the state is limited to provision of essential resources, then autonomy and self-management among dwellers can be enhanced rather than imperilled.

The principle of user control assumes, though, that users are sufficiently motivated and educated to participate. Proudhon acknowledges this when he envisages the principle of federation: 'ruling every people, at any given moment, by decreasing the sway of authority and central power to the point permitted by the level of consciousness and morality'.[86] In other words, he sees the power of the state as in inverse proportion to the political maturity of the people. Unlike Mill, he sees such political maturity as taking power from the state rather than contributing to it, and unlike Marx, he has a fear of the massed 'people'; when they gain absolute power, in their political ignorance they invariably choose a dictator to rule in their name. They are on the one hand the army of liberty and progress, but on the other, potential supporters of summary forms of authority which are deadly to both! The education needed to bring out what Kropotkin would call their 'constructive genius', consists in their becoming conscious of themselves as members of a collectivity, their commitment to goals which are formed out of the collective will, and their participation in the realisation of these goals. Housing co-ops could make a strong contribution to such a political maturation process, and because (as Mill also emphasised) it is a two-way process, they would also be reliant on it for their own survival as direct democracies.

Kropotkin's contribution is again to provide a historical underpinning for such a world-view. He analyses the conditions under which participatory democracy is possible, and begins from the point Engels missed; the tribal society which practises unanimous decision-making, the election of leaders, the federation of small into large units and so on, all made possible by the small-scale, territorially based unit, whose members are pursuing tangible economic and social goals through mutual aid. Even more significant in his view is the medieval city, a federation of both territorial units and guilds, which he describes as: 'an immense attempt at securing mutual aid and support on a grand scale, by means of the principles of federation and association carried on through all manifestations of human life and to all possible degrees'.[87] Kropotkin hopes for a new expression of these principles, which will counter the centralising influence of the state, and restore the people's trust in themselves. This new wave of mutualist institutions would not be the state, nor the medieval city, nor the village community, nor the tribal society, but 'would proceed from all of them, and yet be superior to them in its wider and more deeply humane conceptions'.[88] Were he writing today, it is not fanciful to suggest, he would have identified worker and housing co-ops as key elements in such a movement. Certainly Erich Fromm, in describing the alienated form of democracy in the modern state, and in specifying the conditions under which direct democracy can be restored (through discussion, personal contact, possession of the facts, and a direct influence on decision-making) concludes that both industrial and territorial democracy are necessary. In particular, in a suggestion which has great significance for housing co-ops, he advocates the formation of community councils of about 500 citizens.[89] Similarly Buber quotes Kropotkin as saying that federal communism: 'cannot live unless it creates regional and autonomous life in the smallest of its units – the street, the house-block, the district, the parish',[90] and he goes on to define direct democracy in terms of the active management of what the community has in common.

How, in this decentralised, participatory society would social and economic welfare be guaranteed? Would we be better off than in the individualistic market society, or would we all starve? Firstly, the way welfare must be generated is not by splitting social from economic welfare, but by combining them in free, democratic associations which have simultaneous social and economic dimensions. Proudhon insists that economics and social justice 'ought systematically to be interwoven, justice serving as a law for economics'.[91] There are essentially two ways in which this can be done: Owen and Kropotkin's commune system and Proudhon's mutualism.

The first way involves the integration of town and country, of agriculture and industrial manufacture, which Owen refers to as placing the workman in the midst of his food. He believed, like Marx, that material abundance is possible, given the vast increase in productive power enabled by the industrial revolution (in which as a highly successful mill-owner and philanthropist, he himself had played no mean part). But he did not see the need to retain the large-scale, highly divided labour of capitalist production; given the right conditions, of access to land and tools, a small-scale co-operative community of about 2,500 persons, a maximum of self-sufficiency in each commune, and federal arrangements for the bartering of exchangeable goods and services, production will increase so that all basic needs can be met. Kropotkin spent a considerable amount of time developing technological arguments for the ability of such an economy to produce an abundance for even very large, concentrated populations, given an advanced range of agricultural and small-scale industrial technology.[92] The 'green movement' is only just beginning to put his ideas into practice, and is discovering (a century too late) just how practical his ideas were.[93] Interestingly, Owen had appealed for such a system to be set up for the poor, as an alternative to parish poor relief, and had incurred considerable criticism for it from the liberal, William Cobbett, whose individualistic nature recoiled from such 'co-operative workhouses', and who based his prescriptions for the relief of poverty on the family smallholding. Owen's reply is compelling; that the family is too small an economic unit on which to base human welfare, is too subject to chance, particularly if the head of household falls ill or dies, and it provides no guaranteed mutual support for those in distress. He describes the market individualist view of welfare as not only inhumane, but also highly inefficient in guaranteeing the general welfare: 'All are individualised, cold and forbidding; each being compelled to take an hundred-fold more care of himself than would be otherwise necessary; because the ignorance of society has placed him in direct opposition to the thousands around him.'[94] Nevertheless, it is difficult to find successful concrete examples of the commune system, without citing (as do Kropotkin and Buber) various religious sects such as the Doukhobors or the Hutterites. Buber regards the Israeli kibbutzim as the best example of what he calls the 'full co-op', but calls it not so much a success as a 'non-failure'.

Proudhon's alternative is less rigorous; a much looser, modified market economy, in which access to credit, sound money based on real productive capacity, and mutual exchange, guarantee to the producers (whether individual producers, small farmers or worker co-ops) a fair return on their labour. He believes that the elements of order are there in the market economy, but that these must be organised around a system of mutual credit, the building up of large-scale organisation through the principle of federation, and the use of mutual agreements between associations.[95] Fromm has described the basic form of association thus: 'an industrial organisation in which every working person would be an active and responsible participant, where work would be attractive and meaningful, where capital would not employ labour, but labour would employ capital.'[96] Social welfare would then be provided through similar mutual organisations; insurance and friendly societies, building societies, housing co-ops and so on.

Such a dizzying vision is apt to make the head spin, but it can be brought into sharp focus by the example of 'Mondragon'. In the co-operative movement of the Basque region of Spain, centred around the town of Mondragon, is a thriving, broadly based co-operative economy. The basic unit is the worker co-op, but the central development agency is the co-op bank, which channels the savings of workers and local people into mutual credit, and lends to co-ops in order to finance greater productivity and new enterprises, which in their turn enable the creation of more wealth. A consumer co-op with thirty branches organises distribution, while six education co-ops and a research and development centre organise the skills and new products necessary to continued expansion of the industrial co-ops. Because under Spanish law, worker co-op members are considered to be self-employed (and therefore outside the state social security system), a social security co-op has been formed, which uses funds drawn from the producing co-ops to finance a range of welfare benefits: family allowances, medical insurance, sickness benefits, maternity endowments, invalidity benefits, widows' pensions, and retirement pensions. Benefits are generally much more generous than those provided by the state; pensions for instance, are fixed at 100 per cent of final salary. Unemployment is dealt with, by guaranteeing that anyone laid off is retained on 80 per cent of salary. Five housing co-ops have so far been built, again with finance and development coming from the bank; these illustrate concretely how housing co-ops could become part of an integrated co-operative economy.[97]

CONCLUSION

If the policy-makers, developers and managers of housing in Britain were communitarian socialists, they would be promoting housing co-ops as not one form of tenure among others, but (alongside worker and consumer co-ops) as the cell structure of an ultimately stateless society. If they were liberal pluralists, they would be promoting co-ops along with housing associations, as intermediate institutions between the individual and the state. If they were collectivists, they would be defending council housing, and trying to organise its tenants into a hammer with which to beat the capitalist state. However, if they were susceptible to feminist and 'Eurocommunist' influences, they might be engaged in a reappraisal which brings them closer to the communitarian socialist position. And if they were market individualists, they would see co-ops along with housing associations as a way of avoiding the channelling of funds into the public housing sector. More likely they are none of these, but interpret housing issues in the light of vaguely felt and not easily articulated beliefs, derived from such world-views as these, and in particular from an older Victorian version of market individualism, which still pervades many housing departments and old-style housing associations.

But what of co-op members themselves? Are they liberal pluralists, seeking self-development and political efficacy? Are they marxist collectivists, seeking to extend the class struggle and build socialist reality within the sphere of social reproduction? Are they communitarian socialists, seeking to nurture the seeds of a new society, growing within the decaying body of the old? Or are they, more narrowly, convinced co-operators, drawing from co-operative principles and practices all that they need for committed participation? More likely, they are merely people who want a decent home, and are prepared to put in a minimal level of participation in order to secure and maintain it. But if they do wish to explore co-operative principles, to seek to understand and justify the kind of work they are doing, then the pluralist and communitarian world-views are a source of weak and strong arguments respectively, for such a task.

FOUR

CO-OPERATIVE HOUSING IN BRITAIN: THE EARLY STAGES

To the materialist, the numerical insignificance of the British housing co-operative movement means that it can be treated with contempt. To the policy analyst, its statistical insignificance means that it can be treated with indifference. Yet in the long term, both may even in their own terms be proved to have been short-sighted. The textbooks of ten years ago are now embarrassingly outdated in their assessment of the significance of the housing association movement, which has grown at a phenomenal rate since the 1974 Housing Act placed it on a sound financial footing. Co-ops are part of that growth, and from a standing start have also grown at a remarkable rate, until there are about 500 of them, in addition to the 250 or so co-ownership co-ops which have not been dissolved since the 1980 Housing Act.[1] They are only small, owning or managing anything from 3 to 250 dwellings, but together they make up a significant minority tenure.

However, there is an easier way to impress the materialist; from an international perspective, co-ops are a major housing tenure in their own right. For example, 19 per cent of all Norwegian housing, including 45 per cent of housing in Oslo, is co-operative, averaging only 60 units per co-op, but cumulatively owning over a quarter of a million homes.[2] 16 per cent of all Swedish housing is co-operative, with over half a million (583,000) dwellings.[3] Since the War, co-ops have undertaken 35 per cent of Czechoslovak housing, 17–19 per cent of Hungarian flats, and a third of all new building in Sweden. Or to change the statistical impression slightly, there are 11,000 housing co-ops in India, and over 23,000 in Italy. In Pakistan, an entire co-operative township has been built, and in Poland there are 100 'reconstruction' co-ops in Warsaw alone.[4] Even in the USA, with its dominant image of a nation dedicated to individual property ownership, there is a small but significant sector, which even before the

British movement began had 200,000 dwellings housing an estimated one million people.[5] Co-op City in New York must be the largest co-op in the world, with 15,000 dwellings. Clearly, one can talk without exaggeration of a mass movement which is worthy of even the most hard-headed of policy analysts' attention.

However, even if this point is accepted, the British housing co-op movement may be in greater difficulty still from what follows: Why, then, if co-ops are so strong in other countries, particularly in Scandinavia, has the British movement taken so long to develop, and why is it still numerically so weak? The Rochdale Pioneers, generally regarded as founders of the world-wide consumer co-op movement in the 1840s, had as one of their aims: 'The building, purchasing or erecting of a number of houses, in which those members desiring to assist each other in improving their domestic and social conditions may reside.'[6] But housing co-ops did not generally emerge at this time; in fact co-operators had to wait for the 1975 Housing Finance Act before any kind of movement could begin. The point is enlivened by a paradox; that although in the middle of the last century the Scandinavian co-operative movement took its original inspiration from the British consumer co-op movement,[7] in the middle of this century British enthusiasts had to visit Scandinavia to find out what housing co-ops were all about.[8] One of them, John Greve, explained it like this: 'as in many other fields, while the original, impulse-giving effort faltered and then faced away in its place of origin, the transplanted ideas took root and flourished elsewhere.'[9]

But this still begs the question of why the ideas did not take root and flourish in Britain. To continue the horticultural analogy, what was it about the soil, climate or cultivation method which allowed the seed to die? Or to be more precise, what are the key variables which affect the development of housing co-ops? We can identify at least five:

1 Housing needs, not being met in other ways.
2 Appropriate co-operative structures, which work in practice.
3 Promoters: both charismatic individuals and organisations.
4 A favourable, or at least not unfavourable, legal/financial environment.
5 A favourable psychological climate.

Obviously, since co-ops are not profit-making enterprises, housing need is the most basic factor which must be present. There must be an appropriate structure for the organisation, which allows it to meet these needs in a co-operative way; this was the great achievement of the Rochdale Pioneers and their consumer co-operative society that it provided a model which others could adapt to meet different needs. There must be promoters, charismatic individuals who can produce effective development agencies which can then promote the particular co-op form. There must be a sympathetic legislative environment, which allows the co-operative form to be recognised and to grow, and which encourages, or at least allows, financial backing. Lastly the right kind of psychological climate is needed, in which people will recognise the benefits of co-operation, and will help make it work, or at least not stand in its way. Only if all five of these variables are present will co-op development take place on any significant scale. Using this simple model we can attempt to understand the complexities of history.

THE EARLY HISTORY OF HOUSING CO-OPS IN BRITAIN

Any history of co-operative housing has to start somewhere, probably at the point where records started to be kept in the last century. But we must not be fooled into thinking that there was no co-operation in housing before then; it is as old as the first group of *Homo sapiens* who ever helped each other to provide shelter. As Colin Ward reminds us: 'Most of the world's people feed, clothe and house themselves, usually in co-operation with their neighbours, sometimes with the help of their rulers, sometimes despite them, and take some pleasure in doing so.'[10] Bearing in mind this cautionary point, let us try to trace the early history of housing co-ops in Britain.

At the time of the earliest experiments in consumer co-operation, historians are agreed that there was certainly a range of dire housing needs to be met.[11] Throughout the nineteenth century the pace of population in Britain grew too fast for the builders, and persistent poverty made working-class housing unprofitable. Rents rose much faster than wages, and unemployment and illness made any improvement in most people's standard of housing liable to be temporary. The legislation introducing proper sanitation and water supply and preventing overcrowding simply increased the cost of housing, and so after 1876 there was a drop in building, which by 1921 had led to a deficit of 805,000 homes. Clearly there were needs not being met by the private market or by philanthropy. What structures were to hand, then, by which co-operators could attempt to provide for such needs?

Co-operative housing: the early stages

The first structural development in working-class mutual aid was the friendly society; these had a million members by 1815, and were, as E.P. Thompson describes them, 'authentic evidence of the growth of independent working-class culture and institutions'.[12] Out of these grew the trade unions, and the consumer co-operative societies; the Rochdale shop was actually modelled on a 'sick and burial' society. It was natural that the earliest method of co-operation in housing should be the terminating building society, a mutual savings club similar to the friendly societies, but without the actuarial complications of insurance. The earliest building society for which there are records was at the Golden Cross Inn, Birmingham, in 1775, where members subscribed regularly until one by one they were allocated enough money to build houses.[13] Another early form was the building club (what we might now call a self-build co-op), which provided mutual help with the actual building work; one of the earliest recorded examples was at Colinburgh in Scotland, where in 1826, 6 blocks of 8 flats each were built.[14]

Such experiments were by their nature short-lived. In the building society, unlike the friendly society or the consumer co-op, membership was limited to those who had joined at the beginning, unless newcomers were able to contribute a lump sum in order to catch up with the other members' payments. In both the building society and the building club, once members were all housed the society was wound up. They were also dependent on the fluctuating fortunes of a working class in the making, which was suffering all the vicissitudes of labour in a rapidly changing market society; periodic cycles of unemployment made it impossible for all but a small minority to plan for the future. There was eventually a favourable legal environment, in the form of the friendly society and then the industrial and provident society acts, and among the working class there was undoubtedly a positive psychological climate for mutual aid, but, until the consumer societies began to amass surplus capital towards the end of the century, there was a chronic shortage of available finance. Furthermore, inefficiency, coupled with greed and even fraud on the part of the middle-men who often arranged the building of houses, made the outcome uncertain. Enid Gauldie notes that 'Most of the genuinely worker-inspired societies did not survive the first half of the (nineteenth) century.'[15]

Those which did survive, did so by making fundamental changes in their structure, at the expense of co-operative principle and working-class character. For instance, building societies did not so much decline as metamorphose into a permanent financial institution. The key structural change was the break-out from mutuality: the discovery that borrowers and investors need not necessarily be the same people. Permanent societies then grew rapidly, and in the process, since they were able to employ professional staff, became much better at business management and the oversight of building work; in 1873 there were still 959 temporary societies listed as opposed to 540 permanent ones, but the latter were vastly different in size and level of organisation.[16] The new structure may have made the investment safer, but it excluded all the working classes but the artisan elite from both the chance of becoming home-owners, and (since meetings were now held in the mechanic's institute rather than the pub) from the democratic running of the society. In Gauldie's judgment, by 1871 'the middle classes played a bigger part in the building-society movement than the working class for whom it was designed.'[17] A similar fate may have befallen the other main co-operative form, the building club. If it evolved at all, it was into commercial co-ops, such as the Edinburgh Working Men's Building Association and the Co-operative Building Co. Ltd, founded in 1860 and 1861. These were rare in being both genuinely worker-inspired and commercially viable; they were owned by building workers who by 1895 had built over £500,000 worth of housing for sale to working people with building society finance. However, the Co-operative Building Company was misnamed; its structure was really that of a Building Productive Society, or 'working-class limited', in which profits were divided by share-capital as in a normal joint-stock company.[18]

Why did housing co-ops not emerge at this time? The appropriate structure was to hand in the Rochdale principles, which by the middle of the century were being extended from retailing into wholesaling and even primary production, but it had simply not yet been adapted for co-operation in housing. What was missing was a promoter who had the vision to see how the principles could be adapted, and the practical sense to promote the idea successfully. The first great promoter was, of course, Robert Owen, who in 1813, long before the Rochdale experiment, had had a vision of integrated villages of co-operation in which all needs would be met co-operatively, and housing would be built in a parallelogram of buildings enclosing a courtyard.[19] The high cost (an estimated £100,000 per village of about a thousand people) meant that the plan hinged on massive support from the wealthy; not surprisingly, despite his appeals to the ruling classes of Britain and

Europe, this support was not forthcoming. He then turned to the promotion of experimental communities which would demonstrate more conclusively the rationality of his plans; their comprehensive nature and Owen's total lack of financial realism necessitated the use of large estates, which were vulnerable to the vagaries of ownership; the Ralahine community in Ireland was evicted when the owner gambled away the estate, and Orbiston was lost when the owner died. However, the grandiosity of Owen's plans was also to blame; another co-operative community at Queenwood was bankrupted by Owen's over-ambitious building plan. It is ironic that some of the Rochdale Pioneers lost money invested in the last scheme, through the extravagant refurbishing of a mansion at a time when they did not have the resources even to house themselves properly. It is not surprising that after such unrealistic promotion, the idea of co-operative housing received a setback.

When the retail societies eventually did try to provide housing for their members, it was not in a co-operative form at all. By the mid-nineteenth century they had built up substantial capital reserves, but there was need for high liquidity because members had grown to expect a high dividend even in bad trading years; the result was that they under-invested in their *own* fixed assets and even put surpluses into government stocks. When they did invest in housing, it was in the conventional form of owner-occupation and private rental, and the psychological climate was circumscribed by arguments over which of these two tenures were the most principled; retail co-op ownership was seen as a kind of 'community on land', but private ownership was seen as the promotion of self-reliance. The main initiative was the founding in 1884 of the Co-operative Permanent Building Society, which grew slowly until the First World War, before experiencing spectacular growth. Some retail societies were also heavily involved; by the turn of the century, mortgages had been lent to members on 23,940 houses, 8,247 houses had been built by societies and were being rented to members, and 5,080 had been built and then sold to members.[20]

Many of the co-operative productive societies established towards the end of the century also provided help with housing for their members. Equity Shoes at Leicester provided loans to enable members to build 60 houses, including some built by a co-operative building association. Kettering Boot and Shoe Society solved a problem of having too much capital by building 100 houses and renting them out to members, and buying land to sell in individual plots. However, probably the only society which actually practised co-operative principles in the management of its housing was the Anchor Boot and Shoe Society in Leicester, which formed a tenants' association to run an estate of 96 houses (including a block of shops, a meeting room and recreation room) through co-operative self-management.[21]

How, then, did the idea of fully co-operative housing emerge and become promoted? It was not until 1880 that a possible structure for co-operative housing was suggested, and then it was by a Frenchman, M. Godin. His idea was noticed and taken up by an active co-operator, Owen Greening, in an article written in *Co-operative News*. Greening said, 'I am in favour of a society building and owning houses for its members, and letting them on real co-operative terms.'[22] He thought that it would simply entail payments to a building society, as in owner-occupation, but with each member's contribution credited towards not the individual dwelling, but an equivalent shareholding in what we might now call a co-ownership co-op. The idea was elaborated further by Benjamin Jones, London manager of the Co-operative Wholesale Society, who, having seen how working-class people had been made homeless by slum clearance, was determined to apply the 'Rochdale system' to the problem. In 1883, he mentioned his idea to Henry Broadhurst, Under-Secretary of State for Home Affairs, and was asked to draw up a scheme for the consideration of the London Trades Council. The pamphlet which he wrote in response spelled out the structure of a workable housing co-op, but it did not at first get much support. As Yerbury says, it was difficult to get over the prejudice in favour of owner-occupation, and 'much time and energy had to be devoted to the necessary propaganda before a body of workers could be brought together to put principles into practice.'[23] In fact it took four years of promotional work before Tenant Co-operators Ltd was eventually founded in November 1887, and it is interesting to note that it was not work among the working classes which paid off, but the persuasion of powerful men like Henry Vansittart Neale (son of the great co-operator Edward Vansittart Neale, and later to be knighted) and Walter Hazell (later to become MP for Leicester and Mayor of Holborn). We are no longer in the realm of the building club or society meeting in the local public house.

The idea was to buy or build houses all over London, let to tenant members at local rents, and financed through a nominal £1 minimum share taken up by tenants, plus loan stock taken up by small investors, and a loan from the Public Works Loans Board. The rents would have to cover maintenance, 4 per cent interest on the shares and loan stock, and the government mortgage, but surplus profits would be returned as a dividend, credited to each tenant's share account. The aim was for the value of the dwelling to be set against the member's share capital in a book, and for the account to grow until in the end the tenant owned the equivalent in shares of the value of his or her own dwelling; working-class people would then own their houses, but instead of having to sell up when they moved in search of work, they could transfer to another co-op tenancy and take their shares with them, or sell the shares back to the co-op. In other words, the co-operative would begin with a large stake by outside shareholders, but would gradually move towards full co-ownership, though it is unclear whether shares would be redeemable at full market value. (We can probably assume that they would be.) Even before this, though, it was expected that tenants would be in majority control, because of the principle of one member one vote. Reflecting their consumer co-op model, the Tenant Co-operators were to set aside 2½ per cent of net profits for an education fund, and were to be a member of the Co-op Union.

With £4000 invested by 100 people (who we are assured were mainly working class), the Co-op began with the purchase of 6 houses at Upton Park, and then went on to build 24 cottages at Penge. The idea must have been commercially sound, for it soon paid out a dividend of 1/6d in the pound (and divi continued to average 6 per cent), but progress was slow; by 1909 it had only succeeded in building 122 houses and tenements (210 dwellings in all) at five sites around London.[24] As Yerbury explains in his history, two badly designed schemes dogged the co-op throughout: flats at East Ham were compared by residents unfavourably with cottage property available in the area, and they had to be refurbished at heavy cost before they could be fully let, while at Epsom, over-building in the town meant that rents had to be reduced to attract tenants.[25] Time and money were taken up in large quantities in dealing with these problems, and so education was neglected. Slow growth meant that each site remained isolated and small and could not support a local meeting place, and that the ratio of tenants to investor-members remained unbalanced; by 1911 there were only 51 tenant shareholders to 293 other individuals. Not surprisingly, tenant involvement remained minimal. In fact, in 1901, when the committee had to raise the rents at Penge to cover increased rates charges, the tenants took the co-op to court! At East Ham and Epsom, despite the nominal £1 share, it was found necessary to admit non-member tenants, and then to make all the tenancy conditions compatible so that the co-op had to do all internal repairs, and this put even more strain on the co-op's finances. The committee readily admitted that for the idea to work, not five but fifty estates were needed. Nonetheless, in its modest way, this first housing co-op was a success; as Aneurin Williams noted, it had provided good housing at cost price, though it had not succeeded in gaining the interest of the members. 'Whatever the cause, the society, admirable as it is in other ways, is in effect more a public-spirited association for supplying workmen's dwellings than an organisation of working men co-operators.'[26]

The next stage of development, the Co-partnership Housing Societies, had no shortage of promoters, both institutional and individual. It arose out of two social movements, Labour Co-partnership and the Garden City movement. These converged to provide, respectively, the idea of co-partnerships in housing, in which tenants would own shares along with other shareholding 'partners', and the idea of a totally planned neighbourhood, in which middle-income people could obtain by co-operation the kind of amenities previously reserved for the rich. In 1901, some building trade members, interested in the labour co-partnership movement which had recently set up several fairly large productive co-ops owned jointly by consumer co-ops, trade unions and workers, applied the same model to housing, and formed Ealing Tenants Ltd. The structure of the new society differed little from that of the Tenant Co-operators Ltd, except in two vital respects. Firstly, it demanded an ultimate take-up of £50 in share-capital by tenant-members, payable in full or in instalments of £2–5 and then 2/6d per month. This limited the concept, catering, in the opinion of the Tenant Co-operator Yerbury, 'for the well-to-do classes equally, if not more, than for the poorest of the workers'.[27] Secondly, despite the inclusion of 'Pioneer' in its title, it was not an isolated society attempting to develop the idea alone, but was simply the first of 15 daughter societies to be developed by means of a federation which was also the central developer, the Co-partnership Tenants Ltd. This organisation, with its salaried officials, its departments for finance, accounts, trading, architecture and education, as Yerbury noted rather sourly, was in complete contrast with the small, over-worked and unpaid committee which was still struggling to keep the Tenant Co-operators afloat.

Backing the new movement were certainly some heavy-weight figures. At first there was the umbrella of the Labour Co-partnership

Co-operative housing: the early stages

Association, and then by 1905 the movement's own promotional organisation took over, the Tenant Co-partnership Housing Council. Souvenir booklets issued by the Ealing and Hampstead societies are full of ingratiating references to aristocratic sympathisers, and of photographs of the Duke and Duchess of Connaught opening the Ealing estate, King George the Fifth and Queen Mary visiting Hampstead, and so on.[28] Henry Vivian, the chairman of the movement, became an MP, while Raymond Unwin, consultant architect to the schemes, was virtually the founder of town planning in Britain. The method was quite simple, to buy up land on the outskirts of towns and cities at under £300 per acre, then to call a meeting of possible members, explain the details and take names of those interested, and then, when the likely demand was known, to plan out the land on sound town planning principles. The rules would be registered, a prospectus issued, subscriptions to share and loan stock invited, and then the federation would do the building, acting as architect and builder, employing its own workforce to do well-designed, good-quality work. Ealing Tenants eventually took up 60 acres and built 700 houses, with 12 acres of playing fields, 5 acres of allotments, a school of gardening (for experimental intensive horticulture on lines suggested by Kropotkin!), a club and institute, a school of handicraft, a kindergarten school, and so on. Expansion was rapid; by 1912, 14 societies had built 6,595 houses on 652 acres, for a population of 30–35,000.

The First World War brought the movement to a halt. Then there came a determination to build 'homes fit for heroes' which led Raymond Unwin to turn against his co-operative roots, and recommend in the Tudor-Walters Report to Lloyd George's government that local authorities should be the main means by which social housing should be provided. Thereafter, the co-operative idea was buried for a long time. There was no reason why local councils could not have chosen to meet their commitment through the promotion of co-ops, except that the psychological environment which prevailed reflected the overwhelming dominance of council housing and owner-occupation; the co-operative form was simply forgotten. Even within the consumer co-operative movement, the dominant forms of tenure prevailed; the Co-operative Permanent Building Society began to expand rapidly, and became the third largest society in Britain. Some retail societies continued to manage rented housing, the largest being the Well Hall estate at Eltham, built by the government for munitions workers during the First World War, and owned by the Royal Arsenal Co-operative

Society. By the late 1920s, over three million pounds were still invested in housing for rent, but the problem of capital was by this time going into reverse; embarrassing surpluses had turned into shortages, and there was criticism of societies for allowing capital to be locked into such an immovable form.[29] From then on, activity by retail societies diminished.

One or two isolated experiments kept the idea of housing co-ops alive. The Dronfield Health and Housing Society was formed in 1946, financed by a 10 per cent stake taken up by the tenants, and a loan from the Public Works Loan Board. In the same year, some retail co-operative societies sponsored the East Midlands Housing Association, which began to experiment with tenant-controlled estates. Reg Freeson, later to be Minister for Housing and enabler (through his 1975 Housing Finance Act) of the current wave of housing co-ops in Britain, took the opportunity while a local councillor, in 1958, to promote the Adys Lawn Association; 12 flats financed by a 90 per cent mortgage from Willesden Council. Two further small co-ops (Rutland Park Gardens Association and Neptune Housing Society) followed. However, these were hardly a challenge to the two dominant forms of housing tenure; when in the 1960s, new alternative tenures were finally sought, the co-ownership co-operative structure had to be imported from Scandinavia. Until then, and for the most part until the mid-1970s in Britain, there was no real challenge to the two dominant models of housing; the psychological environment precluded even awareness of co-operative alternatives. In order to understand just what might have been possible had the environment been more congenial, had there been strong promotion of co-ops by the consumer movement and a clear grasp of the advantages of the co-operative form, we have to turn for comparison to the history of co-operative housing in Scandinavia.

HOUSING CO-OPERATIVES IN SCANDINAVIA

What is it about the early history of housing co-ops in Scandinavia that led to their expansion into a major form of tenure, while in Britain the whole movement ground to a halt after the First World War? Being predominantly rural, Norway and Sweden did not experience acute housing needs until much later than in Britain, but by the First World War both countries were suffering from shortage of urban housing, speculative building and the inability of the private market to respond appropriately to needs. Perhaps it was the sheer scale of the problem, though, which led the British policy-makers to advocate a large-scale solution via council housing. On the other hand, in Scandinavia early experiments in co-ops did provide models for the setting up of large-scale promotional organisations which could both cope with the crisis of housing need and foster genuinely co-operative solutions.

Sweden

For instance, in Sweden a Workers' Housing Association was established in the 1880s, but it was a later co-op, the Stockholm Co-operative Housing Association (SKB), formed in 1916, which really began large-scale co-op development. The structure of SKB is curious. It is one large, growing common-ownership co-op, organised into four districts, three geographically based around Stockholm and one made up of prospective members. Local block councils have limited influence, but tenant members elect representatives to an elected SKB assembly, which then elects a board. Management and maintenance are organised centrally, so that there is no direct influence over it by members. Because it is a centralised organisation, rent pooling is possible, and rents are fixed not by historic costs but by use value. SKB now has 25,000 members and owns 4,270 flats.[30]

Then in 1923 the HSB (Tenants' Savings Bank and Housing Association) was formed by the National Tenants' Union. It started in Stockholm, then expanded rapidly into a national federation. It was an innovative co-op developer, insisting on providing bathrooms for all dwellings, then in 1926 beginning to build in community laundrettes, and in 1929 inventing the refuse chute.[31] It is set up on three levels, a national society, 65 local societies and individual housing co-ops. Its 'mother-daughter' structure, whereby prospective co-op members first have to join the local society and save with it before being offered a place in a new co-op, has enabled the efficient, continuing development of new co-ops; the HSB mother society responsible for promotion of a local co-op claims 2½ per cent of the cost of production, and 1½ per cent goes into a guarantee fund for assistance in covering the losses of any 'daughter' co-op which gets into trouble. Yet its federal structure has enabled genuine democratic control by existing and prospective co-op members over the local and national societies. Local co-ops need only accept financial services from the mother society, and are free to arrange their own management. HSB has provided its own design and build, extending back by vertical integration into the building and supply industries. Its production peaked in 1965 at 18,000 units, but is now producing 7,000 per annum. It has produced about 275,00 co-op dwellings to date, for 430,000 members in 65 societies, but it has also built 110,000 dwellings for the municipal housing companies and 25,000 houses for owner-occupation. It even builds holiday homes.

Finally, in 1940 the third main co-operative development organisation was formed, Riksbyggen, sponsored initially by the Swedish building trades unions, who were concerned about very high unemployment among their members. It is jointly owned by the unions, the consumer co-op movement (the Co-operative Union and the Wholesale Society) and the local housing co-ops which it has developed; these last own 30 per cent of the society. It has no membership structure, and its local offices are controlled by the national organisation, and so it has been freer even than HSB to diversify into other building and design activities. Flats are simply 'sold' to purchasers who can pay the co-operative deposit. It provides services to the local co-ops which it sponsored, but they are free to choose whether or not to enter into management agreements. Riksbyggen is currently diversifying into the management of rental housing in general; it manages 180,000 dwellings for co-ops and municipal housing companies.

Given such powerful promotional and service organisations as HSB and Riksbyggen, co-operative development has been dramatic. Greve estimated in 1971 that co-ops had undertaken 25 per cent of all post-war housing development in Sweden, out of a massive new building drive which has provided 65 per cent of the total housing stock. Since then expansion has been checked, since flats have tended to become less popular, and owner-occupation has become more desirable. Even so, Cronberg estimates that HSB and Riksbyggen co-ops between them control 375,000 dwellings.[32] Yet they could not have achieved so much without a very sympathetic legal and financial environment, and what we have called a favourable psychological climate. For instance, individual ownership of flats has been illegal in Sweden, and so co-ops have been the only way, apart from straight rental, to promote multi-occupied dwellings. Secondly, in a system for subsidising new building established in 1942, while nearly all of new build housing has been subsidised by the state, co-ops and municipal housing have been specially favoured. All developers have been able to get a first mortgage for 70 per cent of the cost with a subsidised interest rate, and a second mortgage through the state loan system, but this takes co-ops up to 99 per cent of building costs, but other developers only to 92 per cent. Short-term bridging loans have solved the problem of financing the early stages of a scheme, and deferred payment loans have made initial rents more economical.

The psychological climate has been consistent. Social democratic governments have recognised that co-ops are inherently socialist, in that they encourage communal living, and avoid social stratification. Municipal housing has been disliked because of its bureaucratic and less democratic nature, and many municipal companies now buy their management direct from HSB or Riksbyggen, or have transferred their stock to co-ops. Local authorities have exchanged land for nomination rights in co-ops, and have made them part of their total strategy. Their current interest in tenant participation and decentralisation of services leans heavily on the co-op model. In fact, in 1982 a law was passed enabling tenants to buy their own buildings from the landlord, whether public or private, and to form a co-op, assisted by special state loans.[33] The climate is not entirely warm, though. Riksbyggen is currently attempting to develop new types of co-op, designed specially to replace council housing; the 'limited type co-op' limits membership to the municipal waiting list, and restricts sales of shares so that people can enter the co-op without needing a large down-payment; however, its restriction on sale of the right to occupy was declared illegal in a recent court ruling. Another type, the 'housing rights association', is a kind of tenant management co-op, but it has met opposition from the National Tenants' Union, which backs a 'co-determination' model of decentralised, estate-based housing management, similar to the Priority Estates Projects in Britain. On the individualist right, there is a call for a more market-based sale of co-operative rights to occupy, and on the collectivist left, a call for a broadening of tenant participation in municipal housing management, rather than the 'tenants take-over' by co-ops – much the same spectrum of opinion as exists in Britain.

Norway

In Norway, housing co-ops developed comparatively late, after 1917. It is interesting to note that the first development was a co-operative garden village, inspired by both the Rochdale Pioneers and the Garden City movement. In 1929 the largest secondary or 'mother' co-op OBOS was founded, again by trade unions, and modelled on the Swedish HSB. In 1935, the Oslo Commune agreed with OBOS that it should carry out all future municipal housing, taking over the council's waiting list, and becoming the dominant housing agency for the city. In 1947 it went even further. After tenants demanded a rent reduction of 20 per cent, because of years of under-maintenance of their properties, Oslo decided to sell 5,000 homes to a holding company. When over 50 per cent of tenants on an estate decided in favour of forming a co-op the company transferred ownership to a daughter co-op. The commune provided loans for purchase, and a grant for maintenance work. In 1957 the holding company was transformed into a new mother society, OBF.

As in Sweden, trade unions, the consumer co-op movement and tenants' unions have all played their part in promoting housing co-ops; the National Federation of Norwegian Housing Co-ops, for example, is backed by OBOS, the trade unions and the Norwegian Union of Tenants. In fact, by 1950 co-operation between these interests reached an international level, with the founding of the Scandinavian Organisation of Housing Co-ops, which has rationalised production and distribution of building materials, as well as providing a forum for exchange of information, across the boundaries of Sweden, Norway and Denmark. But to return to Norway; there are 106 mother associations in membership of the Norwegian Federation, and 3,400 daughter co-ops, with between them 215,000 dwellings. OBOS has provided 62,000 dwellings, and the next largest mother society, USBL, 7,000. There are yet more co-ops independent of the Federation; Cronberg estimates another 70,000 dwellings.[34] Altogether, the co-operative sector makes up about 19 per cent of the total housing stock, and in Oslo 45 per cent.[35] One interesting new development is the formation of the Oslo Urban Renewal Co-op, whose job is to buy out landlords and form daughter co-ops in rehabilitated property.

Also as in Sweden, the state has, since facing a severe housing shortage in 1947, given active support to the co-operative method. The state housing bank funds almost all co-ops, with low-interest, long-term loans, and even with loans to individuals for the down payment, which since prices have been allowed to float on the market, can now average £17,500. The initial 60-year, low-interest loans covered up to 85 per cent of the development costs, and a grant covered another 10 per cent, but subsidies have been steadily reducing in the last decade. Co-ops have received continued support from the Labour party, which sees them as being strongly associated with the labour movement; the climate of opinion is one which questions the need for state ownership and control of social housing.

Co-operative housing: the early stages

It was the sale of those 5,000 dwellings to co-ops by the Oslo Commune which attracted the attention of some British academics, and laid some of the ground-work for the current revival in housing co-op fortunes in Britain; when the next phase of co-op development began, with the co-ownership societies of the 1960s, it was not the example of the old British co-partnerships which was most influential, for these had been completely forgotten. It was the Norwegian pattern of mother and daughter society which was adopted.

CO-OWNERSHIP HOUSING SOCIETIES

It was in the unlikely setting of a Conservative government's interest in promoting new forms of private rental housing, and steps towards owner-occupation, that the next wave of co-operative housing was made. The 1961 Housing Act made available £25m for the development of housing societies for cost rent or co-ownership. The idea of the first was simple: to build for rental, charging rents which would cover all the costs of a private but non-profit landlord. The idea of the second was much more complex, and was taken, with some crucial and, as we shall see, fateful modifications, from the Norwegian co-ownership co-operative.

The idea was that a sponsoring 'parent' society would carry out the development and then manage a housing scheme, while ownership would be vested collectively in the occupiers, who would appoint a management committee to oversee the work of the managing agent. The members would be co-owners because they would own the dwellings collectively, but be individually tenants. They would pay a rent which had to cover the entire cost of mortgages and services, but their payments would gradually build up an interest in the collective property; not a share of the equity on the individual dwelling (as in a shared ownership co-op) but of the collective equity (as in a co-ownership). When they left, if they had stayed for a qualifying period of 5 years, they would receive a premium payment calculated as a percentage of the mortgage pricipal repaid by them, plus a percentage of the rise in value of the dwelling, calculated not on the open market, but on a notional rise in building costs; the sum total of these percentages would rise slowly according to the number of years in the scheme. In practice this complicated scheme was soon modified because re-let rents had to cover the cost of the premium paid to outgoing members; if a dwelling could not be re-let at the appropriate level, then the premium was reduced. Looked at from this angle, there was, therefore, an element of 'market value' in the premium which members would receive when they left. Unlike the Swedish and Norwegian system, though, members would not have a 'right to occupancy' which they could sell to the incoming member. Nor did the sponsoring societies have to be co-ops, owned and controlled by prospective members; in practice, most consisted of self-appointed professionals, including architects, property developers and the like, who stood to gain from the work they were generating. This meant that there was no provision for educating members to take on the running of their co-ownerships, and no safeguards if things went wrong.

The first 3 societies (HL Score, SE London, 102 houses in all) were formed with loan capital provided under the 1961 Act. Unfortunately, the £25m was almost exhausted before a legal structure could be found to enable co-ownerships to benefit from it. The 1964 Housing Act then established a Housing Corporation which was to provide loan capital for part of the cost of schemes, and loan guarantees to encourage building society investment on the rest. The Corporation was also obliged to do a nominal amount of education work: 'to publicise, in the case of societies providing houses for their own members no less than in the case of societies providing houses for letting, the aims and principles of such societies'.[36] With an initial fund of £100m, the Corporation was able to underwrite all the schemes which could be promoted, and the number of societies grew rapidly, particularly when, in 1967 under a Labour government, option mortgage tax relief was made available on their collective mortgages. Promoters of cost-rent schemes which had also been encouraged under the Act, but with a traditional landlord-tenant structure, switched to co-ownership in order to benefit from the tax relief. Also in 1967 changes were made to the structure of co-ownership, to make it easier for people to become members: the lease was reduced from 99 years to 3 years or less, deposits reduced from 5 per cent of the cost of the dwelling to no more than the equivalent of 6 monthly payments. Whereas in 1966 there were 94 societies, by 1977 there were 1,222, owning over 40,000 dwellings.[37] However, by 1974 the boom was over: rising interest rates and building and land costs had priced such housing above what prospective members were able to pay in rent, and so few new schemes were attempted.

The story does not end here, though. There were many problems associated with the management of the schemes, which led to the formation in 1976 of a federation, the Council of Co-ownership

Co-operative housing: the early stages

Housing Societies. By tracing the history of the federation, we can find out just what was wrong with the initial structure of co-ownership, and the way it was promoted. The Society was never really strong. It was helped initially by a grant of £7,500 from the Housing Corporation, but then had to try to become self-sufficient, relying on subscriptions from member societies to keep it going. This meant that the membership fees were heavy, based on the number of units in each member society, and though it needed 500 in membership to break even, only 231 joined. The executive tried to encourage regional groupings, but with limited success, and by 1978 a financial crisis necessitated the redundancy of a field officer who had been hired to develop the Council to the point where it could become self-sufficient. Nevertheless, though it never reached its full potential, the CCHS produced a quarterly magazine called *Co-owner*, and 3 or 4 guidance notes per year, giving advice on a variety of very complex problems which were besetting individual societies. We can tell from these notes what the problems were. They were certainly very grave; by 1978 46 societies were in 'loss-rent' status, which meant that they were not able to pay their mortgage to the Housing Corporation, owing to inability to make rental income cover outgoings; the cost of development work on later schemes had risen drastically through inflation, mortgage interest had risen steeply, and several societies were beginning to experience crises due to bad management and latent defects. In 1979 a Labour government offered a chance to convert to a new structure, co-ownership equity-sharing, in which Housing Association Grant would be made available along with a reduced premium payment, so as to enable the societies in trouble to become viable. Only 3 had converted by the time the option was withdrawn by the Conservative government in February 1981.

Minutes show that at first delegates to CCHS annual meetings were in confident mood, defending the concept of co-ownership by returning large majorities against the idea of pursuing the right to sell their societies off to the members. But by the 1979 AGM the mood had changed; they were asking whether co-ownership had failed, through internal problems within the societies, and the failure of the premium payment to enable members to raise a deposit towards owner-occupation. There were 83 votes against 65, that if the terms were right, they would buy their own dwelling.[38] An incoming Conservative government had raised hopes that the right to sell might be granted; a survey done by CCHS showed a 2 to 1 majority in favour among

Co-operative housing: the early stages

co-owners, amid growing pessimism about rising interest rates. The minister had at first excluded co-ownerships along with other mutual co-operatives, but individual societies, including some in the Prime Minister's own constituency, were lobbying for the right to sell,[39] and eventually it was granted. By May 1981, 9 societies had sold up, and 300 more had permission to do so from the Housing Corporation. There remained the problem of minorities who did not wish to buy. The initial ruling was that unless there was a viable society remaining (meaning at least 7 co-owners who could register as an Industrial and Provident Society) societies would not be able to sell. Gradually, though, pressure was brought to bear and societies were allowed to sell against the minority's wishes, and to set up management societies and other devices in order to offload those who refused to buy. The CCHS, in advising societies about sales, and trying to remove impediments, contributed to its own demise; in July 1983 it was wound up. Profits were usually in the region of £8,000 to £20,000 per dwelling, depending on the age of the society, but some profits were spectacular; in one Regent's Park society members bought their flats for £20,000 and sold them immediately for around £150,000. One further problem remained; some 33 loss-rent societies were unable to sell because of financial problems or latent defects.[40] The CCHS had helped 'several dozen' societies over latent defects, and Housing Corporation loans had been made available for court action against builders and architects, and for remedial work. In June 1981 the minister gave loss-rent societies an ultimatum to begin charging an economic rent by August. In ignoring this, and trying to sort out their problems on an individual basis with the Housing Corporation, these societies remain a residual problem. Together with others which for one reason or another have not made the decision to sell, they make up a total of about 250 societies which have survived the sales programme.

How should we evaluate this rather short-run experiment? Firstly, it did meet the housing needs of those it was aimed at: 'better paid skilled workers, lower managerial grades, young professional people and small traders',[41] who did not have a deposit on a home and needed to be both housed and encouraged to save for eventual ownership, and of those who because elderly or self-employed could not get a mortgage. Full waiting lists have witnessed to this, right up to the time when societies have been sold off. Secondly, though, its structure is generally agreed to have been too complex, forcing members to rely too much on their managing agents; capital values had to be computed and new rents

Co-operative housing: the early stages

fixed every time mortgage interest changed, premiums and rent levels were difficult to calculate, and when members transferred to another dwelling, or loss-rent status changed premium entitlements, the formulae became too much even for the experts! But it is the promotion of co-ownerships which has been most to blame for the difficulties encountered throughout its history.

The Scandinavian model required a mother society, controlled by prospective co-op members, which would carry out the development of the daughter co-op. However, the market individualists, who for their own purposes promoted co-ownership in Britain, did not understand or care much about this; the 1964 Housing Act split the promotional and development functions, allocating the former to the Housing Corporation and the latter to independent societies of professionals, interested in living off the income generated by development and management allowances. The role of the Corporation was supposed to be educational and advisory, but in practice it was both bureaucratic and autocratic. It was intended explicitly that sponsors, some of whom were benefiting commercially from the work entailed, should become founder-members of each society, then become its managers, even secretaries of the management committee; a triple set of overlapping interests which was never questioned.[42] The Corporation's oversight of the initial development was very much at arm's length and heavily reliant on the self-discipline of the professionals, but management was subject to the need for all sorts of approvals (over rent levels, premiums, changes of managing agents and so on) which hampered the elected management committees in their attempts to gain control. Management agreements were signed by the founder members, who were also in many cases the managing agents, for up to 7 years, for 'continuity of management and administration'[43] so that co-owners were tied to contracts they had never been party to. Before the management committee were elected, the agents were expected to run the society for 6 months, and to 'bring the committee into consultation and to provide a continuing method of liaison'.[44]

In practice, though, many agents continued to run societies for years without informing the co-owners that they were anything more than tenants of the agent! The Corporation staff were clearly worried, not about this flagrant breach of co-operative principle, but about its possible application; they recommended in uncharacteristically expressive language, that: 'the Managing Society should be permitted to carry out the duties in the Agreement without pettifogging interference or being required to report on the minutiae of its tasks.'[45] The co-operative nature of this form of tenure was played down, and mentioned only where it absolutely had to be, in the model loan agreement and rules, while the role of the professionals was enhanced; the following extract from an educational leaflet is typical:

> practical experience has proved that the initial work of setting up a Society, of finding a site and developing it, and of dealing with lettings and estate management generally, is best undertaken by a sponsoring or parent society which has the necessary professional skills at its disposal.[46]

In view of the latent defects and bad management later uncovered by many societies, this appears very complacent, but the accompanying assertion that 'all the problems will have been ironed out by the professionals' comes across as unforgivably naive.

Such attitudes, when expressed in print, are merely irritating. In practice they were disastrous. The CCHS complained that the Corporation officials would deal only with the professionals, did not even know who were the elected chairmen, and did not send information to them. This extended to what looked like positive covering up of mistakes. 'In a number of instances', elected management committees were discouraged from going to law to remedy the professionals' defects.[47] The Corporation staff were uncomfortable with the co-operative nature of co-ownership, and wanted to off-load their educational function on to the federation without, however, giving it the resources to do the job. In its submission to the Campbell Report, the CCHS identified three problem areas: promotion, finance and management. Firstly, new and untested designs, inadequate site supervision, use of inferior materials, were all beginning to show up. The Council stated boldly that 'the promotion and development of co-ownership housing societies contained many improprieties [for which] individual co-owners ultimately have to pay', and that the 'ingenuous approach to the activities of professionals and ... failure to ensure effective supervision' by the Housing Corporation were partly to blame.[48] Secondly, since the beginning of the co-ownership experiment five sets of model rules had been issued, and co-owners had become confused about the structure of their societies and about the working of the premium system. Thirdly, managing agents were extracting maximum fees on a managing agreement which they had signed for both parties, and were expected to negotiate solutions to defects which they as sponsors had caused. Even then, in 1974, control had not passed to an elected management committee in many societies. Nor could the CCHS carry out its job properly, since some agents were advising co-owners not to join their federal body. We might add a fourth problem, that the legal environment had been far from sympathetic. There had been no clear legal status for co-owners, who had fallen between owner-occupation and tenancy, unable as tenants to qualify for security of tenure or rent allowances, or as owners for insulation grants. Lastly, the psychological environment can be deduced from the way in which the schemes had been promoted. It was made even worse by the lack of sympathy for those societies left in loss-rent status in 1979, which was shown by an incoming Conservative government. Within each co-ownership society the psychological climate is hardly better; with some honourable exceptions, those societies which still survive are lacking in tenant participation and any sense of community, caused by ignorance of their co-operative nature.

Is there a future for this type of co-op? The CCHS was optimistic, providing the premium system were simplified in a move towards a market-value type co-op, with premises based on district valuations.[49] The Campbell Report suggested new subsidy scales which would allow for various levels of equity stake, so that rents could be brought within members' capacity to pay. Mortgages could be extended in order to finance premiums, which would be simplified to a predetermined proportion of market value, and available after a reduced qualifying period of 6 months. Real education, advice and assistance would solve the problem of ignorance and lack of participation. However, Campbell recommended the much simpler structure of shared ownership (what he called community leasehold), in which individual titles would be held to part of the dwelling, and Housing Association Grant would be available on the rental portion. Anyone who has struggled with the complex calculation of premium payments in a co-ownership would almost certainly agree.

FIVE

CO-OPERATIVE HOUSING IN BRITAIN: THE LATER STAGES

PRECONDITIONS FOR GROWTH

When a new form of co-operative organisation emerges, it usually does so not out of the blue, but because of work done behind the scenes for a number of years, by a rare breed of co-operator who manages to combine both visionary power and patient determination to succeed. We have seen how the Tenant Co-operators Ltd had Benjamin Jones working for them, who when he saw the chance of putting his idea into practice calmly provided start-up capital by personally borrowing £100 at 5 per cent interest, and re-investing it in the co-op at 4 per cent. Similarly, Henry Vivian promoted the idea of tenant co-partnership, the Canadian co-operator Dr J.J. Tompkins the house-building co-op, Alex Laidlaw the more recent wave of Canadian common ownership co-ops, and Abraham Kagan the early trade-union-sponsored co-ops in New York. In the case of the current wave of common ownership co-ops in Britain, it was Harold Campbell and the Co-operative Party who did the ground-work. Harold said in one of his regular pamphlets on the subject, that the Co-op Party 'used every platform at its disposal in and out of Parliament to demand legislation that would give such co-operatives the legal and financial framework on which to build'.[1]

In the case of tenant management co-ops, again the Co-op Party as early as 1959 responded to a Labour Party policy of municipalisation of privately rented housing with a dissenting plea for devolved management and then in 1970 began to argue for a transfer of ownership and control on local authority estates.[2] In 1973 the Liberal Party Assembly resolved that a gradual handover to tenants' associations was needed, and Councillor Trevor Jones wanted to begin the process in Liverpool. Then in 1974 Colin Ward's powerfully argued book *Tenants Take Over* began to arouse interest, and with it the

Co-operative housing: the later stages

working example of the tenants' take-over in Oslo.

It is not always enough, though, to have promoters; they need powerful friends. In this case, Reg Freeson, one of the few Labour politicians who really appreciated and had first-hand knowledge of housing co-ops, became Minister for Housing in the new Labour government of 1974. He turned immediately to Harold Campbell to set up a working party. The brief was to report to the Minister on ways by which the formation of housing co-ops could be promoted, as well as on the idea of tenant self-management on local authority estates, and on the problems currently facing co-ownerships. The aptly named 'Campbell Report' which followed resulted in amendments to the 1975 Rent and Subsidies Act being rushed through so that co-ops could benefit from the grants and loans offered the previous year (in the 1974 Housing Act) through the Housing Corporation to the housing association movement.[3] Common-ownership co-ops were thus enabled to 'piggy-bank' on legislation which had ensured the rapid expansion of housing associations as the 'third arm' of British housing policy. That they were only to be a finger on the third arm, or perhaps to change the metaphor, a fledgling form of tenure nestling under the protective wing of a larger one, was not at the time thought to be a disadvantage. At the same time, amendments to the same Act allowed local authorities to hand over management of estates to tenant management co-ops without losing central government subsidies.

Another precondition for the growth of a co-operative form seems to be the promotion of actual experiments which both demonstrate its worth and show what difficulties lie in its way. The tenant co-partnerships were able to point to the older Tenant Co-operators Ltd, the co-ownerships to OBOS in Norway, the management co-ops to the Oslo tenants' take-over and the Canadian co-ops to the 'dogged efforts' of the founders of Willow Park Housing Co-op, Winnipeg. The current wave of common-ownership co-ops benefited similarly from experiments. Student Co-operative Dwellings began in 1968 to plan the provision of new-build student co-ops, but legal and financial problems delayed the first building scheme until 1973.[4] In 1972 the Holloway Tenant Co-operative, a neighbourhood-based co-op, was formed by the North Islington Community Project and began to administer property owned and improved by Circle 33 Housing Trust. It experienced great difficulties; a year after it began to administer the housing association's property, it still had no legal status, and had to have a 'major showdown' over continuing lack of control. It took five years before it was able to buy houses in its own name.[5] In Liverpool the Shelter Neighbourhood Action Project sponsored the Granby and Canning Co-ops, which began to use grants to housing associations available under the 1969 Housing Act to buy and improve whole streets of terraces, but without being allowed to become fully mutual co-ops.

Such experiments show the need for enabling legislation. John Hands says in comment on this difficult period, that 'The machinery has been geared to process a different animal, and if a housing co-operative managed to get into the machine, it was usually either rejected or mangled.'[6] Now, when most types of co-operative become established, they tend to create their own legislation to ratify what they are already attempting to do. A whole series of Industrial and Provident Society Acts in the last century were sponsored as a result of the growth of consumer co-operation. Where housing is concerned, though, the problems can be so formidable as to require legislation before a start can be made at all. Sometimes new forms of co-op have been almost completely 'children of an act'; the co-ownerships of the 1960s, for instance, or the 'Section 213' co-ops in the USA. Significantly, both of these were exploited more by developers out to make money than by genuine co-operators. More usually an act clears the way for a form which is struggling to emerge; in Canada, co-ops had been promoted from 1965 by 'bending' the existing National Housing Act, but they only became officially sanctioned in a 1973 amendment. A similar situation existed in the USA until, after several attempts, an Act was passed in 1950. In Britain, then, the 1975 Act was a clearing of the way, so that SCD, Granby and Holloway could become the rule rather than the exception, and so that tenants on council estates could enter into agency agreements with their landlords.

THE STRUCTURE OF THE CO-OPS

Before we continue with our history, it is worth digressing to find out more about the structure of these new types of co-op. We can distinguish three main types of primary co-op: common ownerships, tenant management and short-life, but a few shared ownership co-ops have been developed, and there are some privately funded co-ops which have a variety of structures, including common, shared and co-owernship. Community housing associations have also grown rapidly in Glasgow and Belfast, and share some of the features of the co-ops, with the important exception that though tenants can be members, they do

Co-operative housing: the later stages

not have to be; unfortunately we shall have to ignore them for our present purposes.

(a) Common-ownership co-ops

The structure of the largest group, the common-ownerships, is indicated by some of the titles they have been given. For instance, they are referred to as 'par value co-ops' because members have to take up a nominal £1 share which they may receive back on leaving at par value, without any element of individual gain. Or they are called 'non-equity' to distinguish them from co-ownership (where equity builds up in the entitlement to premium payments), or 'fair rent' co-ops, because they come under the Housing Corporation's system of grants and loans to housing associations, which necessitates as part of the grant calculation the fixing of a 'fair rent' by an independent rent officer. Because Housing Association Grant is paid, they are even sometimes called inelegantly 'HAG' co-ops. The important point is that the property is held in common; individual members are tenants but also common owners, without an individual stake in the equity. There are also a few privately funded common ownerships, but we can ignore them for the moment, and concentrate on the 'HAG' co-ops, so-called because the shortfall between actual development costs and 'fair rent' income is made up by a once-only Housing Association Grant. Most of them are mutual, that is, only tenants and prospective members can be members; happily (from the co-operative point of view) this excludes them from the right-to-buy clause of the 1980 Housing Act which allows council and non-charitable housing association tenants to buy their homes. Generally the co-ops are small, and one with over 100 households is rare. The smaller ones are sometimes managed by general meeting, the larger most often by an elected management committee, but some larger ones have a system of sub-groups which involve nearly all the members in some kind of decision-making.

(b) Tenant management co-ops

Management co-ops are voluntary associations of tenants who enter into an agency agreement with their landlord (a housing association or a local authority) to carry out housing management and sometimes rehabilitation on their estates. The range of responsibilities varies, but usually includes allocations and transfers, the drafting and enforcement of tenancy agreements, repairs and maintenance, and in England (but not generally in the Scottish co-ops) rent and rate collection and arrears chasing. In return, the co-ops receive a management and maintenance allowance, out of which, if they are efficient, they can make a surplus which may be used to build up a reserve against future maintenance needs, or to provide enviromental or housing improvements. They tend to be larger than the common-ownerships, and one or two have up to 250 households.

(c) Short-life co-ops

Short-life co-ops are also management co-ops, in that they are granted a lease on empty dwellings from landlords such as housing associations, local authorities, private landlords and property-holding agencies such as British Rail and the Department of Transport. The lease is usually only a licence to occupy, as the dwellings are scheduled for eventual demolition, improvement or conversion. They are sometimes eligible for 'mini-HAG' funding, whereby the Housing Corporation gives a small grant and loan for temporary repairs and improvements which will ensure a productive life for the property until it is repossessed. They tend to be smaller than the average common-ownership, and more informal, managing by general meeting.

(d) Shared-ownership co-ops

Shared-ownership is a concept developed recently by housing associations and means that a dwelling, usually new but occasionally rehabilitated, is offered part for rent and part for purchase. The owner-tenant chooses to buy 25, 50 or 75 per cent initially, and rents the rest at a fair rent, which has received housing association grant subsidy. The Greater London Secondary Housing Association, which under Harold Campbell's direction was active in promoting new forms of co-op until it was wound up recently, promoted the Glenkerry Housing Co-op in a tower block in the East End of London, with a complicated formula whereby the local authority own the freehold, the co-op a community leasehold and the flat-dwellers 50 per cent of the value of their dwellings. They do not have the right to buy the rest of the equity, and so the co-op will continue to supply low-cost home ownership to those just starting on the owner-occupied ladder. GLSHA also exploited the shared ownership concept to develop a 'staircasing' co-op. CDS Co-operative Housing took over this first scheme, and has now produced four new-build shared-ownership co-ops. These are slightly different from the original housing association model, in that owner-tenants have to buy from 50 to 75 per cent of the equity initially, and then can 'staircase' their way to full ownership in leaps of at least 10 per cent. As the dwelling is sold leasehold, presumably some kind of co-op will remain even if 100 per cent of the equity is eventually taken up. Unusually, prospective members are not involved at the design stage, and are selected according to their ability to pay the monthly mortgage and rent. When they leave the scheme, either they must find a buyer for their share of the property, or must buy the whole of the equity on the same day that they sell it on to the new member. If the latter method is often used, one would expect that the scheme would become quickly less of a co-operative and more an ordinary owner-occupied estate.

THE ORIGINS OF THESE CO-OPS

The origins of common ownership co-ops have been extremely varied. At first, before the idea of co-ops was generally known, some (e.g. Seghill Housing Co-op, in Northumberland) were formed by housing associations or secondary co-ops in the same way as co-ownerships, in that a group of members were selected after the co-op was formed, with the developers as founder members. This method is becoming rarer, though, and is generally avoided; CDS in London still use it, because they promote new-build co-ops which take a long time to develop. Others are formed in this way, but with some members selected at an early stage so that design participation can be ensured. The majority are formed by the consumers themselves, groups of people in great need of decent housing. Some (e.g. Seymour Co-op in London) have grown out of the squatters' movement of the 1960s and 70s, when groups were given an amnesty, took on the management of short-life property, and then evolved as they gained experience and confidence into the promotion of long-life co-ops. Others (e.g. Heathview in N. London) have grown out of tenants' associations formed in privately owned mansion blocks, who have eventually bought out the landlord. Others (e.g. Saint Andrew's St in Beverley, East Yorkshire) have formed to fight redevelopment plans and rehabilitate terraced housing, or (e.g. Weller St in Liverpool) to keep control of the new-build process when their old homes have been demolished.

Some have been formed by very disadvantaged groups, such as

Co-operative housing: the later stages

Bengalis in Tower Hamlets (Spitalfields co-op) and Chinese in Liverpool (Greenleaf Co-op), who have suffered from discrimination in the allocation of council housing, and others have been formed by pressure groups representing single-parent families (Liverpool Gingerbread Co-op) and elderly people (Huyton Community Co-op). One or two have even branched out into providing services for other even more disadvantaged groups; the Princes Park Housing Co-op, which provides homes for single-parent families, is building a hostel for women who have suffered from domestic violence. Perhaps the most interesting of these varied origins is that of the Coin St co-ops in Waterloo, London, where over ten years the local community have fought 'one of the most effective and sustained community campaigns ever seen in Britain', to make sure that housing for local people is built on a 13 acre derelict site.[7] They took on some of the most powerful forces one can imagine; property companies who wanted to put up a £200m wall of offices a third of a mile long, and who were supported initially by the Greater London Council. Having won the battle, the local people have set up in Coin St Community Builders, a non-profit company which is to develop the site, and build 400 co-operative houses. The local Labour council has been won over to the co-operative method because it ensures that the tenants' right to buy council housing is circumvented. But the local people are committed for more solid reasons; as one commentator says: 'For a community that has fought so hard and so unitedly for its future as Waterloo has done, co-operation comes naturally.'[8] With such origins in acute housing need, these common ownerships have housed some of the most disadvantaged people in Britain. A recent survey shows that of 100 co-ops surveyed, 50 per cent of members have net incomes of less than £80 per week, and 74 per cent of less than £120 per week. 8 per cent are single-parent families, 20 per cent are Asian, African, Black British or non-white British, and almost all had left bad housing conditions; 11 per cent had had no bathroom previously, while 34 per cent had had to share one, and so on.[9]

Management co-ops originate in one of three ways. Firstly, there is pressure for joint management and eventual autonomy by active tenants' associations (e.g. Speirs Co-op in Glasgow, or Cloverhall in Rochdale). Secondly, there is the new-build management co-op, where tenants of a brand-new estate are selected for their desire to be in a co-op, and are educated in the running of it before and during the move in (e.g. on the Elthorne Estate in London, where four co-ops have been formed on an estate of 400 houses). Thirdly, there is the new co-op formed in a rehabilitated formerly hard-to-let estate from which the original tenants have been transferred.

Short-life co-ops originated out of the squatters' movement, when mainly in Labour-controlled areas, councillors realised that their plans had outstripped the funding for new building, and that the dwellings they had condemned would have to stay up for a long time. Licensed squatting led to the more organised response of specialists such as Islington Community Housing Association, who used their charitable status to achieve rate reductions. Such housing associations have been more or less co-operative in form, depending on their size and whether or not they ask all tenants to be members. Other groups (e.g. Leytonstone Co-op in East London) have at first tried to provide permanent co-op housing, but then, because of spending cuts, fallen back on short-life.

THE STARTING-UP PROCESS

How easy has it been for groups to promote their own co-ops? With common ownerships, the process is complex and long-drawn-out, and the outcome is uncertain. Firstly, founding members have to register their co-op as a friendly society, and then to attempt to register with the Housing Corporation as a housing association. Registration depends on there being enough grant and loan finance available for the Corporation to give the co-op an 'allocation', and on the co-op's willingness to use an approved secondary co-op or housing association as development agent. The procedure is far from automatic; in one survey, 5 out of 45 applications for co-op registration were found to have been rejected by Corporation officials.[10] Then, when they have leapt over this major hurdle, they have to cope, together with their development agent, with all the complexities and uncertainties of the Housing Corporation's funding system, which lays down 'total indicative costs' which a project must not exceed, and requires several stages of loan approvals. When the housing is built, or bought and rehabilitated, the co-op members have to enter the next stage, of self-management. Because of the receipt of housing association grant, they are obliged to charge the correct 'fair rent' on each property, and to allocate their dwellings on the basis of need, but otherwise they are autonomous, the smaller ones doing the work through volunteers, the larger ones hiring their own staff or buying services from a secondary co-op or housing association. In fact, in 1986 there were over 200 staff working in secondaries or as direct employees of primary co-ops. They do all their own allocations, but often have to take a proportion (usually 50 per cent) of local council nominees, though being able to choose between different candidates to find those most committed to the idea of being co-operators.

With management co-ops the process is simpler, but it can still take a long time before it produces the desired housing. Short-life co-ops can get moving fairly quickly, as their housing is temporary and can be brought quickly back into use. Tenant management co-ops ought to find the process equally simple, but the negotiation of a management agreement can take years. At Cloverhall Co-op, for instance, a tenants' association was formed early in 1981, and members entered into joint management of the estate with the council until their management agreement was signed late in 1984. Even more protracted have been the negotiations between eleven management co-ops and the London Borough of Islington, which have just been concluded after six years; six of the co-ops (on newly built estates) have been managing their property without any legal status even as secure tenants, while four others had an agreement with the GLC, which they had to renegotiate when the latter was abolished. Apparently, it is quite common for co-ops to operate without agreements, or in an interim period after a former agreement has expired; during this period they run the risk of being disbanded for holding out on issues they feel strongly about.[11]

THEIR PROMOTION FROM 1975 ONWARDS

(a) Common-ownership co-ops

Now that we have begun to understand the character of these co-ops, we can return to our history, and the 'watershed' year of 1975. As far as common ownership co-ops were concerned, Reg Freeson did not just sit back and wait for them to emerge, but backed up the Campbell Committee's findings and his legislation with no less than four Department of the Environment circulars.[12] Following the Campbell Report's recommendation, a Co-operative Housing Agency was set up very quickly in late 1976 as a division of the Housing Corporation. There was criticism of this move from tenants' and co-op representatives, since it placed the Agency within a bureaucracy which for them was already discredited by its handling of co-ownership. Yet the advantage was of speedy growth, with the hope of a later conversion of the Agency to control by the co-operatives. It suited no one perfectly;

Co-operative housing: the later stages

Corporation officials saw it as being too independent, co-op groups as being too tied to government bureaucracy, and it never shook off the problem of having to both promote and regulate the new movement. However, under the Agency's vigorous promotion, co-ops were formed rapidly; early in 1977 there were only 17 registered primary co-ops on the Corporation's books, but by July 1980 these had grown to 128, and then by August 1984 to 216.[13] It is difficult to pin the movement down to figures, but Table 5.1 is probably as accurate and up-to-date as one can get.[14] There are marked regional variations; in 1980 about half of all co-ops were in London, and a further quarter in Liverpool, but as the table shows, by 1987 co-ops were beginning to develop in other regions as well.

TABLE 5.1: Common-ownership co-ops by region, 1987

	HAG co-ops	Pre-HAG co-ops	Co-op h/assocs	Unclassified co-ops
London and Home Counties North	70	2		28
London and Home Counties South	40		7	5
Merseyside	39			4
North-east	20			3
Lancashire and Yorkshire	20			11
The Midlands	18			5
The West	7			10
South Coast	3			0
Scotland	6			0
TOTAL	223	2	7	66

Source: *NFHC Directory.*

The Housing Corporation's provisional allocation for co-ops in 1984–5 shows a continuing emphasis on London, but a steady growth throughout the other regions; out of the total allocation for housing associations in each region (both in new-build and rehabilitation), London and Home Counties North received 8.2 per cent, London South received 11.2 per cent, and the other regions of England around 2–3 per cent each.

The active promotion of housing co-ops after years of neglect can, of course, bring its own problems, of over-ambitious planning, the forcing of a pace which can only go as fast as a genuine educational process will allow, and possible disillusionment when the movement does not live up to unrealistic expectations. Something of the sort happened in Quebec, where 40 projects were started in the late 1960s, but where because of a lack of genuinely democratic, decentralised promotion, the whole idea had by 1972 'come under a cloud'.[15] In the British case, the Co-op Housing Agency also started off in a comparatively big way; 14 staff, including 6 specialist officers and researchers, were appointed who ran weekend courses for co-operators and local promoters, assisted primary co-ops with educational work, granted secondary co-ops the funds to employ education workers, enabled the employment of development workers for isolated co-ops and so on. Yet it was closed down in February 1979 by the Minister, ostensibly because of the failure of the sector to grow quickly enough to use the 10 per cent of the Housing Corporation budget allocated, but really because of internal management difficulties within the Agency. It was replaced with a central co-op unit of 3 people within the Corporation headquarters, and specialists within each region. Again the promoters had to wait for co-op development to catch up; some regions did not appoint specialists, because it was felt that there was not enough activity to justify them. Then, with reorganisation of the Corporation in 1981 into generic regional teams, only one co-op specialist remained, based at headquarters; co-ops have been subsumed under housing association work, with no further commitment by the Corporation actively to promote them.

(b) Secondary co-ops

Nevertheless, the activity of the CHA, over-ambitious though it might have been, enabled secondary co-ops to emerge; from only 2 in 1977, they had grown by 1987 to 14. Table 5.2 shows their distribution around the country. Not surprisingly, the distribution of primary co-ops mirrors that of the secondaries. The latter were a necessary development (perhaps more necessary even than the CHA), because the Housing Corporation required that registered co-ops have a development agreement with a secondary or a housing association, to steer them through a complex system of approvals for funding; as early as 1977, figures showed that nearly all primary co-ops to date (92 per cent) had been promoted by an approved agency, either a secondary housing co-op (67 per cent) or a housing association (22 per cent), with 3 per cent being supported by independent consultants.[16] It was vital that promotional bodies should develop in a way which enabled an efficient service to be given to primary co-ops, controlled by and accountable to them. Secondary co-ops have either been set up from the start as consumer-controlled organisations (in which each member co-op has voting rights, either on a 'one co-op one vote' basis, or weighted by the number of members in each primary co-op), or have begun with a non-elected management committee and slowly worked towards greater primary co-op involvement, as the latter have become established. These secondaries have been able to provide a comprehensive range of services and skills needed by primary co-ops, relying on the development and management allowances paid to the latter by the Housing Corporation. The best of them offer to primary co-ops one individual who is a generalist worker, who works from an accessible, local office, and steers the co-op through the whole development process, helping its members to become mature and independent so that in the end they can become completely self-managing.[17]

TABLE 5.2: Secondary Co-ops by region, 1987

	Secondaries	Local federations
London and Home Counties North	4	3
London and Home Counties South	3	2
Merseyside	3	0
North-east	1	1
Lancashire and Yorkshire	2	0
The Midlands	1	0
The West	0	0
South Coast	0	0
Scotland	0	0
TOTAL	14	6

Source: *NFHC Directory*

They also employ education workers, who do not necessarily do the educating, but identify needs, plan courses and provide back-up material so that the generalist, and the specialists who he or she calls on at various stages, can themselves take part in the education process. They have found it hard, though, to fund this vital educational side of their work. One way of doing this has been to employ in-house architects and to recycle some of their fee-income. The commitment of

Co-operative housing: the later stages

several secondaries to a collective method of working and an equal wage structure has also helped. Another method has been the educational grants which the 1974 Housing Act allowed the Corporation to make; £149,000 was given in 1979 for this purpose, but the figure has declined, until in 1985 it was only £90,200, spread over a much larger number of agencies. Happily, the grant increased in 1986 and may do so again slightly in 1987. At the same time, secondaries have come to recognise more and more that education work is absolutely essential to both the short-term effectiveness of co-ops and their long-term survival. As one researcher concluded recently, 'it is a pervasive activity, which is at the heart of the way the secondary operates.'[18] Co-operators are not born; they have, at considerable expense in time and energy, to be made. An increasing need met by a declining amount of grant aid is not a recipe for success. Furthermore, in 1984, a Corporation monitoring report on primary co-ops criticised them for poor record-keeping, and emphasised the need for further training, particularly in financial management; the left hand criticised the co-ops for what the right hand had to some extent been taking away. However, recently a special extra co-operative promotion allowance has been agreed with the Department of the Environment; officials have recognised at last that co-ops are not cheap to produce, and are certainly more expensive initially than an inappropriate fee system, geared up to the needs of large housing associations, had allowed for.

(c) Tenant-management co-ops

While common-ownership co-ops could be promoted to some extent outside the existing housing systems, using the new housing association grant and Co-operative Housing Agency, tenant mangement co-ops relied for their development on sympathetic support from local authorities and tenants. The Campbell Report recognised this by spending time arguing the case, and inviting comments from interested parties. There was an argument from first principles: 'tenants should be directly involved in decisions which affect their home and local environment, and should be free to make such rules as they consider necessary within that environment.'[19] And there were several more practical arguments about the tenants' ability to assess design of estates, to contribute local knowledge, their desire to reduce vandalism and improve the appearance of estates, their wish to improve their homes, and so on. Yet the psychological climate was at that time still fairly hostile, the crisis in housing management which Colin Ward had prophesied was only round the corner, but was still not in sight; the Association of Local Councils asserted complacently in their reply, and against all the evidence that Ward and others had produced, that:'Local authorities generally provide a responsive and local management.'[20] In their submissions to the Report, local authorities expressed reservations: that there was no real demand from tenants, and potential conflict between them, and that they would impose over-rigid controls on each other's behaviour. If co-ops were successful, though, they would enhance status differences between estates, creating a different class of tenant; it seems that co-ops could not do right, whatever they did! Tenants (represented by the Association of London Housing Estates) were wary of local authorities trying to off-load their problems on to them, and were worried about top-down promotions, preferring the initiative to come from well-informed tenants' associations. Yet despite their worries, their support for management co-ops was elsewhere expressed forcefully:

> there is a need to move from consultative to management roles and that legislation should recognise the importance of tenants being given a firm programme of participation leading to the stage where they will achieve total control on the estates where they live.[21]

Labour government support led to encouraging circulars,[22] and the Green Paper of 1977 declared: 'all local authorities should take steps to explain to their tenants what housing co-ops involve, and to find out whether they would be willing to take part in such schemes.'[23] Such support was reinforced by a general rethinking of the landlord–tenant relationship; the promise of a tenants' charter which would give secure tenure, powers to sub-let and to improve council housing, the right to be consulted about changes in management practice and so on. The incoming Conservative government then confirmed the new status of the tenant in the 1980 Housing Act, while shifting the emphasis to individual purchase of the dwelling, but at least allowed management co-ops to remain on the agenda.

More was needed than gradual changes in the climate of opinion. Promotional agencies were set up, but only in London and Glasgow. The Greater London Council helped to set up the Greater London Secondary Housing Association, to create a series of co-ops on the Elthorne Estate, while in Glasgow the City Council set up its own

Co-ops Unit, which began by promoting the Summerston Co-op, and the Tenant Participation Advisory Service provided general advice to tenants. However, the idea has been spread more widely by the Priority Estates Project, set up by the DoE to work in England in 1979, and later extended by the Welsh Office to Wales in 1983. The 'PEP' aimed to develop estate-based management and maintenance on problem estates, but regarded tenant self-management as one option, albeit the most challenging one, whereby such estates could be improved; a management co-op has been developed at Cloverhall, Rochdale.

TABLE 5.3: Tenant management co-ops by region, 1987

	Local authority TMCs	Housing Association TMCs
London and Home Counties North	21	9
London and Home Counties South	8	18
Merseyside	0	0
North-east	0	0
Lancashire and Yorkshire	2	0
The Midlands	2	0
The West	0	1
South Coast	0	0
Scotland	11	0
TOTAL	44	28

Source: *NFHC Directory*.

By 1979 about 'two dozen' serious attempts were known to the DoE, but lack of agreement with the unions representing housing management staff had held up progress in Liverpool and Lambeth. By 1981 12 management co-ops based on local authority property had had their agency agreements approved by the Secretary of State, but if housing association developments and prospective co-ops are taken into account this figure increased to over 40; the 1981 Directory of Housing Co-ops included 28 groups in London, 2 each in Birmingham, Liverpool and Glasgow, 1 each in Milton Keynes and Lichfield, and 4 in Glasgow. By 1982, evidence was available which showed how effective such co-ops were: a DoE paper claimed that there were *no* inherent disadvantages in tenant management co-ops, merely potential difficulties to be guarded against, and that there were many proven advantages; tenancy agreemenets reflected members' real preferences, and breaches of rules were being handled effectively. Selection of tenants was not excluding those in housing need, even though the need to select good co-operators was primary. Repairs services were quick and efficient, estates well cared for, with virtually no vandalism, and savings on allowances were enabling improvements to be financed, and in 3 of the cases monitored by the DoE study enabling rents to be reduced. Co-ops were found to be socially satisfying, with mutual aid, care for the elderly and children, and so on.[24] By 1987, the situation was as set out in Table 5.3. Progress has undoubtedly continued to be (as the DoE study described it) 'fairly slow', but it is at least steady; there are 9 more co-ops currently being considered in Scotland.

TABLE 5.4: Other co-ops by region, 1987

	Short-life co-ops	Long-life co-ops also doing SL.+	Privately-funded
London and Home Counties North	65*	14	9
London and Home Counties South	56	12	1
Merseyside	0	0	0
North-east	0	0	1
Lancashire and Yorkshire	2	0	7
The Midlands	0	1	5
The West	4	0	1
South Coast	2	1	0
Scotland	0	0	7
TOTAL	129	28	31

Source: *NFHC Directory*.
 * = including 4 short-life users' groups
 + = already counted as HAG co-ops in Table 5:1

(d) *Short-life and privately-funded co-ops*

As Table 5.4 shows clearly, short-life has mainly grown up in London, where the high cost of conventional housing, the ineligibility of childless couples and single people for council housing, and the large number of empty properties have combined to make it attractive.

Recently, the development of co-ops has slowed, owing to a variety of factors; mini-HAG funding has been hedged about with restrictions, local authorities have been buying fewer houses for slum clearance, community care schemes have been competing for those houses that are available, and the growth in homelessness has meant that councils are using their own short-life dwellings for homeless families. However, in 1985 the funding because less restricted; mini-HAG rules changed, and the DoE gave a grant to the Lambeth Federation of Housing Co-ops of £190,000, which will enable about 30 houses to be brought into use, and a worker to be appointed. Even more recently, two new National Federation workers have been appointed with London Boroughs funding to concentrate on short-life developments in North and South London.

Privately funded co-ops have been inadequately researched, and it is difficult to generalise about how they have developed, or the form they have taken. They usually require either a 'windfall' benefactor, or substantial personal capital to set up, though in some cases these have been supplemented by building society and bank mortgages, loan capital from friends and relations, use of improvement grants and 'sweat equity'.[25] A few HAG-funded co-ops have experimented recently with additional schemes involving improvement grants and building society mortgages, but the going has been very difficult. However, as we shall see below, this form of co-op may be set for a major expansion in the near future.

THE DEVELOPMENT OF A FEDERATION

The true measure of the maturity of a co-operative sector is in its ability to sponsor and support a federal organisation. We have noted the way in which Scandinavian co-ops have organised at national and even international levels, and the difficulties which the co-ownership federation had in Britain, before being wound up. At first, the National Federation of Housing Associations provided support to common-ownership co-ops, with a working party and a Co-op Management Project, yet its main aim has always been to represent a different type of organisation. For this reason, co-operators saw it as imperative that, in the words of Peter Clarke: 'Housing co-operatives have got to develop their own identity rather than, as they are at the moment, always tugging at the coat-tails of housing associations.'[26] In 1977 an embryonic National Federation of Housing Co-ops failed to get off the ground, but the NFHA sponsored Standing Conference of Housing Co-ops, reconvened after the demise of the CHA, helped the movement to try again. By 1981 there was sufficient interest, particularly in those regions which had sufficient primary and secondary co-ops, to ensure that this time it survived. Officially there are 8 regions plus Scotland, which though it has its own Scottish Federation of Housing Co-ops, sends four representatives to the national Federation. At the time of writing, there are seven fully constituted regional federations: Merseyside, North-East, Lancashire/Greater Manchester, Yorkshire/Humberside, London North, London South and the South Coast. The East and West Midlands and Wales/West regions are still being developed. They are autonomous, and control the policy-making of the Federation via a twice-yearly congress; the national committee to which they each send two representatives is more of an agenda-setting body.

Like the co-ownership federation, they have had trouble persuading all the primary co-ops to join; by November 1985 there were 160 affiliates. They have also had to rely totally on voluntary workers, until 1986 when the Department of the Environment has signalled the Government's renewed interest in co-ops, by funding two full-time workers. The London Boroughs Grant Unit has just matched this with funding for the two workers mentioned, who will work on short-life housing. The Federation's activities and influence have been out of all proportion to its size. Working groups have been convened on Housing Corporation monitoring of co-ops, private mortgage finance, management co-ops, short-life co-ops and so on, and an editorial and production group has produced a regular magazine called *Around the Houses*. Having achieved consultative status with the DoE, the Federation has campaigned against cuts in the education grant, in favour of the special co-op promotion allowance, against very high fair rent increases, and so on. New regions (such as the South Coast and Merseyside) are being formed, and existing ones underpinned with more local federals; co-ops in the London boroughs of Brent, Camden, Newham and Tower Hamlets are now forming their own umbrella organisations (see Table 5.2). It is a rather confusing picture, since those secondary co-ops which are area-based cannot help also acting as federations for their own primary co-ops, but it is a much livelier one than it was a few years ago.

Co-operative housing: the later stages

FUTURE PROSPECTS

(a) Common-ownership co-ops

An advisory committee which claimed in 1977 that 'obstacles remain which are hardly less formidable than those which followed the 1961/4 experiments'[27] is probably exaggerating, but for common-ownership co-ops some large problems do remain as yet unresolved. Firstly, there is need for a more favourable legal environment. A proper co-operative tenure should be defined in law, enabling members to have a 'right to occupy' status not based on inappropriate landlord-tenant law, but on a recognition of the common interests of co-op members as individuals and common owners. There are other legal irritants, including the restriction in the 1980 Housing Act on payments to committee members, which ironically, in finally stopping the abuses outlined in the last section on co-ownership, also stops co-ops from rewarding their hard-working officers with an honorarium. Secondly, there is a need for a more favourable financial environment. The same advisory committee described the Housing Corporation funding system as 'terrifyingly complex and incomprehensible'. It certainly causes confusion among co-op members, demoralising delays and enforced changes in design, which during an unnecessarily long development process makes it difficult to keep up the morale and involvement of all but the most dedicated co-operators. A simplified system, perhaps based on subsidised interest rates rather than on a once-for-all grant, would be easier to understand, and allow greater financial autonomy. But by far the biggest problem is that the total level of funding has been reducing steadily; housing corporation allocation has halved, and will continue to fall in real terms; the 1986 figure of £685m for housing associations is to be repeated for the next two years, with no allowance for inflation, while local authority funding has almost completely ceased. When the Greater London Council was abolished in 1985, secondary co-ops had to make almost superhuman efforts to save many co-ops which were threatened, even in some cases when work was on site. Then in London, soaring prices have this year made it almost impossible for secondary co-ops to acquire property at all. If the demand for new co-ops is to be met, there will have to be at least a restoration of the 10 per cent co-op allocation for Housing Corporation funding, and a continuous review of cost limits.

Yet despite these continuing problems, the climate of opinion has been generally favourable. Support from the Labour government of

1974-9 turned for a while to indifference among the Conservatives, but not to outright deterrence; the 1980 Housing Act at least ensured the movement's survival by excluding mutual co-ops from the 'right-to-buy' legislation. Recently an all-party consensus on co-ops seems to have emerged, from Conservative housing and environment ministers to Liberal and Social Democratic MPs and Labour front-bench spokesmen, all of whom have been out-bidding each other in singing the praises of the housing co-op; in fact, the only real opposition has come from the militant collectivists of the Liverpool Labour party.

Nearer the ground, though, the going is still tough. In an annual report, one secondary co-op reports that the will to help form co-ops is there in some areas but not in others, and that 'The lack of widespread recognition of the potential that the co-op model has to offer is very frustrating.'[28] Some Housing Corporation staff, other housing professionals and local councillors remain reserved about co-ops, questioning whether members will safeguard housing need in their allocations, and whether they are competent to handle large sums of money. Yet on these criticisms co-ops can hardly win; the criterion of competence to some extent contradicts that of housing people in genuine need. From the co-ops' perspective, the main aim must be to satisfy their members, not the Corporation or the local council, to control the professionals, not to give them more power. The problem of reconciling participatory democracies of mainly working-class people with the huge representative democracies of so-called 'local' councils, and with the large quasi-governmental bureaucracy of the Housing Corporation is an inherently difficult one, and requires, paradoxically, a high degree of professionalism in the way the amateurs approach the professionals. Such a growth in knowledge, confidence and commitment takes time to emerge, but it is emerging; primary co-op members are beginning to take a leading part in determining not only their own future and that of the secondaries, but through their federations, that of the whole movement.

(b) Tenant management co-ops

At first sight, there are no legal impediments to tenant self-management, because it is limited to control and not ownership of property. Yet over the crucial legal document, the management agreement, there have been continued difficulties. We have noted how it has taken years of negotiation for co-ops to reach the point where all parties are prepared to sign, particularly when there are outstanding defects to be remedied before the co-op will take on responsibility for maintenance. The National Federation's Management Co-ops Group is working on a model management agreement which, given goodwill on the landlord's side, should remedy the situation.

Another impediment to the development of management co-ops has been the patchy nature of their promotion, by agencies limited mainly to London and Glasgow. Yet such agencies are vitally needed. The development process is not as complex as that faced by common-ownership co-ops, but it still takes an initially heavy input of resources for the education of tenants, and sometimes for community development work, before co-op members feel confident enough to take over the management of their estates. Employment of a skilled manager where co-ops are large enough to afford one, does reduce the burden on members, but they still need to be able to manage the manager. Either out of lack of confidence in their abilities to sponsor co-ops, or out of a disinclination to commit scarce management resources, many local authorities have in the past fallen back on less exacting and more 'tokenistic' strategies for tenant participation. Others, notably Sheffield and some London Boroughs, have put their faith in decentralising and thereby hoped to improve the quality of traditional housing management. The 1986 Housing and Planning Act should change all this, for two reasons. Firstly, councils will have a duty to consider proposals for a tenants' take-over, and give a reasoned response; their reasons why it should not happen will have to be sound ones. Secondly, grant aid will be available to promotional agencies specifically for the education of tenants in the self-management option. Secondary co-ops are hoping to extend into this field, and a National Federation working party is to submit a package of proposals for funding. A joint conference with the DoE on the subject has recently been held, and one of the Federation's new full-time workers is to deal exclusively with management co-ops.

It would seem, then, that tenant management co-ops are, after a slow start, heading for a major expansion. The climate of opinion is very different from that shown by respondents to the Campbell Report over a decade ago, and hardly anyone is now arguing for the retention of council housing in its old form. The Housing and Planning Act received all-party support when it went through Parliament recently, and politicians seem to be trying to out-do each other in co-op promotion; an opposition amendment (sponsored by the National Federation of

Housing Co-ops) which would have given tenants the right to self-management whether or not the local authority agrees was defeated, but only on the grounds that some consensus would still be needed if an agency agreement were to be signed.

(c) Privately funded co-ops

There is no reason why private funding should not be used for co-operative development. In the USA and Canada credit unions and mutual insurance societies, both of them a kind of co-op, have been involved for many years in funding housing co-ops. Building societies and pension schemes in Britain and even one or two banks (the Co-operative Bank and Unity Trust) have some co-operative features, or are at least non-profit societies. Scandinavian co-ops owe their success at least in part to their second-tier co-ops being also mutual savings banks. In fact, the term 'private' finance is incorrect; these sources of funds can be placed on a continuum from private capitalist to mutual or co-operative.

There are several reasons why in Britain, at present, the tapping of the gigantic reserves of capital built up in these institutions is being explored by, among others, the housing association movement, the Housing Corporation and a National Federation of Housing Co-ops working-party. HAG funding provides all sorts of restraints on co-ops, including the need to gain permissions at every stage of the development process, regular monitoring of performance when in management, the inability to set their own rent levels and liability for 'claw-back' charges on surpluses made. At the same time, HAG funds are becoming harder to obtain, and being channelled away from general housing needs to special needs and shared ownership. Fair rents are, after several steep rises, no longer necessarily cheap rents. Short-life housing has contracted, while the private rented sector continues its steady decline, and there is a desperate need for more rented housing. Publicly funded housing does not cater for single people and childless couples, and so on.[29]

Yet co-ops have some built-in advantages; they are mutual housing societies, and so members do not have legal security of tenure and the right-to-buy, both of which would frighten off the private lenders who would want to be able to repossess a property if a mortgagee defaulted on payments. Yet they provide collective ownership of the property, which brings with it mortgage tax relief and exemption from

Corporation and Capital Gains Taxes. A combination of low-start or deferred payment mortgages and tax relief could, in theory at least, mean that rents would be low enough for people in housing need to afford.

Already there have been some housing association schemes using building society mortgages and public subsidy. Two pilot projects are going ahead. A 600-home green-field site in Cardiff will be funded by a combination of a 70 per cent mortgage, Housing Association Grant and land provided by the city council in return for nomination rights. A massive 4000-home building programme by the North Housing Association will raise £100m on the money markets, topped up with £12m of the association's own resources.[30] The Housing Corporation has commissioned some feasibility studies of a new 'assured tenancy', which would combine a mutual society with mortgage tax relief, a 30 per cent HAG subsidy, low-start index-linked building society mortgages and rents at about 10 per cent above current fair rents.[31] With agreement from the Treasury not to count such funding as public (which strangely it does at present), and to sanction 'dual-source subsidy' (entailed in giving mortgage tax relief to occupiers as owners and allowing housing benefits to them as tenants), it could lead to an output of 15,000 homes per year. This is all very well, but, despite the need to form a mutual society in order to gain tax relief, they would not necessarily be co-ops; only one of the five feasibility studies, submitted by Co-operative Development Services (Liverpool), is planned as a co-op. The rest are conventional housing association schemes which set up the mutual society merely as a device for obtaining tax relief. As in 1963, when a previous Conservative government wanted to boost the rented sector and started co-ownership, the commitment to co-operative practice is thin; there is no provision for member education or real democratic structures. One housing association developer has described the mutual society candidly as 'a thing of straw'.[32]

There are opportunities and pitfalls, then, in the future development of housing co-ops with private funding.

(d) The Glasgow District Council 'Community Ownership' scheme

Lastly, there is one scheme which, though it is just getting off the ground, may become a major new method of co-op development. This is the Glasgow Community Ownership scheme. What do you do when you are the largest municipal landlord in Europe, have 41,000 on the

Co-operative housing: the later stages

waiting list, with 5,000 new households expected to be formed in the next five years, can afford to do no new house-building, and have a massive problem of disrepair and hard-to-let estates? Bailie James McLean, the city's Convenor of Housing, describes it as the worst crisis of the century,[33] caused by the wholesale clearance of tenements in the inner city, and their replacement with high-rise flats, and large windswept estates on the periphery. The Housing Support Grant from central government has been cut by 63 per cent from £69m in 1980-81 to £25.7m in 1984-85, and the Housing Revenue Account from £197.5m to £153m, yet the immediate repair bill from estates is reckoned at £180m; the cost of keeping stock wind and weather-proof alone in 1984 was £64m. Altogether, the Director of Housing estimates that over £1600m would be needed for capital investment to 1990.

The plan is to sell thousands of homes to community ownership co-ops. But what can co-ops possibly do about such a disastrous situation, except shoulder a responsibility which no one in their right minds would take on? It is not so wild a suggestion as it seems at first sight. Co-ops, as non-public forms of social ownership, are eligible to tap into considerable funds which Glasgow holds, but which the Conservative government will only allow to be spent on the private housing sector. They can apply for private finance to buy the dwellings and for council grants to improve them. Nor is the plan as opportunist as it seems; the new type of co-op fits into an existing strategy of maximising the use of stock by improved housing management and tenant participation, which has already produced 11 management co-ops. At first, 14 groups of tenants expressed an interest, and 4 were chosen for feasibility studies. The studies showed that viability hinged on low acquisition costs from the council, improvement and environmental grants and promotional grants to set the co-ops up, low-start building society loans with tax relief on the interest, and government loan guarantees. The resulting cost rents were estimated to be feasible, except in one scheme, where a very low acquisition cost would be necessary. The council were prepared to second staff, carry out repairs and improvements on an agency basis, provide the grants and so on. The Housing Corporation agreed to provide training and financial support for staff, the banks and building societies offered competitive lending terms, and the only disquiet shown was from the trade union, NALGO, whose members feared job losses.

Eventually 6 potential co-ops emerged, but after two years of negotiations, the central government's Scottish Office still withheld

Co-operative housing: the later stages

approval, on the grounds that the schemes were more expensive than necessary, and that the Treasury would not allow 'double subsidy' of housing benefit and mortgage tax relief; in fact, this last problem has also held up the fully mutual housing societies planned by the Housing Corporation. Instead, the Scottish region of the Housing Corporation has agreed to fund three of the co-ops, two as ordinary 'HAG' type common ownerships and one as a community housing association, and these are now going ahead, at Easterhouse, Castlemilk and Broomhouse. The very latest news is that the three other potential co-ops will probably also go ahead with private finance and cost-rents as originally planned. The dual-source subsidy problem has already been resolved in England and Wales, and the ruling could easily be extended to Scotland. However, even without the ability to combine collective mortgage tax relief with individual elegibility for housing benefits, the schemes are financially sound. The Housing Corporation has agreed to register the co-ops, and, with only a few minor points outstanding, the Scottish Office is expected to approve the transfer of ownership by Spring of 1987. It will have taken 13 years for Colin Ward's vision of the 'tenants' take-over' to have become, for at least six groups of Scottish council tenants, a reality.

SIX

CO-OPERATION IN PRACTICE: SIX CASE HISTORIES

So far, we have been breathing the rarified atmosphere of co-operative philosophy and the rather stale air of housing co-op history. What is needed now is to present to the reader some living examples of co-operation in practice, some case studies of real communities who are living under co-op principles.[1] The following six case histories are no more typical of housing co-op practice than any other six cases might be, since every co-op is to some extent unique. Yet they do cover a wide range of organisational types, and at least show the diversity and flexibility of the form. They are chosen mainly because they are among the oldest established of the co-ops formed since 1975 in Britain, and so have a longer story to tell. We will draw some lessons from them in the next chapter, but for the moment will be content just to introduce them to the reader.

ST ANDREW'S STREET
(a rehabilitation-type common ownership co-op)

Beverley is a bustling East Yorkshire market town, which used to be one of the most important centres of commerce in England. Through the wealth of its medieval guilds, it boasts a parish church, St Mary's, which the guide-book describes as 'one of the largest and finest parish churches in the land'. And through royal patronage it has a yet greater church, the Minster, which is reckoned 'one of the great churches of Western Christendom'. If you travel from St Mary's through the ancient market square along a narrow street of fine Georgian terraces up to the north door of the Minster, and stroll round to the other side, your gaze will most likely travel uninterrupted from the great east window to the south-east transept and the flying buttresses of what is unanimously regarded as one of the most glorious sights of medieval architecture in Europe, the south front. It would be understandable if you failed to notice across the road a more mundane feat, the newly improved houses of the St Andrew's Street Housing Co-op. It must have been a shocking sight until recently: a narrow street of small unimproved Victorian terraces blighted by a redevelopment plan, mostly boarded up and semi-derelict, but with some stubborn residents refusing to move out to the council housing that was being offered them. Now the street is being converted by the co-op into a mixture of rehabilitated and new-build housing which, with its steeply pitched, red-tiled roofs, and dormer windows, will form a fitting contrast on a more human scale, to the soaring perpendiculars of the Minster.

When I visited in 1983, the co-op had just finished the improvement work to 26 small terraced houses, and had begun demolition of those too unfit to be saved. Two new-build sites were planned, to start on site in 1983-4; site A consists of 36 sheltered flats for the elderly, a warden's house and communal room, to be built on a vacant plot opposite the south-east corner of the Minster, and site B, 12 houses and 5 flats which will utilise the spaces created by clearance on the street and some allotment land bought from British Rail. It is a compact, high-density site, with opportunities for regular social contact between members via a residents' car park, back gardens and the narrow street. Members acknowledge these advantages; in the survey, residents contrasted the street with council estates, which were left to be too big, and spoke warmly of the advantages of living in a small community. The site is very near the town centre, and yet curiously isolated from other residential areas; bounded to the north by the Minster and a busy road, to the west by a field whose status is protected against building uses, to the east by a railway and to the south by a stream, it is a natural small community. It should remain so when the co-op is complete, because members on Site B will continue to use the street for access, car parking will become communal, the street will be pedestrianised and environmental works should make the whole area more attractive. The elderly members on Site A will have a common room which will be available to all members, and so the committee will not have to put up for too long with meeting in a cold, damp house scheduled for demolition.

Of the present 25 households 17 are original members, who were either owners or sitting tenants whose houses were sold to the co-op. They had to be decanted while their houses were improved, but they are all now settled, for the first time in many years in a decent home. A once-strong community will be restored, through the co-op's explicit policy of favouring people as members who had lived in the area but who, through planning blight and the uncertainty and environmental decay which accompanies it, had moved out; the remaining 8 houses have recently been let in this way. Nine out of the 37 members are on the management committee, including the honorary secretary and treasurer, but the chairman is a local butcher who lives just around the corner, and the company secretary is an architect who has seen the co-op through from its earliest stages, when as an architectural student, he was involved in promoting it. Members do their own rent collection, but are as yet heavily dependent on their agent York Housing Association for all development and most housing management functions. Though the co-op was registered with the Housing Corporation by October 1977, it had only just, early in 1983, reached the stage of managing an improved housing stock with registered rents, and a full complement of tenant members. One might ask why it took five and a half years to improve 25 houses, and why the new-build schemes are still not on site. The answer will be found in the peculiar history of this co-op, which arises out of, and is only matched in uniqueness by, the peculiarities of its setting.

In 1958 planners identified the area as one of 'declining housing', and it was designated for clearance and use as open space. Subsequent development plans of 1961 and 1966 continued to blight the area, but as these were rather slyly designated as 'informal briefs', neither public participation nor ministerial approval was needed. At this time (under the 1957 Housing Act), environmental health officers only had to do a cursory inspection in order to declare as unfit housing which, though basically sound, lacked modern amenities. Sometimes, one suspects, they never even bothered to get out of their cars to do a proper inspection, and they certainly hardly ever asked the natives what they thought. As so often happened in such cases, questionable fact became self-fulfilling prophecy, and after the withdrawal of improvement grants and the boarding up of property bought by the Beverley Borough Council, the area did begin to decline. The letting of houses to temporary tenants imported 'social stress' into what had been a strong and close community, and, while two-thirds of the houses had been owner-occupied, by 1974 three-fifths were in council ownership. What one commentator called 'a deliberate policy of devaluation'[2] had enabled the council to buy up houses cheaply, without as yet resorting to compulsory purchase. Ironically, though, the informal nature of the plan, which had originally allowed the council to avoid local consultation, also allowed local people to argue that the policy could easily be reversed. When the Beverley Civic Society called a public meeting in April 1977, the remaining residents responded strongly to the idea. With only ten days to go before the council was to confirm the clearance of the street, a residents' association was formed with a committee of six people, five of whom were to become the nucleus of the housing co-op's management committee. The Beverley Civic Society had invited a lecturer and 4 students from Hull University School of Architecture to comment, and they argued not only for rehabilitation but for a co-operative form of ownership and control of the scheme.

At this point, three authorities had to be won over, the Housing Corporation and the Department of the Environment for funding, and the Beverley Borough Council for a favourable planning brief. The York University Design Unit produced for the co-op a feasibility study which, by combining rehabilitation with new-build, presented what the architect called 'a consistent development worthy of the setting',[3] in conformity with the planners' latest planning brief. It solved a key problem for the planners, of how to blend the south-east corner of the Minster with its surroundings, by proposing that the co-op build a sheltered housing scheme. By October 1977 the co-op had registered with the Housing Corporation, funding had been set aside and Department of Environment approval gained. This was a promising start; in the words of the co-op's honorary secretary, it had 'broken all records' for registration time. However, the DoE was not convinced about the feasibility of rehabilitation and it was only after the first block had been completed over three years later that full commitment was made to a '30 year life' for a total of 26 houses. Uncertainty also continued through delays in acquisition of properties, which were existing under a variety of ownerships. The co-op had entered into an agency agreement with York Housing Association, and in June 1978 a development officer was appointed, to work almost full-time on the scheme. Despite an abundance of professional help, 1979 was a year of crisis. In April one resident applied for an improvement grant, and the co-op members took this as a signal that the whole scheme might collapse, with householders seeking individual solutions, and thus imperilling the local authority's commitment to rehabilitation. In the end their fears were proved groundless, since all but that one owner-occupier eventually sold to the co-op. By August 1979 members were recording their concern over lack of progress, and wondering whether they had made a mistake; the prospect of over-wintering again in unfit

Six case histories

homes had produced an 'explosive' situation.[4]

To talk of 'interminable delays' is to understate the problems faced by this co-op. A start was made on the first house improvement in February 1980, and by May of that year all house purchases were under way, apart from one whose title of ownership could not be proved. This resulted in Phase 2 of rehabilitation being delayed. Phase 3 was to be substituted, but just as it was to go out to tender, a government moratorium stopped all further progress. The Department of the Environment had at first refused to sanction an over-cost limit approval on Phase 1, but after visiting the finished block of houses its officers were won over; though perhaps unmoved by arguments concerning the social benefits of improvement schemes to their occupants, they had at least seen the architectural merit of the scheme. Phases 2 and 3 finally went on site in 1981. The new-build sites were progressing independently, and received the all-clear from the funding authorities by June 1980. Site B depended on the purchase of land from British Rail, and though both sides were willing, negotiations become protracted, and then threatened to reach stalemate when the District Valuer undervalued the site at £1,000 below the agreed purchase price. The land was finally conveyed in January 1982, after nearly 4 years of negotiations! Site A seemed at first to be be trouble-free; the local authority owned the land, but sold it to the co-op, inserting a covenant into the sale that it *should* be used for housing. Then as the land was zoned for this purpose, the Housing Corporation underwrote the sale, and planning permission was expected to be no more than a formality. Local amenity societies had been consulted previously, when the council's 1977 planning brief was published, showing a clear policy of enclosure of the south-east corner of the Minster by housing. Unknown to the Co-op, a storm was about to break.

In March 1979 a local preservation society asked for an emergency meeting to discuss the new-build site, and the co-op was warned informally to get its planning application in quickly before opposition built up. An adverse press campaign led the planners to advise a 'major publicity effort', and in July 1980 the plans were submitted, with a three-dimensional model of the scheme, and much publicity. The outline application was considered by the planning sub-committee of the council, and after a split vote it was referred to full council for a decision, and in November 1978, approved. Opposition continued, though the Beverley Civic Society was fairly evenly split on the matter; aesthetic judgments, of whether a closely blended housing scheme or open space was a more fitting environment for the south front of the Minster, were difficult enough to make, but overlain with deliberate distortion of the extent of the scheme (many people assuming it ran the whole length of the south front) and inaccurate media coverage, the debate became very confused. It also became incredibly high-powered; letters in *The Times*, a debate in the House of Lords, two Ombudsman's reports which confirmed mal-administration by the Borough Council, and other revelations culminated in a High Court injunction being taken out by objectors, against the local authority. By November 1982 an unsuccessful High Court case had been fought; Site A is finally going ahead, and co-op members can at last settle down to the more mundane, but certainly more peaceful, task of learning how to do their own housing management.

SEGHILL
(a new-build common-ownership co-op)

Seghill is a Northumbrian mining village, about eight miles north-east of Newcastle-upon-Tyne. It would be easy to miss it as one drives through to the next village Seaton Delaval, since the mine has closed, and the village is now mainly a dormitory for people working in the steel, coal and chemical industries ranged northwards along the coast, Driving through from Newcastle one sees a bus shelter, a school, a few shops, some nondescript council housing, all strung along the main street, and then suddenly on the left are the very distinctive Swiss-chalet style houses of Seghill Housing Co-op. They are tall, semi-detached, built in a light yellow sand-coloured brick, with white render to the upper story, and roofs which pitch not towards front and rear but unexpectedly towards the side, giving them a continental appearance. There are 38 houses, all with three bedrooms, but varying from '4-person to 6-person dwellings in size,' laid out in a cul-de-sac known as Forest Way. On the south side gardens turn a tidy face to the main road, but on the north they stop at the embankment of an old mine railway, beyond which a hummocky, wild-looking landscape reminds us of a tougher life-style, of old terraced housing and the mine. All reference to those long rows of terraces is avoided, though; the houses on the south side all have their main entrance facing on to a court which serves groups of 4 houses, placed in such a way that each court is fairly private, but encouraging social contact between adjoining members. Four houses are classed as for disabled people and have car ports, but the

Six case histories

rest have on-street parking in bays set at right-angles to the street. The continental style is underlined on the north side by south-facing sun balconies on the upper storey, which lead out from the living room, so that every house has one or two downstairs bedrooms; it has taken some getting used to, and the boarding of the balconies has had to be replaced with something stronger to keep out the driving Northumbrian rain, but on the whole the residents like it. The south side has a more traditional layout, with downstairs living rooms facing on to gardens and the main road. All houses have their own private garden, but looking inwards to the cul-de-sac they have been designed deliberately to be open-plan; a feature which, with communally maintained flower-beds, shrubberies and grass verges, also encourages regular social contact.

Of the 38 households, 32 are original members who moved in when the scheme was completed, while 6 have been chosen from a waiting list to replace families who left. The co-op is run by a committee of 15 members and a finance sub-committee, but there are two further committees for gardening and social activities which are independent of the management committee. Committee and general meetings are held once a month on alternate fortnights and there is plenty of business to transact; the co-op is fully self-managing. Members do their own allocation, rent collection, book-keeping, routine maintenance and void repairs on a voluntary basis, and contract out only central heating maintenance and cyclical or major repair work.

In contrast to St Andrew's Street, Seghill's history has been nearly trouble-free; from registration to full ownership took little more than a year. Almost as soon as legislation was passed to enable housing co-ops to be promoted, North Housing Association staff took up the challenge of creating the first one in the north of England. They decided simply to convert a new-build scheme which was still at the design stage, and in May 1976 they called a public meeting, which along with a good deal of press, TV and radio coverage, resulted in a nucleus of 17 households who were keen to join. Work started on site in October 1976, and so prospective members were not able to influence the design process. They were, however, consulted on choice of kitchen units and bathroom colours, the finish and layout of courtyards, and were given the chance to buy extra radiators, lobby doors and as there was only one door planned, a back door. At first, a steering committee consisting of 7 members and representatives of the housing association and local authority, handled all business, but this gave way in September 1977 to an 'informal committee' of 12 members; while the steering committee had been volunteers, these 12 were elected from six specialist study groups which appointed two members each. The groups had begun working on areas important to members: co-op principles, maintenance, finance, legal matters, secretarial, rent collection and tenant selection. They gained the basic knowledge sufficient for them to tackle with confidence these complex areas of co-op organisation, by means of a 'long and detailed education programme', set up by the association's community development officer, and consisting at first of six monthly talks from housing experts, and then of professional and administrative support for the study groups. From early on, tenant selection had been done by the original nucleus of members, and then allocation of individual houses was carried out along agreed guidelines (matching houses to household size), but with as much choice as possible being exercised by individuals between the houses available.

By October 1976, 36 member households had been selected, with a reserve list of 12. But the education programme must have weeded out those who just wanted a house and were not keen on the idea of a co-op; by March of the next year several had resigned, because, as the steering committee minutes put it, 'they were unable to accept the degree of involvement which the Scheme requires'. However, those who survived those first few months of intensive study and discussion moved into Forest Way between October 1977 and March 1978, having waited around 18 months for their house. Compared with the history of St Andrew's Street, that of Seghill is remarkably calm; a relatively short wait for a house was followed by 'temporary tenancy' status and then full ownership, so that by October of 1979 the chairman could say 'We are now owner-occupiers of Forest Way.' The informal committee was succeeded in May of 1979 by an elected management committee, and in practice the scheme has been self-managing from this date, three years exactly from the public meeting at which it had been launched.

FAIRBRIDGE
(a new-build tenant-management co-op)

Fairbridge is the name given to a co-op situated at Bridgeton in the east end of Glasgow, and grouped round a pedestrian way called Fairbairn Path; hence 'Fair ... bridge'. To get there, you might travel eastwards through the famous Gorbals, depopulated and redeveloped, with hardly a tenement to be seen, and with all the signs of that ill-considered 1960s

Six case histories

housing which leaves medium- to high-rise flats set randomly in an urban wasteland. If you come in from the west, you would see an empty scene of another sort, the monumental Parkhead Forge, shut-down and eerily silent, a dismal reminder of the heavy industry on which Bridgeton's men used to rely for a lifetime's employment. Yet if you come in from the north, you will see some impressive signs of life – the Glasgow East End Renewal Scheme is revitalising Bridgeton Cross, aiming at the 'rejuvenation of this traditional centre of shopping and commercial activity',[6] which had become badly run down. Walking south from the Cross you pass reclaimed land, planted thickly with trees and bushes, and then see along the Dalmarnock Road the new small factories and workshops which the Scheme has built in the hope of encouraging new industries. The most impressive development is also that which is most on a human scale: the tall, narrow, well-built red brick houses which line one side of the road, built by the Scottish Special Housing Association, the far end of which forms the frontage to the tenant management co-op. Turning into Fairbairn Path, you would see behind the first block three more long rows of houses set in an open plan estate, but with each house having that most valued of assets (in the city of the tenement), its own small back and front gardens. They contrast markedly with a tower block which looms behind, a reminder that in Glasgow it has only recently become possible for tenants to have their own 'back and front door'.

There are 63 dwellings in the co-op, consisting of 10 'three apartments' (4-person houses), 42 'four apartments' (6-person houses), 5 very large 'five apartments' (8-person houses), and 6 flats. Though very roomy inside (being laid out to standards which are much more generous than in England), they are built on three storeys, with narrow frontages and small gardens. All houses have a kitchen and bedroom on the ground floor, and as at Seghill, members have had to get used to first-floor living rooms. The landscape consists of three small play areas, footpaths, beds of trees and bushes, benches and car parking, all attractively laid out between the terraces. But because the site is at one end of a larger development, with access to each terrace from different directions, regular social contact is limited to members of the same block, or to people living opposite each other. There are 118 members, mainly families with young children, but including some pensioners, mostly in the flats. Nearly all have lived here from four to five years since the estate was built. The co-op provides repair and maintenance, environmental upkeep and internal management on an agency basis agreed with the landlord, the 'Scottish Special'. An annual allowance is received, which covers the costs of these, and enables the co-op to hire a part-time administrator who works from an office in a nearby community centre owned by the same housing association. Members did not want the responsibility of doing their own allocations, and so these are made by Glasgow City Council from its waiting list, though the co-op has first choice of vacant houses for transfers, and has to agree to exchanges. The housing association retains ultimate responsibility for the fabric of the houses, and handles all rent collection, accounting and arrears chasing. All of the co-op's finances, apart from a £100 imprest account, are kept within the association's computing sytem, thus freeing members from having to handle and account for large sums of money. Co-op members are, therefore, by their own choice, handling a fairly restricted range of responsibilities, mainly repairs and the upkeep of the environment. Decision-making is by a general meeting held every two months and an 'office bearers' committee which handles day-to-day business. However, this simple structure has not always been in place; it has evolved out of practice over five years from something quite different.

The history of the co-op should be as straightforward as that at Seghill, since it also was promoted after a new-build estate was already on site, and by a housing association. Fairbridge is not quite the oldest established tenant-management co-op in Scotland; that distinction goes to Summerston, which was developed by Glasgow City Council in 1975. It *was* the second, and the first to be developed by a housing association. SSHA put forward the idea in November 1977, and the Glasgow City Council agreed to nominate prospective members. Then in March 1978 a meeting was held, attended by 60 people, which according to the SSHA officials was 'far greater than our wildest expectations'. By April a steering group of 20 families had been formed, and as (like Seghill) Fairbridge was to be based on an existing new-build development, tenants were housed quite soon; the 63 households moved in between November 1978 and May 1979. The association made available an allowance of £112 per house, and for the first year seconded the assistant who had developed the co-op to become its administrator. The allowance was made up of four elements: cyclical maintenance, jobbing repairs, external (environmental) maintenance and management. Though it was set at a lower level than that at Summerston (where it was £135), the co-op members could transfer money between the four categories, and were invited to renegotiate it annually. At the annual meeting in April 1979 the meeting was formally handed over to elected office-bearers, who after only one year's development work were expected to take on full responsibilities. By October 1980 they had appointed their own part-time administrator. At first they hired an office worker, but when she left they redefined the job, in favour of a man with more practical building experience; while needing both clerical and practical support, the co-op's officers chose to emphasise as more important the task of ordering and checking on repairs by maintenance contractors. This seems to have worked, since they have been able to build up a surplus on their allowance, without even renegotiating it annually. Already new front doors have been fitted, and expenditure on porches and extra radiators is planned. When some of the central heating boilers proved defective, causing great damage and upset when they suddenly burst, the office bearers acted decisively and, against the advice of the housing association, replaced all the boilers of that type out of their allowance.

In an early handout the development worker had advised: 'The co-op may decide that a slow but steady build-up of its activities is required, and therefore take on a relatively few functions in the early days of its operation.' Following this advice, members first formed three sub-groups. From April 1978 a repairs group discussed policy on maintenance of houses and landscaping, set up a system of repair cards and monthly monitoring, and wrote information on all these for a projected members' handbook. A management group prepared the missive of let (tenancy agreement), and rules on the internal management of disputes and complaints among tenants, and also contributed to the handbook. Later, the group dealt with the setting up of an office and its equipment. Between them, these groups also helped to draft a constitution, and the agency agreement with the housing association. Thirdly, an allocations group decided on the matching of houses to tenants, offering some choices and then weighing up the merits of each case if people's choices clashed. Then an information panel was set up, consisting of two people from each sub-group, designed to meet prospective tenants, answer their queries and tell them about how the co-op was run. Each sub-group made recommendations to members at monthly general meetings; major decisions were then made by the full co-op. In October 1978 suggestions were made for more sub-groups, since new members were being drawn in who could not simply be expected to swell the numbers of the three original groups. A finance group was set up in February 1979. This was the heavy-weight group, made up of volunteers who felt able to cope with such a demanding subject, who not surprisingly made up the majority of the first set of office-bearers two months later. A social sub-group was then formed among those latecomers who had not had a chance to participate, and they organised dances to enable members to get to know each other, investigated the availability of local shops, found out details of local voluntary organisations and planned a summer playscheme.

The structure of the co-op was set up by the housing association deliberately to enable the maximum involvement of members in decision-making; the office-bearers had only an agenda-setting function, and sub-groups had some delegated powers, but they had to take most decisions to monthly general meetings. Given the subsequent decisions to take on only a restricted range of responsibilities, it proved to be a cumbersome and time-consuming system, and in September 1981 the sub-groups were abolished in favour of a more traditional structure, in which a management committee (the office bearers) holds delegated powers from the general membership, who now meet every two months. On the one hand, the history of this co-op is a rather uneventful one, with the planned handover of powers from housing association to management co-op being effected very quickly and smoothly. On the other hand, there has been a complete reshaping of the co-op's democratic structure within two and a half years of its first annual meeting.

SPEIRS
(a rehabilitation-type tenant-management co-op)

There are two roads leading north-west out of Glasgow. From the trunk road, tourists might just catch a glimpse of the tall cranes which signal the famous Clydeside shipyards strung out along the north bank of the Clyde, but they will hurry on to be more fittingly impressed within a few miles, by the grandeur of Loch Lomond, the gateway to the Highlands, the Scotland of the brochures and souvenir shops. But if you take the old Dumbarton road, the one the locals use, which runs right along the edge of the river, the other Scotland forces itself into view; on the left, the proud façade of the shipyards, behind which only one is still working, and on the right a jumble of post-war council housing stretching away into estates, or filling up old bomb sites. The road itself is lined with what remains of the old Victorian sandstone tenements, some improved and looking grander than ever, in contrast with the fading glory of the tower blocks and the damp dejection of the flat-roofed system-built 1960s housing. Yet, despite the uniquely Scottish architecture, the shops and bars on the ground floor of the tenements have that depressed air familiar to all inner cities. Passing through Scotstoun into Yoker, about 5 miles out of the city centre, you will see set back from the main Dumbarton road, Langholm Street, an impressive estate of three-storey tenements, which, faced in imitation stone and with new windows and freshly painted 'closes', is at first difficult to date; neither as old as those Victorian sandstone tenements which are left standing, nor as young as the ubiquitous system-built council housing which has replaced them; this is pre-war housing, built in 1938, and newly improved through the Glasgow District Council's Improvement and Repair Programme. And very grand it looks too, with the broad sweep of the long tenement blocks of flats curving round to run parallel to the main road, pausing for a moment to admit a small park, and then continuing on until they meet the sandstone tenements of the main road again. They provide 338 dwellings in all, with roughly 6 'houses' (or apartments) to each staircase or 'close'. It was recently declared an area of 'multiple deprivation', and the top end of the street, notwithstanding the improvement scheme, looks sadly neglected, its gardens a waste-land of dirty grass, old prams and car tyres. The middle and bottom end are however, a surprise; neatly tended lawned gardens at the front, clean, freshly painted closes and stairs, newly grass-seeded back courts, with 'middens' (bin stores) and washing lines; this is the Speirs Housing Management Co-op.

The co-op is so-called in memory of a local benefactor, Hagart Speirs, who donated a community hall (since demolished) and tennis courts to the street. It comprises 200 dwellings, mostly three- and four-apartments (3 bedrooms) but with a small number of two- and five-apartments. The flats are roomy, the back courts spacious, the road is wide and there is plenty of play space available in an adjacent park. There is a lot of street life; both adults and children tend to congregate outside, round the closes, on the pavements and in the park. Because the street is very long, though, contact tends to be limited to either the middle or end of the street; this may be reflected in the original decision (later overturned), to form two co-ops, Mid-Langholm and Speirs. There are three types of co-op member: ordinary membership is limited to one person per household, and confers full voting rights; associate membership is open to all people over 18, but without voting rights;

and waiting-list membership is open to those on the waiting list, but again without voting rights. The management committee consists of a maximum of 22 members, but in practice settles down each year to about 16 to 20. Up to 16 members are elected from sub-groups, based on the closes, and the other 6 are elected by the annual meeting. If anyone drops out, up to 6 people can be co-opted during the year. General meetings are held monthly, and committee meetings weekly, and the chairman is elected by the annual meeting, the other officers by the committee. The system seems complex, but in such a large co-op it provides for a mix of geographical and general representation, and ensures a large committee which can absorb a high proportion of interested members. Like Fairbridge, Speirs receives a management and maintenance allowance from its landlord (the Glasgow City Council), but this finances a wider range of functions: maintenance of exterior painting, interior repairs, the environment, management of the missive of let, and all allocations. Being so large, the co-op has its own administrator and office secretary, who work from an office on the street, converted from a flat. Besides these functions, the co-op has the distinction of being the first ever instance of council tenants managing their own improvement programme, which has just been finished. This points to an interesting historical development.

Langholm Street was scheduled for full modernisation in 1979, having been designated a priority area; it had become hard to let, owing to a bad reputation, and a deteriorating environment and housing stock. There was an unbalanced population; a pre-improvement survey found that there were 222 children under 16 in 124 households surveyed, that 47 households (38%) had 5–10 people in the family, 42 (33%) had children under 5, and that only 19 (15%) were elderly.[7] Thirty-one households (25%) were affected by medical problems, which were mainly related to lungs (bronchitis), heart (angina), and disability. The flats were in a bad condition, made worse by the gradual clearance of some closes in anticipation of the need to decant people when the street was modernised; vandalism and fire damage had resulted. Established residents tell of a gradual deterioration in both the environment and the image of the street, until it became difficult to obtain loans or even to hire a television with a Langholm Street address; the modernisation plan was eagerly awaited. There was what officials describe as a 'spirit of self-help' on the street, already manifested in, among other things, a local residents' association, which had organised a successful campaign to save the Yoker Ferry across the River Clyde.

Six case histories

When a local councillor and an official from the council's Co-op Promotions Section suggested the idea of a management co-op, these active residents formed two steering committees and began to work out constitutions and a draft agency agreement with the local authority. When spending cuts forced the cancellation of the modernisation scheme, they sent a delegation to the City Chambers, and were invited to consider running an alternative Improvement and Repair scheme themselves. They were determined to fight for the maximum help, and to give value for money by also adminstering a Tenants' Grant Scheme, which gave individual tenants a grant towards a new bathroom, kitchen and heating. Fear that further delays would mean more cuts led to a petition, which was sent, as the minutes put it, 'to let them know that we are prepared to go ahead on our own', because then 'at least we would know for sure that the work was going ahead, and were not just listening to empty promises'.[8] Yet the council was more than willing, and by January 1980 gave authority in principle, and promise of full professional back-up. By March, the co-ops had amalgamated, for, as they put it, 'strength in going forward to the GDC with our request to carry out the Improvement Programme ourselves'.[9]

£3-3500 was earmarked per house for repair and improvement, and £1750 for each tenant grant, and the co-op fought for and got a £900 environment grant for each back court, and a decorating allowance of £156 per house. The co-op was also asked to do the conversion of 6 closes to smaller dwellings, so as to improve the mix of households. A setting-up grant was given of £3500, which enabled the co-op to set up its office and to hire a development officer and office secretary. The social work department was asked to provide rest centres for members whose houses were on site; unfortunately, the co-op was unable to negotiate decant accommodation, and members had to stay in the houses, while new kitchen and bathroom equipment, new windows, heating systems, and rewiring were put in, repairs carried out to the roof, downpipes, chimney heads and stairs, and new lighting, railings, close back doors, bin stores and paths were constructed round them. It was not an easy time, and if it had gone wrong, the co-op might have got the blame. But by appointing their own development officer, exercising great control over the professional staff and builder, and insisting on tenant choices of colour schemes and standard extras from the tenant grants package, they made the scheme both bearable and highly beneficial.

The work was begun in November 1981 and completed by the end of

1982. Meanwhile, the co-op was running into danger from another direction; tenants were beginning to expect the co-op to take on maintenance and emergency work, yet they could not do this without a proper agency agreement. On the other hand, the Council officials expected to sign the agreement only after the improvement scheme was complete. A compromise was reached, whereby the co-op took on each house as it was completed internally, having signed the agreement in December 1981. This might have caused even more problems for the co-op if there had been repair work outstanding, but through persistent pressure based on accurate information about the need for repairs, the co-op was able to get these incorporated in the improvement programme. Internal repairs were only done if absolutely necessary, but were done properly; the co-op insisted that replacement front doors should be solid ones, and so on. So successful was the co-op in extracting extra grants that when further problems were encountered with the parapets of oriel windows, it was allowed to tender an additional contract to finish the work. A communal aerial system was installed, and maintained at the co-op's expense. At the same time, policies were agreed for management and maintenance, a missive of let (or tenancy agreement) drawn up, a handbook prepared, and all the vacant apartments let to new tenants, picked by the co-op's allocations panel. Though the original promotional grant had been exceeded early on, a grant of £25,000 for the cost of running the improvement programme, and a maintenance allowance of £195 per house, have put the co-op on a sound financial footing. Plans have already been drawn up for cyclical maintenance; closes will be washed down annually, gutters cleaned every 2 years, and external cleaning done every 4 years. By July of 1983, a permanent administrator had been appointed, who, unlike the previous development officer, will be concerned with longer-term management and maintenance of the street.

ABBEYVALE
(an old-style co-ownership housing society)

Macclesfield is in Cheshire, but it belongs to those old industrial towns which cling to the valley-sides of the steep hills outcropping from Derbyshire, rather than to the prosperous dormer-towns which sprawl over the flat, lush landscape of the Cheshire Plain and the Manchester commuter-belt. It is a world of old silk mills and nonconformist chapels, and when one thinks of housing in this context it is of long

Six case histories

rows of tiny terraced houses in General Improvement Areas. Yet Abbeyvale Housing Society consists of three modern blocks of flats, in the corner of a new private estate, right on the edge of Macclesfield overlooking the wild Bollin Valley, a ribbon of open country which divides the town from the beginnings of the Manchester conurbation. A thick cover of bushes and trees hides the entrance, which slopes quickly to a car park and the rather functional blocks, each of which includes 14 flats (10 of one bedroom and 4 of two) and on the ground-floor, 6 built-in garages. With a total of 42 flats, it is, compared with other co-ownerships, quite small. The ground slopes steeply away to the valley, and this allowed the architect to build on three storeys at the front and five at the back, thus avoiding the need for lifts. A rather drab entrance leads by stairs both down and up, and north-facing flats have a picture window which allows full appreciation of the magnificent view. The construction is in load-bearing cavity walls and on the five-storey side concrete columns, and with pre-cast concrete floors and under-floor electric central heating. Originally, like so many of these old co-ownerships, the blocks had flat roofs, with access from their staircases via penthouses, but recently sloping roofs have been added. At the back, a large tract of the Society's land slopes to ill-defined boundaries, and a covering of scrub vegetation denotes poor drainage.

Being average-sized flats, built on a large site but with the three blocks crowded together at one end, they are high-density, but because members make little use of the open land, have no communal facilities other than the car park, and see each other only occasionally on the stairs, social contact can be described as very occasional. Joint membership is allowed, but there are only about 54 members, as there is a preponderance of single people. When I interviewed them, most peole had been there less than 2 years, and hardly any were original to the scheme. The society's management is done by an estate agent, who receives an agreed allowance, and decision-making is by an annual members' meeting and a committee whose membership fluctuates from 7 to 12, and which meets several times per year as and when meetings are needed.

Like other blocks of flats on the same estate, distinguishable by their flat roofs, Abbeyvale was built as a co-ownership society. Yet, unlike them, it now has a sloping roof and remains a co-ownership, the rest having been sold to their members since being given the right to sell under the 1980 Housing Act. The roof is a clue to the society's continued existence, as its peculiar history will make clear.

Six case histories

In 1972 the Society was registered on paper by its founder members, who in accordance with the normal method of co-ownership promotion included the staff of a housing association and some of their business acquaintances. They already had a site, sketch proposals for what to do with it, and Housing Corporation approval, and were able to go on site in 1973. By April 1975, the scheme was completed and then gradually let, but it was not until August 1978 that it was handed over to a committee of resident-members, and the founder members resigned; even then the Chief Executive of the association remained as secretary of the co-ownership society. From the beginning, the scheme was dogged with problems.

Firstly, 'difficult and damp ground conditions' were reported as early as December 1972, and by October 1974, the site was still 'extremely soft' and 'completely water-logged'. The builder could not lay paths, and when the architect wanted the land regrading and sowing with grass seed, claimed he had already done as much landscaping work as was allowed for under the contract. By May 1975 the architect was commenting that 'the appearance of this land at the rear of Willow Court is most unsatisfactory and the cause of much irritation to the residents'. The builder was supposed to have produced a level plateau, but the ground was found to slope the wrong way, and it was only after a 'seven day letter' had been issued, threatening to get others to do it and to charge the builder, that the job was done. The original top soiling had been washed away, though, and 'ponding' soon appeared, and when the residents consulted a public health inspector, it was found that not enough silt chambers had been put in; another seven day letter was issued, but the builder maintained that omission of these had been agreed. By May 1976, a letter from residents described the land at the rear as 'rapidly becoming a weed-filled eyesore', and the association were approaching the Forestry Commission to see if anything could be done to improve such poor land. Worse was to come, because in August a 'permanent odour of sewage, that pervades all three forecourts, and greets everyone arriving or departing' was reported, and the drains suspected of being inadequate. Nor did the hand-over to a residents' committee help; they were refused a loan from the Housing Corporation of £3000, because, as the latter put, 'poor design and supervision' rather than a lack of money were to blame. Finally, the fact that one of the blocks had been built three feet too low, in this marshy landscape, leads one to expect problems of dampness, but these exceeded anyone's expectations.

Six case histories

Water penetration and condensation were reported as soon as the first residents moved in, along with defective windows and cracked brickwork. A long catalogue of reports followed throughout 1976. Electric faults appeared in the central heating and extractor fans, condensation worsened, cracks were discovered in supporting pillars, and so on. Already by March 1976, six flats had become unlettable, owing to leaks from the flat roofs. Reading back into the minutes of site meetings and correspondence between the professionals, one can see the inevitability of all this. In 1972 the Housing Corporation had pointed out inconsistencies in the roofing design; was it to be covered in asphalt or fibre-glass? A consultant, hired to comment on the design, queried whether the roof covering and drainage outlets were adequate. By the end of 1973, the builder on site was also asking for definite instructions on the covering material, and when the asphalt surface was finally laid, it was inadequately sloped, and eventually cracked. The consultant also criticised the north-north-east aspect of the 'special' type of picture windows, asked for construction details, and recommended that they have condensation grooves; the mullions began to sag as soon as they were fitted, and the architect became involved in a long dispute with the manufacturer. Also, their aspect did, as the consultant suspected, create condensation problems. But by far the most serious fault was discovered in May 1976; the builder had omitted to install cavity trays in the wall of the penthouses, thus allowing water to seep through to the landings below. Accepting responsibility, he installed the trays, but the water penetration problem still continued. Later investigation by an independent consultant showed that the positioning was faulty, as was that of other cavity wall trays in the upstand walls (between the lower and upper roof levels); they were meant to divert rainwater on to the asphalt skirting of the roof, but because the latter had been built higher than the trays, were feeding it under the asphalt into the flats below. This major problem was the focus of much controversy, the builder claiming that the trays had been installed according to the architect's instructions, the architect claiming that this was not according to his drawings. It was never resolved, because the latter never produced any drawings to verify his claim.

The response of the Society's managing agents to all this was very slow. At first they insisted that 'dampness in walls should dry out in time', and the architect tried to remedy the more obvious faults. But they were hampered by what by then had become very poor relations with the contractor, by mutual fixing of blame between all concerned, and by threats and counter-threats over the withholding of payments due. Mould treatment was applied by a local tradesman, but the problem was completely beyond such piecemeal treatment, and by March 1979 the residents' committee delivered an ultimatum to their agents, to organise 'a comprehensive programme and timetable of work', to include the cavity tray problem, repairs to windows and bathroom fans. Their secretary, who had been both developer (in the form of the housing association) and quantity surveyor (in the form of a private partnership) to the scheme was keen to give the architect more time to resolve the problems. The missing cavity trays were installed, and the committee withheld from the builder and architect the remainder of the sums owing on the contract. They then asked their agent, the housing association, to draw up a comprehensive list of work needed, and to seek legal advice on the windowframe problem. Their exasperation is hardly surprising: by April 1979, 25 letters of complaint from residents had been recorded in the minutes.

The agent eventually sent a programme of works to the Housing Corporation, who requested an independent survey. But the committee had decided to adopt 'a more positive approach which would solve all their problems', as opposed to, as they put it, 'the laissez-faire approach which has now become synonymous with our agents'. (There were by now 5 vacant flats, and 7 more becoming uninhabitable.) The agent announced the need for a report and recommended a particular consultant, but to his astonishment, the committee had already taken control by appointing their own architect, responsible entirely to the committee. Then came another shock to the professionals; the secretary had recommended legal arbitration in connection with the cavity wall problem, but the committee, armed with their independent architect's report, revealed that they had already briefed a solicitor with a view to litigation against *both* builder and architect. They began by slyly offering to release £250 in outstanding fees to the scheme architect if he would supply his drawings, but he refused to comply. Then the court action began in earnest, with claims being registered against the architect and builder, on the basis of 'design faults, bad workmanship, poor materials and a combination of all these factors',[10] and with a counter-claim being received from the latter for his outstanding retention payment. Arbitration was called for by the builder, but the architect refused to be a party to it, and the committee wanted full litigation. The case had to be taken to the High Court. The Society issued a writ for £200,000 damages, and made a detailed statement of claim. The architect claimed that a time-lapse rule enabled him to avoid responsibility for defects which had occurred over 6 years previously, yet the co-owners were able to prove that he knew of the faults from very early on, and was concealing these by blaming the builder. Just for good measure, they added to their major indictments other design faults, such as noisy refuse chutes and negligence over fire regulations. The court action involved committee members, and particularly the chairman, in a huge amount of work, taking statements, following up requests for proofs, deciding which claims to press and which to drop, and sorting through masses of documents made available through notices served on the housing association and architect.

A High Court action would have been expensive; it would have bankrupted the builder just in barrister's fees, and would have added to the co-owners' costs by about £20,000. The builder abandoned his counter-claim, the architect took the advice of his insurers, and by the beginning of 1983 a settlement was made; the Society accepted the builder's outstanding retention money, plus £10,000 which he had set aside for costs, and the architect's offer of £75,000 and £12,000 towards their costs. The eventual cost of the action to the Society was around £30,000. Meanwhile, the committee had called a special general meeting, sacked their managing agent and hired another; the founder members had signed a five-year agreement in 1976, but the agent (who was by this time under investigation by the Housing Corporation for some dubious land dealings, and eventually made to resign from the housing association of which he was chief executive), had had to withdraw from the agreement in March 1980. He had wanted to consolidate his agency work with co-ownership societies by simply continuing the business under a new name, but the committee took the opportunity to make the final break with the Society's unhappy past.

Having borrowed £135,000 from the Nationwide Building Society, they were able by July 1981 to go on site with a major repair contract, which was completed even before the result of the litigation was known; they feared that if the roof remained as it was, the buildings would eventually have to be demolished! Pitched roofs, new double-glazed wooden windows, external wall insulation, upgraded electrics, damp-proofing to ground-floor flats, insulation of garage ceilings and some redecoration were included, but when the scheme over-ran by £17,000, cost reductions were necessary, and the general upgrading of staircases and the landscape deferred. This time there was no leaving of the work to the 'experts'; when an electrical sub-contractor failed to perform satisfactorily, and claimed payment for unauthorised work, the committee took immediate and very tough action, appointing an electrical consultant to check on the work done, and refusing to pay the bill.

In 1979 the Society had gone into 'loss-rent' status, because a poor financial situation in its early life, compounded by soaring interest rates, had made it impossible to pay the Corporation's mortgage; by agreement with the Corporation, loss-rent enabled a society to make reduced mortgage payments, capitalising the debt, and gradually increasing rents half-yearly, in order to get back to financial soundness. The crisis was exacerbated by repair costs and lost rents from the top-floor flats, which the committee had decided it would be morally wrong to let in such poor condition. Yet instead of planning for loss-rent status early on, the agents let the situation continue, and during 1979 simply stopped paying the mortgage, but did not inform the committee, to whom the loss-rent status came later as yet another unpleasant problem to be tackled. With the damages settlement, however, the committee were able to pay arrears and to return the Society to a sound economic footing.

Such a history illustrates all of the disadvantages of co-ownership development cited in Chapter 4. It also shows how, given an essentially co-operative society which had ultimate control over its own destiny, and given immense commitment and determination by the leading committee members, even such a badly planned scheme can be made viable. The current committee are setting about the redecoration of the stairways, the rebuilding of retaining walls in the car park and other improvements to the landscaping which until now they had not had time for. They will make the scheme work despite the failure and culpability of the professionals who planned it.

GLENKERRY
(a unique shared ownership/community leasehold co-op)

If a housing co-op can succeed in a high-rise tower block, perhaps it can succeed anywhere. Glenkerry House is one of three huge tower blocks which dominate the sky-line in the Poplar district of the east end of London, but unlike the other two blocks, it is not owned by a municipal landlord but by the people who live in it. A few miles away in Hackney, the council is running competitions among residents, the prize being the chance to press a button and blow up one of the seven 21-storey tower blocks of the Trowbridge Estate, scheduled for demolition. Here there is no thought of demolishing, because these towers are structurally sound, and the council is learning from the co-op how to make life tolerable for the residents by installing an entry-phone system and hiring a proper caretaker. Glenkerry House is still the odd one out, though, being surrounded by a densely populated triangle of almost exclusively council housing, bounded to the north-west by a canal, the Limehouse Cut, to the north-east by the River Lea, and to the south by the roaring traffic of the East India Dock Road. In addition, the triangle is dissected by the northern approach to the Blackwall Tunnel, along which a daily tide of lorries runs from north to south. Yet despite the constant hum of the traffic, the immediate surroundings are pleasant; bounded on one side by a school playing field, set amongst some of the more successful low-rise council housing, and approached via a courtyard served by a general store, the block is set off to advantage.

It consists of an immense wall of flats, at each end of which is a quite elegant lift-shaft, and it benefits from having been built at the tail-end of the post-war rush to build higher, which had produced so much shoddy housing from untested materials; the architects were beginning to learn from their more obvious mistakes, and the design and building quality are impressive. There are 14 storeys, but only four landings, because from each landing access is given to flats above and below as well as on that level. On the ground floor are 4 four-bedroomed maisonettes, with their own small back gardens, one of which is inhabited by the co-op manager and his family. The rest of the building is made up of 17 one-bedroom, 45 two-bedroom, and 12 three-bedroom flats: 78 flats in all, each with their own balcony. A doctor's surgery is incorporated in the ground floor, which, never having been used for that purpose, is being converted into another flat. In addition, there are two drying rooms, a hobbies room which has been taken over as the co-op office, and a ground-floor extension which provides small lock-up storage units, one per flat. Obviously, such high-rise living is at very high density, but is usually associated also with extreme isolation and lack of social contact. The layout is in this respect about as positive as it can be, since most members have to pass the co-op notice-board to use the lift and one of only 4 landings, and therefore have some opportunity of seeing each other in passing; the result is probably as much as one can hope for in such circumstances, a friendly but reserved community. People in flats which give directly off the staircases and in the ground-

Six case histories

floor maisonettes are more isolated, though, but the shop is a focal point for many. Social contact can be described as occasional.

This is a community leasehold co-op; the Greater London Council is freeholder of the site, the co-op is leaseholder, and members buy a sub-lease which amounts to 50 per cent of the current leasehold value of the flat. New members, once selected by the co-op to go on the waiting list and then given the opportunity to buy, have to raise a mortgage, which usually amounts to 100 per cent of this half value, as determined by the district valuer. The mortgagee has been the GLC Home Loans Department, but now that the scheme has become established, building societies are beginning to grant mortgages. The leaseholder is responsible for the interior of the flat, including electrics and plumbing, but excluding main services, and the co-op is responsible for insuring and maintaining the structure of the building, for providing common services, and for the cleaning and lighting of common areas. But to complicate matters further, the Greater London Council (and now its successor) is responsible for a district central heating system, and for the communal aerial. Members pay their mortgage, and also a service charge which includes the cost of providing insurance, exterior maintenance, heating, cleaning of common areas, lift and entry phone maintenance and so on (and including the manager's salary), and which also includes payments on a residual loan from the GLC, which allowed the co-op to buy the leasehold.

Membership is single or joint, depending on whether members are individual or joint mortgagors, but only one £1 share is held per flat, giving entitlement to one vote. There are about 120 members on average, preponderantly young and single or in couples; only 7 of the present households have children (since the upper storeys are not considered suitable for young children), and only about 6 are middle-aged. Turnover of flats is high; when I visited in 1983, 46 out of the 78 (59 per cent) had been sold again since the first sale, 11 of which (14 per cent) had been sold twice over. Clearly the co-op is achieving its aim of being a stepping-stone for those who cannot initially afford to buy their own house. It is run on traditional management committee lines; general meetings are held annually, but are interspersed with special meetings, and the committee, which aims at a membership of 12 (though the rules allow for anything from 7 to 15 members), meets monthly. There are four sub-committees: finance, member selection, maintenance and information, and these meet as working groups when necessary, and without formal minutes. Between the co-op manager and the committee, the co-op is completely self-managing.

The history of the co-op shows all the advantages of being formed by a committed secondary co-op. Glenkerry House was the last GLC tower-block ever to be built. Unlike the other two local towers it was not immediately let, but stood empty for 18 months, while the Council negotiated its future with the Greater London Secondary Housing Association, with a view to turning it into a housing co-op. The form eventually decided on was community leasehold, which would allow people who could not afford to buy their own houses, either through not having the earning power or the deposit, to build up equity in an investment they could afford, as a stepping-stone to full house ownership. A unique system was devised, whereby members bought 50 per cent of the leashold on a flat, while the co-op retained the rest. They would be able to take away with them the accumulated equity on this 50 per cent when they sold the lease. However, two safeguards were built in to enable the scheme to remain open to those in need; firstly, the agreement between the GLC as freeholder and the co-op as head-leaseholder stipulated that no more than 50 per cent could be bought by individuals, and secondly, sales would not be on the open market, but at the district valuer's valuation, which, as it tends to lag behind the market, would keep rices reasonable. Eventually a deal was worked out, allowing the co-op to buy a 99-year lease; building and legal costs amounted to £1,435,000, but a government grant negotiated through the Housing Corporation for £717,000 and a GLC grant of £144,000 reduced this, as did the sales to members which were expected to bring in about £464,000. The residual amount was then raised through a GLC loan to the co-op (which qualified for option mortgage relief) and charged to members as a ground rent.

The co-op was registered in September 1978 as a friendly society, and with the Housing Corporation, 7 members of the GLSHA board providing its founder-members. Protracted legal negotiations followed, and a district valuation had to be revised upwards, so that 20 members had to pay more for their flats than originally expected. Yet the scheme proved attractive, and GLSHA staff were able to select the resident members (of whom the GLC and Tower Hamlets council nominated up to two-thirds) according to exacting eligibility rules; members had to be in housing need (meaning that they could not afford to buy a house outright), to have local work or social connections, to be committed to the idea of a co-op, and able to meet the costs of a mortgage and service charge. (The local connection rule was later relaxed.) Three potential members helped with the interviewing. A structural survey was done, which found no major defects except the need to support balconies, and the GLC was required to remedy this, to install an entry phone system, and also to give a 2-year indemnity against maintenance defects, and a 10-year indemnity against structural defects. Initial housing management was delegated to the Utopian Housing Association, but GLSHA staff were on hand to follow up further difficulties; a persistent loud knocking in the central heating system was reported by the first residents, and the entry phone system was defective; 'major sources of irritation' which they 'spent many days and weeks dealing with'.[11] The ground was also laid thoroughly for eventual take-over by the members; an 8-member consultative committee was formed from among the first residents, and an educational programme was run by GLSHA staff, attended by 46 members. The first management committee was elected in April 1980. They had wanted to take over even sooner, after the official opening of the co-op in October 1979 (by Geoffrey Finsberg, MP), and it was not long before they were able to terminate the managing agreement with GLSHA, becoming completely self-managing. One of their first decisions was also a very bold one; they decided to give a 25 per cent rebate on the first year's service charge.

They were helped enormously in the aim of being self-managing by a very significant change of policy. Initially, a caretaker had been appointed, but after disagreements with the members, he left and the job was redefined and upgraded as that of co-op manager. The resulting administrative support, as well as the manager's ability to maintain the building and even (having been an engineer) the lift, have been key elements in stabilising the co-op, despite changes in committee membership and in the naturally varying capacities and commitment of its officers. The subsequent history of the co-op has been uneventful, but represents very solid achievements in both policy and practice, gained mainly by hard work. By August 1981 there was still no let up in the pace which the committee had set themselves; meetings lasted until midnight, and even then some had to be adjourned. The impression is of a very thorough initial development by a housing association committed to co-operative principles, and then of a co-op which has built carefully on well-laid foundations, in marked contrast to the crisis-management which members were left with at Abbeyvale. It is unfortunate that such solid groundwork has not resulted in the replication of this type of co-op; the main stumbling-block with the present Conservative government seems to be the way in which the legal framework was deliberately developed to prevent the right of individuals to 'staircase' their way to full ownership of the leasehold.

SEVEN:
A FRAMEWORK FOR EVALUATION

What are we to make of co-operative practice, as exemplified in these six case histories? It is not enough simply to launch into an evaluation without first making yet another excursion into the realm of the theoretical. We only see what we want to see, or what we are trained to see. The way we see determines the value we put on the object, and so it would be a mistake to begin to evaluate co-operative practice without first deciding what is significant about co-ops in general. This does not preclude listening to what co-op members themselves have to say; all that the 'logico-deductive' method does is to enable us to order the masses of material which can be generated from a thorough case-study, in a way which makes sense to us, and also (if we do our job well) to the co-op members. P.A. Sorokin has suggested a simple theory concerning what he calls 'reciprocated altruism', or mutual aid,[1] which ought to be of interest in that it summarises much of what is known about the way co-operative groups behave. The theory has been applied and developed in relation to housing co-ops, and in the process has to some extent taken on a life of its own,[2] so that (with apologies to Sorokin) its main outlines are as follows:

There are six key variables: participation, extensity, duration, adequacy, intensity and purity. The last five vary independently, but the first, participation, is dependent on the rest. Yet as we shall see, participation can act back on the other variables, and they all affect each other in very subtle and interesting ways.

PARTICIPATION

On the surface, there is nothing problematic about this variable; it refers to the hard facts concerning members' involvement in a co-op. Participation can be divided according to *time*: past and present participation levels, and members' expectations about whether they or

A framework for evaluation

other members will take part in the future. It can also be divided according to *function*: involvement in general meetings, in management or sub-committees, in social activities organised by the co-op, in jobs done around the houses by volunteers, in decisions taken over design work, and in work done by members on their own homes. The crucial question is: how committed are members to participate? Are they interested and involved, or apathetic and content to let others run the co-op? Are they willing to engage in mutual help, or are they individualistic, isolated, unwilling to commit themselves? A typology suggested by Homans is helpful; he describes five types of individual response to a group or organisation.[3] Firstly, there are the *true believers*, who are prepared to participate in order to achieve common goals. Then there are the *freeloaders*, who want to obtain the benefits without sharing the costs of participation. Thirdly, *sceptical conformers* do not expect the co-op to be able to provide benefits, do not participate, but otherwise conform. *Holdouts* go further, in refusing to conform but staying in the co-op and withholding their approval of it, and *escapees* are those members who, given a chance, will leave. Naturally, the more true believers there are, the more stable will the co-op be, and the greater its chances of survival over time. The more freeloaders there are, the greater the chances of resentment among the true believers at having to do all the work themselves. The greater the number of sceptics and holdouts there are, the more trouble there will be from innuendo and gossip, which the true believers will find demoralising. The greater the number of escapees, the higher the turnover and the greater the instability of co-op membership.

In fact, though it may be relatively simple to define and measure participation, there is nothing more important or problematic to the future of a co-op.[4] In a democratic organisation, it is ultimately a matter of life or death; the greater the participation, the longer the duration. At all six of the co-ops already described, there is a strong committee, whose members can be relied on to turn out to nearly all meetings; Seghill is highest, with an average of 83 per cent attendance over its entire life-span, at an average of 20 meetings per year. Speirs is the lowest, with 64 per cent attendance, but at 36 meetings per year, they can be forgiven for taking the odd night off. The main problem is always attendance by the general membership at open meetings. Seghill manages a very creditable 55 per cent of members at 13 meetings per year, but St Andrew's Street can only attract 45 per cent of members, and Abbeyvale 31 per cent, to their one annual meeting. The two management co-ops average even lower; at Speirs, 24 per cent attend 10 meetings per year, and at Fairbridge the same percentage attend around 6 per year. As one National Federation member admitted recently:

> Co-ops are full of people who daren't admit publicly what they say privately, that co-ops are not actually full of people in control of their housing, but in fact have too many apathetic and uninvolved individuals who are housed from the sweat of the collective brow of a minority of hard-working co-op members.[5]

Yet this may be an exaggeration, based on the experience of those activits who feel most acutely the 'freeloader' problem.

Firstly, ordinary members do tend to do work for the co-op; at St Andrew's Street, 74 per cent of members had at one time or another done jobs for the secretary, moving furniture, boarding up houses and so on. Secondly, if we examine the networks within which they live, most have a relative or neighbour on the committee, who they can turn to for information and to make any points they need to make; at St Andrew's Street half the households have at some time had someone on the committee, while at Seghill this figure reaches 61 per cent. Thirdly, when compared with, say, attendance at a residents or tenants association meeting, these figures are very good indeed; at Speirs, which used to attract a handful of people to the residents' group, an average of 24 per cent of households is very creditable. Compared also with the involvement of co-op members in other countries, it is also quite high. In Sweden, there are few problems in encouraging members to go on the committee (or local board), but participation in voluntary activities and social events is very variable between one co-op and another. In Norway there is no problem finding board members, because they are paid; the chairperson receives up to £2500 per year. Attendance at annual general meetings varies greatly, but can be as low as 15 per cent, though averages for OBOS of 25-50 per cent and for HSB in Sweden of 15-36 per cent have been calculated.[6] Fourthly, some co-ops (like St Andrew's Street, Speirs and Abbeyvale) start from an existing situation, where a large minority begin by being very sceptical of the whole idea. At Speirs, the figure of 24 per cent has been achieved from a standing start, when the view of many embittered tenants was that the co-op would not even survive.

If we examine the above quotation more closely, we find that there are really two separate issues; how much contribution people make to the work, and how much control they exercise over the co-op. In

A framework for evaluation

Scandinavia, where the two-earner family unit is the norm, members tend not to have much time for doing voluntary work, and so they hire workers to do it. They still keep control, though. At Speirs, a full-time worker takes much of the burden of work off the committee, allowing them time to work out detailed policies. At Glenkerry, again a full-timer does most of the work, allowing the committee to concentrate on arrears problems and financial monitoring. In a situation of high unemployment, it makes sense to generate paid work for local people, rather than relying on volunteers, unless, as happens at Seghill, members volunteer to do all repairs so that they can use the resulting surplus to improve the estate. There is obviously a limit to the amount of regular unpaid work members can be expected to do, unless there is both this communal pay-off and the expectation that others will also pull their weight. There is also a limit in the other direction, though, when payment becomes a sign that members are not willing to co-operate at all; at Fairbridge, which is untypical in putting out to tender everything including the picking up of rubbish from round the estate, two boys had to be paid to tidy an old man's garden. At Seghill this would have been taken as a sign that the co-operative spirit no longer existed, and that it was time to wind the co-op up. There are different expectations, then, of what is to be expected from a co-op member, in different co-ops.

The control issue is more fundamental. If members do not attend meetings, it may be because they are satisfied with the service being given, and feel safe leaving it to others to make the decisions. Yet, as Abbeyvale vividly illustrates, when a crisis occurs, a democratic structure is in place which allows them to gain control. Nevertheless, active members will probably always worry about participation even when they are relatively successful, and they will tend to review their performance regularly. For instance, Seghill publishes an annual summary of members' attendance at meetings, and Fairbridge commissioned a social studies student to interview members and find out why they had stopped going to meetings. Speirs has done the same through a postgraduate student who is doing a thesis on the co-op, and they have convened a participation sub-committee to look at the results of his survey. They are right to be concerned, but probably wrong to be worried.

The problem is seen as an acute one, because of the demoralising effect on the true believers of there being freeloaders, and so most strategies tend to revolve around tempting the latter to take part, by making meetings more accessible or more attractive, combining them

A framework for evaluation

with social events, and so on. Before members are housed, strategies can appeal even more to self-interest; at Battersea Tenants' Co-op for instance, members earn points for attendance and for working on sub-committees, which can be added to their initial priority points for housing need. Such inducements can inculcate habits of attendance in people who will then go on being active members when they are finally housed. However, habit alone cannot be relied on without there being some commitment in the first place; at Fairbridge, a decline in attendance began from the day when the co-op's development officer dispelled a myth that members would be struck off the list if they failed to attend a meeting. This raises the question of whether sanctions should be used to force freeloaders to live up to their responsibilities. At many co-ops, prospective members have to attend a certain number of meetings in a year, or be removed from the waiting list. This strategy is quite appropriate for the induction of members who are still waiting for a home, but once people are housed, sanctions can backfire; at Seghill, non-attenders were denied the minutes of meetings, but then it was realised that this might alienate them further from the co-op, and contact was resumed. At another co-op the same tactic was tried, and it did cause mistrust among members; freeloaders can be made into holdouts or even escapees if they are pushed too hard.

It is not generally the freeloaders who are the problem; they feel vaguely guilty about not joining in, but are generally well disposed towards the co-op. The believers who take on too much work *are* the problem, because if they become 'burned out' through taking on too much, they tend to become not freeloaders, but sceptics or even hold outs, and can then cause far more trouble for the co-op as a whole than do the freeloaders. At Fairbridge, two women talk bitterly of having organised a play scheme for two years running without any help. They no longer go to any meetings because they feel let down badly by the rest of the co-op. Freeloaders *can* become sceptics, but never having made the initial commitment, they do not express such strength of feeling; in fact, when sceptics complain that they do not attend co-op meetings because of a repair job that was never done, or some promise that was not kept, the complaint is often a cover for their own sense of guilt. If it is genuine, it usually does not last for long; at one co-op a woman refused to go to meetings because her house was not improved before someone else's, but her anger is wearing off and she thinks she will go to the next annual meeting.

In a co-op formed completely from new members, if a selection committee has done its job well, there should be no freeloaders at all, at least in the beginning. As Alex Laidlaw says, rather censoriously: 'People who refuse to take part in meetings or assume responsibility or serve on committees are generally not the co-operative type, and are probably better off in public housing or some other kind of accommodation.'[7] Yet, as we shall see when discussing the principle of voluntary membership, housing need is a powerful incentive to prospective members to discover, or even to fake, a short-lived enthusiasm for co-operation. But there is a worse problem in those co-ops which start with an existing set of tenants. A large and vocal minority may be sceptics or even holdouts from the very beginning. Time alone can bring such people round; as one man at Speirs put it: 'At first, five years ago, there was hardly anyone for the co-op; they're nearly all for it now.'

EXTENSITY

This variable refers both to the size of the group and its geographical concentration. Sorokin says that the greater the extensity, the lower the participation; the larger the co-op, the less its members will want to take part in it. Firstly, let us take the question of size. A recent study estimates that in Britain at least, on average common ownership co-ops provide 38 homes, and management co-ops 59; it ought to be remembered though, that the former still have some houses in the development 'pipeline', which will increase the average over time. The largest co-op in Britain may be Cloverhall Tenant Management Co-op, with 241 houses and bungalows. Certainly there are problems over a lack of identification of all households with the co-op, as there are at Speirs, which has 200 dwellings. As we have seen, Speirs gets over this problem by reserving most of the places on the management committee for elected representatives, one from every two 'closes'. The problem can actually work in the opposite way, with some co-ops being too small to ensure that an active committee can be found, or to make social events and shared amenities worth organising. As Yerbury says of the old Tenant Co-operators co-op; 'Each estate by itself was too small to create any feeling of co-operative life or very definite aims or objects for its own social and educational benefit.'[8] Most small co-ops get round the committee problem by not having one, and running all their affairs by general meeting,[9] but St Andrew's Street has a traditional committee which has only just reached its full complement of 10 members since all the houses have been let. With only 17 households at first, the committee had to rely on some elderly and ill members who can now retire.

It is recognised that small co-ops do foster higher participation; in the case of short-life co-ops, they are also cheaper to run, because larger ones need to employ paid workers to compensate for the drop in volunteer help.[10] The Newham Short-life Co-op in London made a crucial decision after reaching a stock of 26 houses, to stop growing and assist new co-ops to form; by 1981, the Newham Community Housing Federation consisted of 7 co-ops, housing 250 members in 100 houses. In Liverpool, Lodge Lane East Co-op grew to over 200 units, and then sponsored a 'daughter', Newleaf Housing Co-op. They are following in an old tradition; the Hampstead Co-partnership Housing Society did not just grow, but formed a 'First Hampstead', 'Second Hampstead' and finally a 'Third Hampstead' as 'the need for extension arose'.

Secondly, there is the other meaning of extensity, geographical concentration. The above-mentioned survey estimates that 57 per cent of co-op homes in Britain are grouped in blocks of flats, or in one or two streets, while 34 per cent is spread through a neighbourhood.[11] The latter type generally experiences greater problems with participation, because of the lack of cohesion of members, and of identification with the co-op.

DURATION

This refers merely to the length of time a co-op has been in existence. With the passing of time, the dangers increase of organisational ossification, and the capturing of leadership positions by an oligarchy. So do the growth of bureaucracy (as the shift of procedural rules from being means into becoming ends in themselves) and the displacement of the original goals, towards organisation maintenance and stability. Member apathy is the other side of the same coin, and so long-term housing management in co-ops may be hard to sustain; other things being equal, the longer the duration, the lower the participation. Happily, though, other things are not always equal, and there are ways of counteracting the effects of organisational ageing. Also, Sorokin did not consider another effect of duration, that of habit. If co-op members begin by habitually acting in a sound manner, to make the co-op effective while preserving co-op principles, then they and their children can come to see their behaviour as being normal; that is, they create co-operative norms.[12]

A framework for evaluation

A second important measure of duration is the length of time people have been members, since it is the members themselves who make up the co-op. A constant turnover of members might counter the effects of an ageing organisation, since it is then being gradually renewed from within. The case histories presented in the last chapter cannot cover enough time to illustrate this point, but they do point out an opposite danger, that of organisational immaturity, caused by a too-rapid turnover of members. This happened at Abbeyvale, where high rents and all the problems caused by faulty design and construction conspired to drive out many members before they could even make a contribution to the society; in one year, just as all the problems came to a head, nine out of ten committee members had to resign because they were leaving the society. However, this case is exceptional, and most co-ops should experience a stable turnover of members. As we shall see, it is not how they deal with time that matters (no one can reverse its onward march), but how they handle the induction and education of new members.

ADEQUACY

This refers to the ability of co-operators to reach the common goals which they have agreed to work towards. It acknowledges the desire of individuals to meet their own needs, while recognising that, given limited personal resources, many people cannot meet even their most basic needs without the mutual strength that comes from co-operating with others. The recognition of common interests is a necessary prelude to co-operation, and expresses and promotes an affective relation between the co-op members. Their concern for adequacy in meeting common goals becomes also concern to meet each other's needs. H.S. Andersen puts it this way, talking about Danish housing co-ops: 'How well they function ... depends upon to what extent they succeed in establishing common tasks and activities that serve the fundamental material and social needs of the occupants.'[13] What sort of needs are they? There are five main areas, which we can summarise thus: development work (including either purchase and improvement of the dwellings or new building), management (including rent collection, arrears chasing, and allocations of homes), maintenance (including running repairs and cyclical maintenance), rule-making and enforcement (including rules about nuisance, tenant damage, home improvements, car parking and so on), and finance (including financial soundness and use of surpluses).

A framework for evaluation

How far do co-ops meet the needs of their members? Broadly speaking, there is a high level of satisfaction among co-op members. In a recent study, the proportion of those satisfied or very satisfied with the co-op's performance varied from 78 to 86 per cent.[14] This was not just true of those who had recently moved in, but of those who had been in the co-op for over five years. 86 per cent were satisfied with the design of the home, 81 per cent with the way the co-op was run, and 78 per cent with maintenance. Taking into account those who were not sure (perhaps because they did not have enough information or personal experience on the subject), we find very low levels of dissatisfaction; 9, 8 and 11 per cent respectively were dissatisfied on these counts, but only 2 per cent were very dissatisfied. Of course, satisfaction is always relative to one's expectations, and expectations in a co-op are often very high. For instance, when asking Seghill co-op members about whether they felt they knew enough about how a co-op was run, I found that far more expressed dissatisfaction with their own knowledge than in other co-ops. Yet they were far more knowledgeable than the members of the other co-ops already; it was simply that their standards were higher, and they failed their own test. Similarly, those who were very dissatisfied with an aspect of a co-op's adequacy in the co-ops I studied were either alienated individuals with a bad personal experience or highly active members who were determined to do even better!

Yet adequacy cannot just be measured in terms of satisfaction, without some reference to comparative costs; co-ops are not only more or less adequate, but more or less in relation to other forms of housing management. Paul Mugnaioni, the pioneering Director of Housing for Glasgow City Council, recognises this comparative aspect when he says: 'As a means of running housing, a co-op must be effective. It must be able to provide a better service for the same price, or an equivalent service for a lower price than its members could obtain elsewhere.'[15] Unfortunately, owing to the inability of professional housing managers to supply estate-level information, comparative studies have been difficult to make.[16] The general case for co-ops as against public housing management is not at issue; the reputation of the latter is just too bad for the comparison to be worth making. When asked whether they preferred council or co-op management, those members of the six co-ops already described who had had experience of council housing simply laughed! One laconic Speirs tenant summed up their previous experience of the council's repair man, calling him simply 'the invisible man'. However, estate-based management by the Priority Estates

A framework for evaluation

Project, and decentralised housing association management, ought to be compared with that of co-ops, as soon as the appropriate measures can be devised.

Even if co-operatives lead the field in rented housing at present, undoubtedly there are areas in which any co-op can improve its performance. Those co-ops already introduced who tackled improvement work to their homes did it superbly well, keeping hold of the design and build process and providing, within the constraints, what their members wanted. They all provide a quick and efficient maintenance service, through paid or unpaid workers who can respond immediately to emergencies and within a few days to ordinary repairs. None of those who collected rents had a significant rent arrears problem and they all managed to build up surpluses with which to do extra repair and improvement work to the houses, or provide rent-free weeks. There *were* disagreements over the making and enforcement of tenancy rules; within every co-op there were factions who were more or less stringent about car parking, control of pets, vandalism, permissions for home improvements and so on. The greatest achievements were undoubtedly in those co-ops, such as Speirs in Glasgow, which had the toughest job to do, choosing to allow some anti-social elements into the co-op, while exercising strong control when violence or vandalism occurred. The worst problems seemed to be, strange as it might seem, in the co-op with the best all-round performance in other respects, where some leading members were trying just a little too hard to protect their homes and environment. As Alex Laidlaw said of Canadian co-ops, we must not expect perfection, and those who do will always be unhappy.

The problems which did occur could well have been ironed out if these co-ops had had occasional help and advice. At the time when these case-studies were done, there was a noticeable lack of continuing education of members by the co-op movement in general, and each co-op seemed quite isolated. Since then, secondary co-ops and the national federation have taken on this important task, and guidelines are now available to help co-ops to monitor their own performance.[17] There is reason to expect, then, that the 'adequacy' of housing co-ops in Britain will be maintained and improved. This will be doubly good news, if the relationship between adequacy and member participation is as Sorokin suggests; the greater the adequacy, the greater the participation. It is not so simple for two reasons. Firstly, participation which aims at adequacy is a means to an end, and once the end is assured, there is no point in participating further. Activists often do not

A framework for evaluation

realise that as a co-op matures, having left behind the hard-working development stage, and having set up management systems and defined policies, the volume of decision-making drops. There is simply less to do, and meetings can become shorter and less frequent. This should be a welcome relief to a previously over-worked committee, but some members feel guilty that they are not putting as much into the co-op. They should not do so, though, and should put the energy they have saved into other things; if they are keen co-operators into federation and the development of new co-ops. Secondly, if members are only interested in adequacy (and not in the values which we shall call intensity and purity), then they may become complacent and decide that their participation is not needed to ensure a high standard of service. Paradoxically, it is only when the standard drops that they begin to reappear at meetings![18]

INTENSITY

This refers to the depth of commitment of members to each other, their sense of community. It is hard to find any literature on housing co-operatives which does not at some point refer to their sense of community, but it is even harder to find references which go further and try to analyse it. Yet the concept can be further divided into four:

1 The *conditions* for intensity, such as smallness of scale, having a meeting room or community centre available, sharing common areas which encourage social interaction, having a settled population who have had time to get to know and trust each other, or having a high proportion of members with relatives in the co-op.

2 The *means* to intensity, such as holding regular meetings at which members can socialise, and organising a variety of social events for different groups, the elderly, children, and so on.

3 The *sense of community*, expressed in phrases such as socialising, getting on with the neighbours, community spirit and so on, which is in fact an end in itself.

4 The *outcomes* from all these in mutual aid and support for the elderly, children and the disabled.

All of these categories are linked in a circular way: social activities are both a means to community and an expression of it, mutual aid reinforces friendships as ends in themselves, while having a community centre can be both a condition for community and an outcome of it, as can kinship relations. The variable intensity can be measured without too much ambiguity, using all these expressions as aspects of the same concept.

In general, co-ops seem to be friendly places to live in. When asked how satisfied they were with the neighbourliness of their co-op, 39 per cent said they were very satisfied, 45 per cent satisfied, 9 per cent were not sure, 5 per cent were dissatisfied, and only 2 per cent very dissatisfied.[19] In the common-ownership and tenant management co-ops which we have met in the last chapter, there is a very strong sense of community, but in the co-ownership and the tower block a much weaker one; in fact, at Abbeyvale and Glenkerry the only groups which socialise regularly are the co-op's committee. This is mainly attributable to the high turnover of members in these co-ops; they were designed originally as stepping-stones to owner-occupation, and high rents and service charges mean that there is financial pressure to move on when they can. Where there is a sense of community, though, it may not always be associated with the co-op. At St Andrew's Street the co-op has been a means of saving an existing community, which until the influx of new members was rather taken for granted; it was not seen as the co-op's job to nurture something which was there before the co-op existed. At Fairbridge, there are strong local ties, but to the wider community of Bridgeton in general rather than to the co-op in particular. Kinship and friendship ties, memberships of clubs and churches all overlap with the co-op, but the initial enthusiasm for co-op-based dances and play-schemes has not been maintained.

On the other hand, at Seghill the members have a very active social life if they want it, based both on formal co-op functions and on informal get-togethers of members, who do feel a strong attachment to other co-op members in particular. Many of them have come from the alienated environment of council estates in nearby Cramlington New Town, and they are determined to be neighbourly. At Speirs, most co-op members are part of a kinship network so extensive that it has to be described as a clan. However, this did not necessarily mean that they saw much of their distant cousins until the co-op began to organise and give them a new sense of identity. And in the busy, sometimes raucous and always vital street-life of the place, in which everyone seems to know everyone else, a substantial minority who do not belong to a clan had always felt isolated until helped by the co-op to come together.

But what of the negative side of intensity? Its disadvantages are expressed in complaints of lack of privacy or of confidentiality, and these would seem to be straightforward measures of the trade-offs which members have to make for a high level of intensity, and which may lead to a desire to lower, or at least not to raise further, the social 'temperature'. More problematic is intensity's opposite, social conflict, which is indicated by, on the one hand, condemnatory attitudes towards vandals, social misfits, problem families and the like, and, on the other, resentments at being treated unfairly, singled out for punishment. Are these evidences of a lack of community, or of a strong sense of community and its obligations? If one draws the boundary of community around all the members, then they are the former, if round only those who act in socially responsible ways, they are the latter. The definition of the boundary of community can be itself problematic and disputed. Yet these instances of disunity can be treated as negative instances of intensity, since they contrast with a positive wish to extend the boundaries further than the co-op.

For instance, at Speirs a small but vocal minority are against the allowing in of known 'problem families', and think that the co-op would be better if it abandoned one block of flats where tenants are troublesome. The majority, though, are determined to maintain the boundaries as they are, to deal with anti-social behaviour firmly but fairly, and if possible to extend the benefits of co-operation to the rest of the street; they have given support and advice to tenants at the other end of Langholm Street who are thinking of starting up their own management co-op. Similarly, though not with the same intensity of feeling, members at Seghill disagree over whether their social events should be open to people from neighbouring streets; some activists are keen to promote a new secondary co-op. Essentially, the question of boundaries is one of confidence; those who believe in the ability of their co-op to deliver both adequacy and intensity have a confidence that tends to spill over into concern for others who are not so fortunate.

Again the proposition is simple: the greater the intensity, the greater the participation. In this case though, participation is not a means to an end, but an end in itself. It can be increased up to the point where it threatens the privacy of individuals and families, at which point people will of course draw back. However, because it has this quality, of being an end in itself, it can increase to take the place of that type of participation which is a means to adequacy, when the latter begins to fall off.

A framework for evaluation

PURITY

This refers to members' commitment to co-operative principles. It seems a straightforward variable, but unfortunately the principles themselves have been the subject of debate and some controversy, which have prompted two study commissions of the ICA which reported in 1934 and 1966. Table 7.1 shows which of the principles have been accepted as definitive at these times. The late listing from 1966 forms the basis on which the International Co-operative Alliance allows co-operatives and their federal bodies to affiliate, and so can be considered authoritative.[20] This means that organisations which meet the ICA-approved principles can be considered co-ops, even if they infringe other principles enshrined in the 'Rochdale' tradition. The important principles are then:

1 Open and voluntary membership.
2 Democratic control, by one member one vote.
3 Fair distribution of economic results, according to labour or consumption rather than ownership of capital; capital should receive fixed, rather than variable interest.
4 The provision of education in co-operative principles and practices.
5 Co-operation between co-ops.

All five principles must apply, unless genuinely inapplicable to some types of co-op.

In addition, the Rochdale principle of purity of goods, that is, of providing the best possible product for the consumer, could be included, but hardly needs to be; in a consumer-based organisation it is surely self-evident, and we have noted under the variable adequacy how co-ops try to live up to it. Buchez's principle on the disposal of net assets when a co-op is wound up to other co-op organisations or to charitable purposes, ensures that co-op members will not be tempted to liquidate the business in order to make capital gains. It just failed to become an ICA principle in 1966, and is enshrined in French and Italian law. If the British housing co-operative movement is to survive in the long term, particularly in the south-east where steep rises in house prices have made co-operative property very valuable, some such law is needed, as well as the current protection which mutual societies have against sales to individual members. The principle of political and religious neutrality is also important, even though the ICA could not possibly endorse it, since so many co-op movements have been formed along political or religious lines. The British consumer co-op movement, for instance, returns members to Parliament in association with the Labour party. However, in a more restricted form it does appear as part of the open membership principle.

TABLE 7.1: Co-operative principles and their origins

Principles	Origin	ICA endorsement	
1 MEMBERSHIP			
(a) Open membership	Rochdale 1844 (some co-ops previously)	1934	1966
(b) Voluntary membership	Rochdale (implicit)	1934	1966
2 DEMOCRATIC CONTROL By one member, one vote	Rochdale (but also (Friendly Socs)	1934	1966
3 ECONOMIC RESULTS			
(a) Distribution according to labour or consumption	Rochdale	1934 (but possibly earlier)	1966
(b) Disposal of net assets on dissolution of society, without profit to members	Buchez		
(c) Limited interest on capital	Rochdale	1934	1966
4 POLITICAL AND RELIGIOUS NEUTRALITY	Rochdale (but also Dr King and 1832 Congress)		
5 PROMOTION OF EDUCATION	Rochdale		1966
6 CO-OPERATION WITH OTHER CO-OPS (Goal of Co-op Commonwealth)	Rochdale		1966
7 PURITY & QUALITY OF PRODUCTS	Rochdale (but only implicit; it was simple self-interest for a consumer-controlled body)		

Source: the ordering of the principles is original, and synthesises the thinking of the various writers.

A framework for evaluation

MEMBERSHIP

> Membership of a co-operative society should be voluntary and available without artificial restriction or any social, political, racial or religious discrimination, to all persons who can make use of its services and are willing to accept the responsibilities of membership.[21]

There are really two principles here: open membership, often referred to as the 'open door', and voluntary membership. *Open membership* can be taken to mean that a co-op should allow absolutely anyone in. In fact, the Rochdale Pioneers required that prospective members had to be approved by a general meeting before being allowed to join; open does not necessarily mean indiscriminate, and co-op members have a right to decide if applicants will make good co-operators. Where they do not do this, a fall in participation can be expected. For instance, the first two blocks of houses at Fairbridge were filled slowly by a housing association's development officer, who took care to offer the alternative of a standard tenancy elsewhere on the estate to those who were not keen on the co-op idea. Then she found that because the area had a rough reputation, the rest of the houses were difficult to let, and she became less stringent; the result was that participation began to decline, as members on the first two blocks became resentful that the rest were freeloading. Because the members then decided not to do their own allocations, the problem will undoubtedly get worse. Of course, the co-ops described in the last chapter are early ones, unusual in that three were promoted by housing associations; secondary co-ops usually demand that a genuine group of co-operators emerges before the housing is found, and that they pay great attention to the selection process.

The 'open door' principle also means that membership is not restricted by considerations irrelevant to the purposes of the co-op, such as political affiliations, ethnic origin, sexual orientation and so on, and that decisions should respect the principle of equity, that (other things being equal) like cases should be treated alike. Recently, the movement has begun to pay attention to this problem, and equal opportunities guidelines have been introduced, suggesting that among other things, co-ops should aim to house at least as high a proportion of ethnic minority members as there are in the wider local population.[22] One secondary co-op, Solon CHS, has gone further, with a 'Co-op Access' project, designed to open up the idea of housing co-ops to ethnic minority groups.

A framework for evaluation

Does this mean that people's economic status should also be regarded as irrelevant, and that co-ops which require a large equity stake (e.g. shared-ownership co-ops) or a high cost-rent (e.g. co-ownerships) are in breach of the open membership principle? This is one of the objections raised by opponents of these types of co-ops, both in housing and, incidentally, in worker co-ops, where the Industrial Common Ownership Movement has steadfastly refused to promote anything other than common ownership. On the other hand, common ownership 'HAG'-type co-ops have to house those in greatest housing need, thus excluding the better off, even if they want to live in a co-op. Both types of exclusion work against open membership, though obviously on other grounds than co-op principles both can be defended. If open membership is to be promoted, then the expansion of the subsidised co-op, *and* the development of new forms of privately financed unsubsidised co-op are needed, to enable people in a wide range of circumstances to opt for the co-operative life-style.

Voluntary membership refers to that precious co-operative value, voluntary association. It means that members are not coerced into joining, but join of their own free will, or out of what the ICA calls 'unfettered appreciation of co-operative values and consideration of ... economic advantage'.[23] This might seem obvious, but the principle is undermined if people in great housing need find that only by joining a co-op can their need be met; they may then feel coerced into joining an association which requires of them more commitment than they wish to give. When members at Fairbridge found out they would not be evicted if they stopped going to meetings, many dropped out; their commitment had been artificially stimulated by the offer of that rare commodity in Glasgow, a house with a 'back and front door'. The only way this problem can be avoided in the long term is by the creation of a housing market which allows genuine choice between tenures.[24]

DEMOCRACY

Co-operative societies are democratic organisations. Their affairs should be administered by persons elected or appointed in a manner agreed by the members and accountable to them. Members of primary societies should enjoy equal rights of voting (one member one vote), and participation in decisions affecting their societies.

A framework for evaluation

The application of this principle seems straightforward. Co-ops are the kind of small-scale organisations which, as we have seen in Chapter 3, liberal and communitarian thinkers have extolled as the ultimate in direct democracy. Even Robert Michels, in his exploration of the 'tendency to oligarchy' says that co-ops 'should incorporate most perfectly the democratic principle'. However, he warns that even they are in danger from 'the existence of immanent oligarchical tendencies in every kind of human organisation which strives for the attainment of definite ends'.[25] There are psychological drives which lead people, even in housing co-ops, to want to keep hold of formal offices and informal positions of power. At first they may volunteer out of a sense of duty, but then continue to exercise their powers out of sheer habit of being in a position of authority, but this can lead over time to the feeling that they have a right to the loyalty of other members in keeping them in office. If they have to stand down, they experience a loss of social status, which can come as a shock. Also, the need for a division of labour in taking minutes, collecting rents, ordering repairs and so on, builds up expertise and experience which become harder to replace the longer an individual carries on doing them. Ordinary members then tend to express gratitude, even veneration of the leaders, seeing them as intellectually superior, and totally indispensable. Yet the more indispensable the leaders seem, the more powerful and independent they become, and so a struggle between leaders and led eventually results.

There are really two questions, or rather two sides to the same question: how members can control their representatives (or in co-ops controlled by general meeting, their informal leaders), and how leaders can encourage their members to be responsible and to participate. There is in fact a variety of tactics available. Firstly, the key to control over leaders and the encouraging of a responsible general membership is in regular general meetings, in which members can question and contribute to decision-making. George Homans has pointed out that 'there is a tendency in repeated exchanges between men for their power to equalise';[26] the more ordinary members have the chance to meet, the more will any concentration of influence be prevented. Those co-ops such as Speirs and Seghill which had regular open meetings where even the most minor committee decisions had to be ratified had no problems about 'them and us' attitudes. There was a general confidence in the leadership, even among members who did not go to meetings, because the opportunity was there to become informed, to criticise and ultimately to control. In one meeting at Seghill, members took a vote and changed the dates of the rent-free weeks which were arranged to coincide with holiday periods, and no one in the committee seemed to mind; they expected to be challenged. At St Andrews's Street though (and by all accounts at Weller Street in Liverpool),[27] a long struggle against the authorities to provide decent housing had led to a concentration on committee meetings at the expense of the general meeting. This resulted in a 'them and us' attitude among members; the committee had had very little time to communicate with the ordinary members, and then, when they did, were easily able to get their way by displaying their expert knowledge. It was not that they particularly wanted to get their way, but some members felt that they did, and that the ordinary members were there to 'rubber-stamp' decisions that had already been made.

Secondly, information can be exchanged in a variety of other less formal ways, via the distribution of minutes, or a regular newsletter, and ordinary members can be encouraged to attend committee meetings as observers. At Speirs, for instance, the newsletter provided a valuable alternative method of communicating with non-participating members. Thirdly, steps can be taken to ensure a regular turn-over of officers; at Seghill, the most far-sighted members were already talking about a rule preventing committee members from standing for more than, say, three years at a time, and 'understudies' had been appointed to work with the key officers with a view eventually to replacing them. Glenkerry went even further, and encouraged the old officers to continue to come to committee meetings to give help and advice to their successors. The way in which new committee members are appointed can be crucial. At Seghill, nominations are not needed, and members can simply ask to be put on the list for voting. At Speirs, the election of committee members by groups of 12 flats encourages people to stand who would not have dreamed of doing so otherwise; there is a high drop-out rate from the committee during the first month or two of a new committee's term, but at least a large number of members get the chance to serve. But the personal approach is the best: at St Andrew's Street, the secretary has very wisely invited new people on to the committee to counter the 'them and us' attitudes. Finally, at Seghill the gardening and social committees are made up of members who are not on the main committee, and so opportunities to serve in more informal ways are created.

A framework for evaluation

ECONOMIC RESULTS

The economic results arising out of the operations of a society belong to the members of that society, and should be distributed in such a manner as would avoid one member gaining at the expense of others. This may be done by decision of the members as follows: (a) by provision for development of the business of the co-operative; (b) by provision of common services; or (c) by distribution among the members in proportion to their transactions with the society.

This is commonly known as the 'dividend principle', but, as the above quotation shows, it concerns the wider principle, that in a co-operative members have the democratic right to decide how surpluses are to be used, whether they are distributed to members as an individual 'dividend', used for communal benefits, or retained within the reserves of the business. The crucial distinction between a co-op and a capitalist company is that capital is hired at a fixed rate of interest, and that variable returns are only made to members in proportion to their labour or consumption. In a consumer co-op, the dividend is better called (as in the American usage) a 'patronage refund'; it is a *return* to the member of over-payments made because of the inability in advance to predict cost-price accurately. It is a kind of fair-price mechanism, which protects the consumer from overcharging. In a housing co-op, it is a return on rents, which ensures that the co-op does not charge members more than the actual cost of their housing, but it can also be used collectively to provide environmental and housing improvements, such as play areas, gardens, central heating or double glazing. Co-ops may even decide to use part of their surplus to support the development of other co-ops.

The ICA insists that: 'in deciding in what forms and in what proportions or amounts the surplus or savings shall be allocated or divided, the members as a body have, and ought to have, absolute discretion.'[28] Unfortunately, common-ownership co-ops which receive housing association grants are specifically barred from distributing to individuals, by section 26 of the 1974 Housing Act, an imposition which threatens this fundamental co-op principle. They are able to fix their own rents only if prepared to forgo consideration for revenue deficit grant in the future, and since 1981 the Department of the Environment is to 'claw-back' any surplus above the level of management and maintenance allowances, calculated *as if* the co-op were charging a fair rent. At Seghill, members have made large surpluses by doing all their own repairs, and they are frustrated by the inability to set their own rents and directly to reward members for their participation. In fact, when I interviewed them, several members were seriously considering whether it was worth their while continuing to do voluntary work in this way.

Tenant management co-ops are in theory able to allocate surpluses from management and maintenance allowances for any purpose, subject to the claims of natural justice. However, some local authorities mistakenly interpret the surplus as a profit (just as governments have often done in regard to consumer co-op dividends), and so some agency agreements prohibit distribution of benefits to individual members in the form of rent rebates; the Islington Council took this view, in taking over the Elthorne co-ops from the Greater London Council.

If some authorities infringe the positive aspects of the economic results principle, some co-ops may themselves infringe its negative aspect; the prohibition of a variable return on capital. When owner-occupiers sell a house, they take a profit which reflects partly rises in building and labour costs, but also, and more importantly, the scarcity value of the dwelling and its location. The latter gains are speculative, in that they rely on an imperfect market in which the supply of new housing is not able to meet demand, or even worse, is artificially restricted by the 'banking' of development land. Co-operative housing was started in Sweden and Norway after the First World War, and in Canada during the 1960s, partly as a result of inflationary spirals in the owner-occupied market. If offers a way of providing housing without adding to inflation, because the co-op members do not gain simply from the increase in value of the dwellings. Yet this is not quite true of co-ownership co-ops, and is certainly not true of shared-ownership schemes, in which part of the dwelling is owned individually. This has led some theorists to deny that such types are real co-ops.[29]

When one examines the issue closely, it becomes extremely complicated. For instance, shared-ownership co-ops can be said to include an element of speculative capital gain, but only in the individually owned part; the co-operative part remains untouched by such criticism. If this argument is accepted, then it also applies to condominiums, where individuals own the entire leasehold interest of their homes, but have a collective share in the freehold. The latter element is still a kind of co-op, no matter how truncated when compared with a full-blown common-ownership co-op. Co-ownerships are more difficult to evaluate. Where sale of the right to occupy is based on a valuation tied to average rises in building costs, no speculative gains occur, but where it is allowed to float in the market, then depending on the state of that market, speculative gains may occur; Swedish co-ops are therefore more co-operative than Norwegian ones. In the case of British co-ownerships, an initial formula for basing premium payments on the rise in building costs was superseded by one based on what the incoming tenant's rent could pay for; the whole issue is so complex, and the sums involved so trivial, that it is probably not worth evaluating.[30]

EDUCATION

All co-operative societies should make provision for the education of their members, officers and employees, and of the general public, in the principles and techniques of co-operation, both economic and democratic.

This principle is in one sense logically prior to the rest, since only by being informed about the co-op principles and being taught to care about them, can people apply and observe them. It was taken very seriously by the Rochdale Pioneers, some of whom were disciples of Robert Owen, and convinced that rational enlightenment was both necessary and sufficient to introduce a new co-operative world order. They provided, almost before their business could afford to, a reading room, library, children's and adults' schools. Education was at first general, since many members could neither read nor write, but by the 1880s it had narrowed, owing to local authority intervention to provide basic education, into the teaching of the specific co-operative business practices and principles.

The International Co-operative Alliance emphasises that: 'The effort to reshape the economic system on the basis of Co-operative principles requires a different discipline from those of either individual or government enterprises.'[31] The collective self-discipline needed to run co-ops effectively is a cultivated growth, which requires: 'acceptance of new ideas, new standards of conduct, new habits of thought and behaviour, based on the superior values of co-operative association.'[32] It includes both what people learn and how they learn it; the use of participatory learning techniques makes co-operative education a method as well as a principle.

A framework for evaluation

In housing co-ops education is particularly important, since they demand a higher commitment and skill among the average member than do larger types of co-ops, and since the members have to learn to live together in close proximity. The education process which normally takes 10–15 years in other types of co-op has to be speeded up to around two years in a housing co-op, and is an intense, often exhausting, activity. Unlike other organisations, they face their greatest difficulties early on, and so the earlier the education, the better. In Norway, 'mother' co-ops provide booklets for ordinary members, and voluntary courses for board members. This does not seem much, but regular exchanges of experienced members between different co-ops ensure a high level of competence. In Sweden, the secondary co-ops (or 'local societies' as they are called) organise regular 1 or 2-day courses for board members, in a range from basic to advanced, and HSB even has its own training college.

Developments in Britain have been much more tentative and recent. We have noted how for co-ownerships there was little educational provision, if any. The members at Abbeyvale had to rely solely on a pamphlet and tenancy agreement supplied by the Society's agent. In consequence, participation was very erratic, commitment uncertain, and the impressive achievements in the sphere of adequacy were mainly due to the sheer determination of two individuals, who later left the Society. In fact, under a later chairman the committee hardly met, and it is open to question as to whether, in the absence of any vetting of new members for their commitment, and any educational work, the Society will continue to function as a democratic body; it may simply lapse into a paper society, run by and in the interest of the agent. On the other hand, a well-organised education course may not produce the goods either, unless it is built around the real needs of members, and is thoroughly absorbed. The account of the Weller St co-op is very interesting in this respect, graphically describing how the professionals failed at first to communicate with the members in a language they understood, and in contrast how much members learned simply from visiting other co-ops and seeing what they had done. The Fairbridge Co-op had a long and well-organised course, in a series of meetings, yet at the end of it they still did not feel confident about running their own co-op. This was partly because hardly any of them had any previous experience even of attending a meeting, let alone running one. The officers did gain confidence, but only after doing the job for a year or two; there is no substitute for learning by doing.

A framework for evaluation

When members do have previous experience of either formal schooling or of similar organisations such as trade unions or voluntary groups, formal courses are more successful. Glenkerry was fortunate in having a mainly middle-class membership, and, with three solicitors on the committee during the first year, could hardly go wrong. Seghill had a mainly skilled working-class and clerical-worker membership, who have been able to draw on work and trade union skills. They may get exasperated by smooth-talking professionals, but are not put down by them. St Andrew's Street members, when I interviewed them, were still struggling with the terribly complex issues surrounding the controversy over the building site at the corner of the famous Minster. As one man confessed, when talking about the professionals, 'It's got too technical, you've got to be well educated to understand it,' and another said even more forthrightly, 'We're thick but they're fully educated.' Perhaps the best educational strategy, though, was provided by Speirs, where education was regarded as an ongoing and cumulative process, based on talks at general meetings, discussions at committee meetings around written policy statements, a regular newsletter and so on.

All six of the co-ops described above suffered to some extent from being pioneers, in that there was no established network of co-ops with which to share experiences. If the best form of education is learning by doing, the second best must be learning by imitation, by other people's experience, and this is what is happening more and more in those areas where co-ops are thick on the ground, and education can be co-ordinated through secondary co-ops and local federations. In fact, courses are now being put on for members of new co-ops using the skills and experience of members of established ones, and specialist courses are being organised for the secretaries or treasurers of several co-ops at once. Delegates to secondary co-op committees are being paired with a more experienced member, so that the always difficult induction period is made as easy as possible. These methods make education truly cost-effective, since they cost less and have more effect than courses put on by professional 'educators'. The professionals have not backed out, but have redefined their role as that of facilitators, organising but not necessarily running courses themselves, providing visual aid material, and a burgeoning library of handbooks, manuals and advice leaflets. But if co-ops are to take education seriously, they will soon have to begin adopting the practice of consumer co-ops, and set aside a proportion of their surpluses for the purpose; secondary co-ops may introduce education subscriptions to make up for the recent short-fall in grant aid, and it will be a test of the maturity and commitment (or in terms of our theory, the 'purity') of primary co-op members, as to whether they pay up. A London-based education workers' group now provides a forum for the co-ordination of training, and a national education group has begun to meet. The ultimate aim must be what the Solon secondary co-op calls: 'a better-resourced, higher-quality, nationally co-ordinated and extremely responsive education and training service for housing co-ops'.[33]

CO-OPERATION WITH OTHER CO-OPS, AND THE CO-OP COMMONWEALTH

All co-operative organisations, in order to best serve the interests of their members and their communities should actively co-operate in every practical way with other co-operatives at local, national and international levels.

There are two ways in which this rule can be interpreted, and it applies to both: that co-ops should co-operate with each other and form federations within each type, and that they should co-operate with other types of co-op. Firstly, Chapter 5 traced the growth of federal groupings of the newly emerging housing co-op movement. At the time when they were interviewed, members of Seghill co-op were ambivalent about the new National Federation of Housing Co-ops, wondering whether it was worth supporting. With a characteristic combination of realism and dedication, they sent a representative or two, withholding judgment about whether it was worthwhile. Then when the regional federation threatened to fall apart through lack of support, they hired a mini-bus and packed a meeting, and the treasurer became a prominent member of the national committee. Though some regional federations still have to emerge as formal organisations, there is no longer any doubt about the viability, or, as it has been so successful, the value of a national federation.

There has as yet been little co-operation with other types of co-op. It would be fitting if housing co-ops could order all their design, building, repair and maintenance work from other co-ops, and the recent phenomenal growth in worker co-ops makes it more likely that these kinds of co-operation will occur. Solon is engaged in an interesting joint development with the Greater London Enterprise Board of joint industrial units and housing in the East End of London, and the

A framework for evaluation

Hunslet Co-op in Leeds has sponsored a worker co-op, but these are as yet isolated examples. Another neglected area is that of credit unions; every housing co-op should have one, providing cheap loans and a modest return on members' capital. One or two housing co-ops have experimented with bulk buy food co-ops; the extensive and highly successful Japanese example of 'Han groups', in which a dozen families get together and co-ordinate all their buying needs, is a useful model. Much more needs to be done, and probably will be, when the more mature housing co-ops are able to pay attention to more than the needs of the moment. To the extent that they do succeed in co-operating with other co-ops, they will be fulfilling an imperative derived from that early Owenite vision; the Co-operative Commonwealth.

CONCLUSION

Armed with these basic variables, we can weave intricate patterns of relationships between them. Firstly, the greater the adequacy, intensity and purity, the higher the participation. If a co-op aims to improve its performance in any one of these areas, participation should increase. However, the greater the purity, the greater the adequacy and intensity. Commitment to co-op principles leads to a concern with meeting common goals and a sense of community. The greater the intensity, the greater the adequacy, since caring among neighbours usually leads to a desire to meet each other's needs. The greater the adequacy, the greater the intensity, since success leads to identification with one's neighbours, and the greater the adequacy, the greater the purity, since success leads to curiosity about what is distinctive about the co-operative form. If a co-op's performance is improved on more than one variable at once, then the combined effect of the improvements will affect participation even more than they would have done if made separately at different times; what the organisation theorists call 'synergy' will occur.

There is more to it than this, though, because there are several intervening variables which also affect participation, all of which revolve around the cost to the individual of taking part. If members have already had experience of working in similar organisations, then the learning process will be less costly. If they are not working shifts, looking after young children, suffering from back trouble or just plain tired, then the personal cost of attending meetings will be lower. Looked at from this perspective, of the cost to individuals, a whole different set of generalisations apply, based on an economic concept of

A framework for evaluation

opportunity-costs. Hold a general meeting on a night when a favourite soap opera is on, or England is playing in the World Cup, and the cost of attendance will be very high indeed. There is much that co-ops can do to make participation less costly, such as making sure that a crèche or baby-sitting service is available for meetings, that rooms are warm and not choked with cigarette smoke. Every individual has a different 'boredom threshold'; in one co-op, two women said of the same meeting 'I could have listened to our chairman talking all night' and 'I was bored stiff after ten minutes; there was no need to go on and on like that.' For the sake of those with a low boredom threshold, it pays to make sure that adequacy-type participation, as a means to an end, is kept to a minimum, and that intensity-type participation, as an end in itself which is also more fun, is increased.

There is much more that can be said and done, using this framework for evaluation of the performance of housing co-ops, but out of respect for the boredom threshold of the reader, I will leave it to another time.

CONCLUSION: A CO-OPERATIVE VIEW OF HOUSING POLICY IN BRITAIN

There are many voices seeking to gain attention in the noisy debate on the future of housing policy in Britain. They seem to be talking in the same language but, as we have seen in Chapters 2 and 3, they are expressing radically different world-views, summed up in competing slogans: the right to buy in a free market, the right to rent social housing, the right to a home. In this debate, the co-operative voice is a small but persistent one, which has only recently come to be heard, let alone listened to with respect and attention. That it has been heard at all is due not so much to the carrying power of the co-operative voice as to the mimicry and opportunism of politicians, though when they have actually visited a housing co-op, they have been genuinely impressed; the quiet confidence of co-op members in getting on with the job has been more eloquent than any rhetoric. The result has been a growing chorus of approval, a consensus, surprising in these times of the embittered clash of political tempers, which has led policy-analysts from all sides to agree, even to compete in affirming, that co-operatives are 'a good thing'. The one exception has been the Militant-led Liverpool Council, which is committed to a municipal-Leninist housing policy which is universally decried, and on which, as we have noted, Lenin himself had a complete change of mind. Not that this consensus has done more than put housing co-ops on the agenda; it has not yet allowed the Glasgow District Council to lease estates to common-ownership co-ops, nor has it produced a replicable privately funded co-op as an alternative to private renting. It *has* produced some key clauses in a Housing and Planning Act which received all-party support, encouraging local authorities to lease estates to groups of tenants, and enabling tenants to have their own plans for co-operative take-overs considered. But it remains to be seen if the swelling chorus of approval leads to anything more than 'sound and fury, signifying nothing'.

Conclusion

What co-operative housing has done already is to burst the bubble of a few long-held myths: that owner-ocupation is the only way in which people can gain consumer control over housing, that council housing is the only way in which disadvantaged people can gain access to decent housing, and that philanthropic housing associations are the only way in which people can gain the advantages of small-scale housing management. What co-operative housing has done is to alter, once and for all, the terms of the debate. It has, simply by becoming a reality, declared the most fundamental right of all – the right to *dweller control*. Once we accept that this is what the debate should be about, then its blurred lines suddenly come into sharp focus.

Take, for example, owner-occupation. It is commonly thought that to own one's home is to have control over it. This is only true for some owners, some of the time. There are the elderly people who cannot afford to keep up the repairs on terraced houses which are, like much of Britain's housing stock, falling into major disrepair; control is for them a dreadful responsibility. Then there are the young couples in London where property prices have recently climbed to staggering heights; they cannot afford to get married and have children, because they need the tax advantages of being single, and two incomes to service a gigantic mortgage into the foreseeable future. Are they in control of their homes, or are their homes in control of them? Then there are those who, through redundancy, ill-health or divorce, are part of that growing band of mortgage debtors who are being evicted for non-payment, and who in many areas of Britain find that the value of their investment has dropped below what they owe; they are simply walking away and abandoning their homes. Then there are the council tenants who have exercised the right to buy, then have got into similar difficulties, or who have found major structural problems with their homes, such that the council has had to buy them back. Then there are the thousands of owners of newly built homes, who each year claim against the National House Building Council for shoddy workmanship, or complain to the Office of Fair Trading; they are paying for having had no control over the design and construction of their homes. Then there are the sizeable minority of owners who suffer from noise or nuisance from neighbours and find that there is little they can do about it except to go to the expense of moving. Finally, there are the leasehold flat-owners, who are at the mercy of freeholder 'landlords' who can neglect the property and at the same time extort massive service charges; these are, of all owners, perhaps those least in control.

Conclusion

None of these people are in control of their housing in the way they would be if they were in a co-op. There are many ways in which co-operative forms can improve on owner-occupation. Elderly people can sell their house to a co-op and either get a co-operative tenancy in return or use their equity to buy part of a flat or bungalow, the rest of which is held jointly by the residents as co-operators. Young people can marry and have children, secure in the knowledge that the rents will not spiral upwards just because there is a housing shortage in the area. People on low incomes and in insecure jobs can get the protection of a rental which is eligible for housing benefit, and a system of rent collection run by people who know what it is like to be poor or in ill-health. People in newly built housing can be in control of the architects and builders, and those who sufffer from anti-social neighbours can appeal to the collective power of the co-op members to impose minimal rules of good behaviour. If given the right to buy their homes from the freeholder (they are getting some new powers in legislation proposed by the present government, but not the automatic right to buy out the freeholder), leaseholders could form a condominium, which is a restricted but genuine form of co-operative. They would then be in full collective control of their homes.

More generally, owner-occupation can be criticised for exacerbating inequalities in society. Firstly, tax relief is made available in a way which is highly regressive, benefiting those on higher incomes and encouraging them to invest in housing not for its use-value but for its eventual exchange-value; they are rewarded for consuming more housing than they need. Secondly, this encourages the build-up of equity which is transferred eventually (and usually long after they need it) to the owners' children, thus exacerbating the already marked disadvantage of the 38 per cent of households who are either tenants or homeless. Thirdly, the consequent attractiveness of owner-occupation and the absence of alternatives fuel house price inflation, which creates a further band of inequality; the owner's initial high mortgage is a kind of tax on youth paid to older people. Fourthly, widening inequalities between different regions, caused by the decline of traditional extractive and manufacturing industries, are exacerbated by the way in which house prices respond to demand, leaving owners unable to sell their homes in high unemployment areas, and unable to afford to buy in areas where their skills *are* in demand. Then there are other, more sweeping arguments which suggest that not only does house price inflation widen inequalities, but it also undermines the long-term viability of the economy as a whole, thus making everyone worse off in the long run. A combination of huge consumer debt to building societies and banks, the siphoning off of equity which ought to be invested in productive industry, and the leaking of the equity stored in housing into the economy as consumer spending, all seem to point to a spiral of economic decline which is for the moment masked by an artificial prosperity based on land and property values.

Co-operative housing is inherently equalising, since it is allocated strictly on the basis of need. But, unlike council housing, it is controlled by the dwellers, who use the rent income to make sure that the property does not deteriorate in value. In common ownerships, there is no equity gain by individuals, and so house price inflation is checked. There are, of course, increases in costs associated with rising land values and building costs, but there are few speculative gains to be made, because the development process is controlled by the dwellers, and then the property is held in common. Where large-scale subsidy is needed, this is because the state is having to pay the price of not controlling the speculation in land, property and finance capital which occurs prior to the co-operative being developed. There are of course, inequalities between co-ops in the amount they have to pay for their housing, but these can be relieved either by a state-funded fair rent scheme such as operates in Britain at present, or by a voluntary rent-pooling scheme operated by the co-ops themselves. What such co-ops do not do, though, is to offer a realistic alternative to owner-occupation in contemporary Britain, for those who can afford it.

Firstly, those who can afford to buy, have to, since the state-subsidised common ownership co-ops can only admit those in housing need. Secondly, even if access is gained to a co-op tenancy, those who can afford to invest in housing later on will become disadvantaged if they do not do so. The answer to both problems is of course a more equitable system of housing subsidy, which benefits all tenures equally instead of bribing people to become individual owners, and penalising those who do not. The co-operative movement can play its part by developing shared ownership and co-ownership co-ops, through which dwellers can make individual investments in their housing without losing the advantages of collective control and a more co-operative life-style. We have noted in Chapter 5 that shared ownership co-ops are being developed, but that they are really designed to lead to eventual owner-occupation, and (unless there is a residual freehold held in common as in a condominium) the dissolution of the co-op. We have

Conclusion

noted also, in Chapter 4, that the old-style co-ownerships were sold off to their members. How can individual equity be encouraged, without it destroying the very existence of the co-operative? There are a variety of ways. Common ownerships can issue loan stock to members at fixed rates of interest, but hardly ever seem to do so. Shared ownerships could, in return for state subsidy, be constituted so that a fixed part of the equity is always held in common, as at Glenkerrry House, described in Chapter 6. Co-ownerships could be formed in a simpler way than before, with members taking up a minimum share-holding, then receiving bonus shares as the value of the property rises and surpluses are made on rents, and (as in the old housing co-partnerships outlined in Chapter 4) being able to sell them to a new member when they leave, or transfer them to a new co-op. This would entail two safeguards; a law (such as France and Italy have already) against the break-up of the co-op for capital gains, and a procedure for valuing the member's shares which discourages speculative gains.

Another way of tackling the problems which owner-occupation brings is by gaining co-operative control of the process by which owner-occupied housing is produced and improved. In Ireland and the United States, house-building co-ops buy land from local councils, and then control the entire development process until the houses are sold to individual co-op members. This cuts out speculative gains, and enables young people to get into the market without falling prey to the property developer. In Canada and to some extent in Britain, such development has included self-build, which enables low-income people to build their own homes. The result is neither a permanent co-op nor an estate of restless, alienated owners, but a group of people who have not just built their own homes, but have at the same time built their own community. What is needed to make such collective control more widespread is a radical change in attitudes among local authorities and financial institutions; they are at present geared up to servicing the developers who make a living out of the dwellers, rather than the dwellers themselves. If local authorities can be persuaded to sell land to co-ops without speculative gains, if credit unions become established in Britain to the extent they have in the USA, and building co-ops to the extent that they have in Scandinavia, then co-ops will be able to finance and build co-ops, in a complete circle of mutual aid which cuts out the need for either capitalist markets or bureaucratic paternalism.

Little more need be said here about the future of council housing. Chapters 1 to 3 contain powerful arguments for the devolution of council estates to tenants. There is a ladder of control, ranging from initial consultation of tenants, to joint management, complete self-management and eventual co-operative common ownership, but tenants are rarely aware of the possibilities, let alone the rung of the ladder they wish to stop at. The new Housing and Planning Act will make available funds for the education of tenants, the formulation of plans for the tenants' take-over, and the training of officers who will be responsible *to* the tenants. Secondary co-ops have the expertise and the will to do the work. However, tenant control is not a cheap alternative, at least not in the short run; defects in construction, outstanding repairs and improvements, all have to be funded if tenants are to agree to take over their homes. Provided such funding is available, all that is needed is an education process which completely changes the world-views of both tenants and housing professionals! As Chapters 2 and 3 showed, this is easier said than done, but it is already occurring, under pressure from a growing number on both sides who have completely lost faith in the old paradigm of landlord and tenant. There *is* a non-co-operative alternative, that of the establishment of estate budgets and a proper contractual relationship between tenant and landlord. It is an admirable alternative because it also tries to sweep away that dreadful old municipal paternalism, by demanding that the landlord be just that, a landlord, responsible to the dwellers for services for which they pay. If it works, it will make council housing more business-like. If it fails, it will renew demands from below, for full dweller control over housing management and maintenance.

From this co-operative perspective, the same argument for dweller control applies to private landlords and housing associations. It may seem strange to lump together Rachmanite dealers in property and charitable housing trusts, but they have this in common, that they both deny the principle of dweller control. Where tenants want to, they should be empowered in law to take over their dwellings, regardless of whether these are owned by a municipal, private or charitable landlord. New initiatives by the present Conservative government to revive the private rented sector include the forming of co-ownership societies by tenants, in order to gain access to mortgage tax relief and thus keep rents down. It is, as we have seen in Chapter 4, a device that has been used before, with sometimes disastrous results; let us hope that this time it produces genuine co-ops and not just paper ones conferring rights of which the dwellers are hardly made aware. If they are to be genuine co-ops, then they must be developed by secondary co-ops for

Conclusion

people who can afford to pay more for their housing than a subsidised fair rent. But if secondary co-op workers are to be persuaded to develop such co-ops, they must be assured that any new form of co-operative tenure will be in addition to, and not instead of, housing for those in the greatest need. The recent change of mind on the part of Treasury officials, who were counting private mortgage funding as public expenditure, is to be welcomed. The future of new forms of co-operative tenure depends on their making another crucial change of mind; to allow 'dual subsidy' of co-ops, so that members can both claim mortage tax relief as collective owners, and housing benefits as individual tenants.

A whole range of co-operative inroads can be made then, into all the other tenures. Whether they will do depends partly on whether new forms of co-op can be produced, and whether the legal and financial environments help or hinder their development. But the main question mark which still hovers over co-operative housing has to do with the psychological climate. Beneath the rhetoric, just how committed are people to mutual co-operation as opposed to market competition or bureaucratic control? The right to buy, the right to rent, the right to a home or the right to collective dweller control – which of these will become the slogan around which housing policy is made and judged up to the turn of the century?

NOTES

INTRODUCTION

1 Michael Young and Peter Willmott, *Family and Kinship in East London*, Routledge & Kegan Paul, London 1957.
2 Solon Co-operative Housing Services *Annual Report 1985–6*.
3 John Hands, *Housing Co-operatives*, Society for Co-operative Dwellings, London, 1975, and Colin Ward, *Tenants Take Over*, Architectural Press, London, 1974.

CHAPTER 1: HOUSING NEEDS AND CO-OPERATIVE SOLUTIONS

1 William Morris, *News From Nowhere*, Routledge & Kegan Paul, London, 1970, p. 10.
2 See John F.C. Turner, *Housing by People*, Marion Boyars, London, 1976.
3 Alexander F. Laidlaw, *Housing You Can Afford*, Green Tree Publishing Co. Ltd, Toronto, 1977, p. 118.
4 David Clapham, Keith Kintrea, Muriel Millar and Moira Munro, *Co-operative Housing in Norway and Sweden*, Discussion Paper No. 4, University of Glasgow Centre for Housing Research, 1985, p. 28.
5 United States Dept of Labour, Bureau of Labour Statistics, *Non-profit Housing Projects in the United States*, Bulletin No. 896, 1947.
6 Clapham et al., op. cit.
7 Vincent Tucker (ed.), *Co-operative Housing in Ireland*, Bank of Ireland Centre for Co-operative Studies, Cork, 1982.
8 Ibid.
9 Laidlaw, op. cit.
10 See, for example, the Report of the Housing Commission of the Conseil de la Co-opération de Québec, *Housing Co-ops in Quebec*, 1968.

CHAPTER 2: HUMAN NATURE AND CO-OPERATIVE VALUES

1. See Peter L. Berger and Thomas Luckmann, *The Social Construction of Reality*, Penguin, Harmondsworth, 1971.
2. Adam Smith, *Theory of Moral Sentiments*, Oxford University Press, p. 119.
3. Adam Smith, *Moral and Political Philosophy*, Harper & Row, New York, 1970, 'Wealth of Nations' section, p. 399.
4. Herbert Spencer, *The Man Versus the State*, Watts, London, 1940, p. 54.
5. Milton and Rose Friedman, *Free to Choose*, Secker & Warburg, London, 1980, ch. 1.
6. R. Harris and A. Seldon, *Not from Benevolence*, Institute of Economic Affairs, London, 1977, Ch. 1.
7. See Herbert Spencer on altruism and egoism, chs. 11–13 of *The Data of Ethics*, Williams & Norgate, London, 1890.
8. J. S. Mill, *On Liberty*, Penguin, Harmondsworth, 1974, p. 121.
9. Ibid., p. 120.
10. J. S. Mill, *Principles of Political Economy*, Penguin, Harmondsworth, 1970, pp. 336–7.
11. Mill, *On Liberty*, p. 128.
12. Ibid., p. 137.
13. G. Watson (ed.), *The Unservile State – Essays in Liberty and Welfare*, George Allen & Unwin, London, 1957.
14. Mill, *On Liberty*, p. 123.
15. F. Engels, 'Origins of the Family, the State and Private Property', in Marx and Engels, *Selected Works*, Lawrence Wishart, London, 1968, p. 519.
16. Ibid., p. 580.
17. Ibid., p. 582.
18. For Marxist views on the early Marx, see Lucio Colletti's introduction to Marx, *Early Writings*, Penguin, Harmondsworth, 1975.
19. Ibid., p. 50.
20. Engels, *The Housing Question*, Progress Publishers, Moscow, 1979, pp. 21–2.
21. Erich Fromm, *The Sane Society*, Routledge & Kegan Paul, London, 1956, p. 264. For a Marxist critique along similar lines, see Andre Gorz, *Farewell to the Working Class*, Pluto Press, London, 1982.
22. But not forgetting his French counterpart, Fourier, and the founder of practical co-operation, Dr William King.
23. A. L. Morton, *The Life and Ideas of Robert Owen*, Lawrence & Wishart, London, 1969, p. 117.
24. Ibid., p. 84.
25. Ibid., Part One.
26. Woodcock calls him the 'Man of Paradox': see George Woodcock,

Anarchism, Penguin, Harmondsworth, 1962, ch. 5. For explanation of the antinomic method, see Edwards' intro to P. J. Proudhon, *Selected Works*, ed. S. Edwards, Macmillan, London, 1970.
27 Ibid., p. 55.
28 Ibid., p. 56.
29 Ibid., Part 5, 'Education'.
30 Ibid., p. 177.
31 P. Kropotkin, *Mutual Aid – a Factor of Evolution*, Extending Horizons, Boston, undated. See also, for a modern reworking of this theme in biology, M. F. Ashley Montagu, *The Direction of Human Development*, Watts, London, 1957. Kropotkin's argument is directed at the social Darwinists, primarily Huxley, but also Spencer, and not Darwin, who had admitted that mutual aid complements mutual struggle.
32 Kropotkin, op. cit., p. xiii.
33 Ibid., p. 277.
34 P. Kropotkin, 'Anarchist Communism', in *Revolutionary Pamphlets*, Dover, New York, 1970, p. 47.
35 Martin Buber, *Paths in Utopia*, Routledge & Kegan Paul, 1949, foreword.
36 Ibid., p. 13. But remember that Buber is writing in the Stalinist era; modern Marxism may meet some of his criticisms.
37 Ibid., p. 8.
38 Gustav Landauer, quoted in Buber, op. cit., p. 58.
39 Fromm, op. cit., ch. 8.
40 A. H. Halsey, *Change in British Society*, Oxford University Press, London, 1978.
41 F. A. Hayek, *The Constitution of Liberty*, Routledge & Kegan Paul, London 1960.
42 Ibid., p. 18.
43 Ibid., p. 85.
44 Ibid., p. 45. For a creative use of the concept, see M. Young and P. Willmott, *The Symmetrical Family*, Penguin, Harmondsworth, 1973.
45 Hayek, op. cit., p. 45.
46 Some Anarchist free-marketeers go even further in denying even the need for state action; individuals can contract in the market for self-protection. See Murray Rothbard, *The Libertarian Manifesto*, Collier Books, New York, 1973.
47 Spencer, *Data of Ethics*, p. 239.
48 Ibid., p. 76.
49 Ibid., p. 146.
50 See discussion in Watson, op. cit., ch. 12.
51 Mill, *On Liberty*, p. 69.
52 Watson, op. cit., p. 17.

53 Mill, *Principles*, p. 140.
54 Watson, op. cit., ch. 4.
55 For detailed policies, see David Steel, *A House Divided*, Weidenfeld & Nicholson, 1980.
56 See discussion on p. 127 of Mill, *Principles*.
57 Mill, op. cit., p. 128.
58 P. Berger and R. J. Neuhaus, *To Empower People*, Washington, 1977, ch. 1.
59 Robert A. Nisbet, *The Quest for Community*, Oxford University Press, 1969, p. 19.
60 Ibid., p. xvi.
61 Ibid., p. 240.
62 Marx/Engels, 'The Communist Manifesto', p. 48.
63 Ibid., p. 53. See also Engels, 'Socialism Utopian and Scientific', p. 426.
64 Ibid., p. 52.
65 Lenin, *The State and Revolution*, Progress Publishers, Moscow, 1965 (revised), p. 96.
66 Lenin 'On Co-operation', in *Collected Works*, vol. 33, Lawrence & Wishart, London, 1966, pp. 467-75.
67 Gregory Andrusz, *Housing in the USSR*, Macmillan, London.
68 Marx, 'Critique of the Gotha Programme', *Selected Works*, p. 321.
69 Ibid.
70 Ibid., p. 325.
71 For such a potential conclusion, see John Cowley, *Housing for People or for Profit?* Stage 1, London, 1979.
72 Marx/Engels, Selected Works, Engels, 'Socialism Utopian and Scientific', p. 397.
73 Ibid., 'Manifesto', p. 45.
74 Ibid., Engels, 'Origin of the Family', p. 576.
75 Ibid., Marx, 'Critique of the Gotha Programme', p. 326.
76 Ibid., Marx, 'Civil War in France', p. 291.
77 Ibid.
78 Ibid., Engels, 'Letter to Bebel', p. 334.
79 Ibid., Engels, footnote to 'Origins of the Family', p. 512.
80 Thus G. D. H. Cole defines social theory in terms of the whole problem of human association, the solution of which demands that universal principles of association be discovered. See ch. 1 of G. D. H. Cole, *Social Theory*, Methuen, London, 1920.
81 C.F. Durkheim's description of tribal society as 'mechanistic', lacking in any sense of individuality. Emile Durkheim, *The Division of Labour in Society*, Free Press, New York, 1964.
82 Proudhon, op. cit., p. 62.
83 Ibid., p. 94.

84 Thus the liberal Nisbet can quote with approval Proudhon's famous saying 'multiply your associations and be free', and the socialist Tawney can make his idea of functional property the basis of his analysis. For fuller definition of a socialist view of liberty, see *Equality*, George Allen & Unwin, London, 1964.
85 Proudhon, op. cit., p. 94.
86 Ibid., p. 44.
87 Cole, op. cit., ch. 12, on 'Liberty', quote p. 189.
88 See R. H. Tawney's *The Acquisitive Society*, Wheatsheaf, Brighton, 1982.
89 G. D. H. Cole and Mellor, *Self-government in Industry*, Hutchinson, London, 1972.
90 In this reliance on rational discourse to promote social order, Owen was influenced by Godwin, who significantly shunned group association, and posited a much more individually self-sufficient society. See William Godwin, *Enquiry Concerning Political Justice*, Penguin, Harmondsworth, 1976.
91 Kropotkin, *Mutual Aid*, p. xvii.
92 For the argument that Kropotkin's main aim is not freedom but 'communal individuality', see Alan Ritter, *Anarchism*, Cambridge University Press, Cambridge, 1980.
93 For a detailed critique of Kropotkin's failure to deal adequately with individual freedom, see David Miller, *Social Justice*, Clarendon Press, Oxford, 1976, ch. 7, 'Kropotkin's Theory of Justice'.
94 Buber, op. cit., p. 145.
95 Morton, op. cit., p. 146.
96 Tolstoyan Anarchists and Buddhists continue to emphasise this primacy of the moral; the arguments can be very strong.
97 Proudhon, op. cit., p. 53.
98 Compare Proudhon's antinomic method to the 'yin-yang' of Taoist philosophy. Quote is from P. J. Proudhon, *The Principle of Federation*, University of Toronto Press, Toronto, 1979.
99 Interestingly, Georges Fauquet takes a similar approach to consumer co-operation, and is an avowed political liberal. See his *The Co-operative Sector*, Co-operative Union, Manchester, 1951.
100 Durkheim (op. cit.) sees the potential for social solidarity of the increasing division of labour, but through his functionalist method infers a formal solidarity which is lacking under capitalist relations of production; he has to come down to earth in Book Three, in what he calls the 'anomic' and 'forced' division of labour.
101 Kropotkin, *Mutual Aid*, p. 54, 58.
102 See Kropotkin, 'Anarchist Morality', in *Revolutionary Pamphlets*. Proudhon also uses the golden rule, but does not explain its origin so

well, in the intuitive individual, conscious of solidarity.
103 Kropotkin, *Mutual Aid*, p. 227.
104 Ibid., p. 284.
105 Buber, op. cit., p. 14.
106 Ibid., p. 139.
107 Ibid., p. 140.

CHAPTER 3: DEMOCRACY, THE STATE AND CO-OPERATIVE WELFARE

1 F. A. Hayek, *The Constitution of Liberty*, Routledge & Kegan Paul, London, 1969, ch. 7.
2 *Roof* magazine, Mar/Apr, 1986, p. 20.
3 See Colin Ward, *When We Build Again*, Pluto Press, London, 1985, p. 56.
4 For detailed cases, see Colin Ward, *Tenants Take Over*, Architectural Press, London, 1974, ch. 1.
5 *Roof* magazine, op. cit.
6 Alex Henney, *Trust the Tenant – Devolving Muncipal Housing*, Centre For Policy Studies, London, 1985.
7 Many of Friedman's arguments can be found anticipated in Herbert Spencer's *The Man Versus the State*, Watts, London, 1940.
8 Henney, op. cit., p. 12.
9 See David Clapham and Muriel Millar, 'Restructuring Public Housing – the Swedish Experience', in *Housing Review*, July/August 1985.
10 Spencer, *The Man versus the State* p. 113.
11 F. A. Hayek, *The Three Sources of Human Values*, London School of Economics, London, 1978, p. 16.
12 See Rhodes Boyson, 'Down with the Poor', and for a more subtle 'cultural pathology' argument, see Keith Joseph, 'The Cycle of Deprivation', in R. Holman and E. Butterworth (eds), *Social Welfare in Modern Britain*, Fontana, Collins, London, 1975.
13 J. S. Mill 'Representative Government', in *Three Essays*, Oxford University Press, Oxford, 1975, p. 152.
14 Ibid., ch. 2.
15 Ibid., p. 168.
16 See C. Pateman, *Participation and Democratic theory*, Cambridge University Press, London, 1970.
17 Mill, 'Representative Government', p. 277.
18 As described so graphically by Norman Dennis, *People and Planning*, Faber & Faber, London, 1970.
19 William Hampton and Jeffrey J. Chapman, 'Towards Neighbourhood Councils', *Political Quarterly*, vol. 42, 1971, 3 pp. 247-54, 4 pp. 414-22.

20 Robert A. Dahl and E.R. Tufte, *Size and Democracy*, Stanford University Press, Stanford, California, 1973.
21 Communitarian socialists try to avoid this tragic outcome, by the principle of federation.
22 Dahl and Tufte, op. cit., p. 140.
23 Robert A. Dahl, *A Preface to Democratic Theory*, University of Chicago Press, Chicago, 1956.
24 C.B. MacPherson, *The Life and Times of Liberal Democracy*, Oxford University Press, Oxford, 1977.
25 Pateman, op. cit.
26 J.S. Mill. *Principles of Political Economy*, bk 4, ch. 7, Section 6. Quoted in chapter 3 of MacPherson, *Liberal Democracy*, op. cit.
27 See Liberal Party Manifesto, 1979.
28 T.H. Marshall, *The Right to Welfare*, Heinemann, London, 1981, ch. 6, 'Value-Problems of Welfare Capitalism'.
29 William Beveridge, *Voluntary Action*, George Allen & Unwin, London, 1948, p. 117.
30 For a sketch of all such developments, see Ann Richardson, op. cit., ch. 3, and for more comprehensive consideration see N. Boaden, M. Goldsmith, W. Hampton, P. Stringer, *Public Participation in Local Services*, Longman, Harlow, 1982.
31 Marshall, op. cit., p. 79.
32 Ibid., p. 112.
33 T.H. Marshall, *Class, Citizenship and Social Development*, University of Chicago Press, Chicago, 1977, p. 301.
34 Ibid., ch. 14.
35 F.J. Gladstone, *Voluntary Action in a Changing World*, Bedford Square Press, London, 1979.
36 R. Hadley and S. Hatch, *Social Welfare and the Failure of the State*, Allen & Unwin, London, 1981.
37 Marx/Engels, *Selected Works*, Lawrence & Wishart, London, 1968, 'Manifesto', p. 37.
38 Nicos Poulantzas, *Political Power and Social Classes*, Verso, London, 1978.
39 Marx/Engels, op. cit., Engels, 'Origin of the Family'.
40 For an action view of Marxism, see Ralph Miliband, *Capitalist Democracy in Britain*, Oxford University Press, 1984.
41 Marx/Engels, op. cit., Engels, 'Origins of the Family', p. 578.
42 Ibid., p. 579.
43 Ibid., Engels, 'Letter to Bebel', p. 332.
44 Ibid.
45 See, Ibid. Engels, 'Socialism Utopian and Scientific' for this argument, p. 424.

46 Ibid.
47 Ibid., Marx, 'Civil War in France', p. 289.
48 Rudolf Bahro, *The Alternative in Eastern Europe*, Verso, London, 1981, ch. 1.
49 This did not stop the East German state imprisoning him as a result.
50 See Marx/Engels, op. cit., Marx, 'Civil War in France', pp. 289-90.
51 Ibid., Engels, 'Origin of the Family' pp. 579, 583.
52 V. I. Lenin, *The State and Revolution*, Progress Publishers, Moscow, 1965, p. 60.
53 Ibid., p. 52.
54 Marx/Engels, op. cit., Marx, 'Wage Labour and Capital', p. 78.
55 Ibid., Engels, introduction, p. 70.
56 Ibid., Engels, 'Socialism Utopian and Scientific', p. 404.
57 Ibid., p. 423.
58 For a penetrating analysis of these problems, see Alec Nove, *The Economics of Feasible Socialism*, George Allen & Unwin, London, 1983, Part 1.
59 See David Miller, 'Socialism and the Market', *Political Theory*, vol. 5, no. 4, 1977, pp. 473-90.
60 James O'Connor, *The Fiscal Crisis of the State*, St Martin's Press, New York, 1973.
61 Ian Gough, *The Political Economy of the Welfare State*, Macmillan, London, 1979, p. 47.
62 Norman Ginsburg, *Class, Capital and Social Policy*, Macmillan, London, 1979, p. 5.
63 Gough, op. cit., p. 144.
64 CDP, *Whatever Happened to Council Housing?*, CDP Information and Intelligence Unit, London, 1976.
65 John Cowley, *Housing for People or for Profit?*, Stage 1, London, 1979.
66 See in particular Marjaleena Repo, 'The Fallacy of Community Control', in John Cowley, Adah Kaye, Marjorie Mayo and Mike Thompson, *Community or Class Struggle*, Stage 1, London, 1977.
67 Cynthia Cockburn, *The Local State*, Pluto Press, London, 1978, p. 80.
68 Ibid., p. 95.
69 See Repo, op. cit.
70 Cockburn, op. cit., p. 101.
71 Cowley, op. cit., p. 92.
72 See CDP, op. cit., and *Profits Against Houses*, also 1976.
73 M. Castells, in Cowley, Kaye et al., op. cit.
74 Stuart Lowe, *Urban Social Movements*, Macmillan, London, 1985, p. 22.
75 Ibid., p. 35.
76 Cockburn, op. cit., p. 182.

Notes to pages 80–88

77 London Edinburgh Weekend Return Group, *In and Against the State*, London, 1979, p.48.
78 Cowley, op. cit., p.146 (both quotes).
79 A.L. Morton, *The Life and Ideas of Robert Owen*, Lawrence & Wishart, London, 1969, p.161.
80 P.J. Proudhon, *Selected Works*, ed. S. Edwards, Macmillan, London, 1970, p.139.
81 P.J. Proudhon, *The Principle of Federation*, University of Toronto Press, Toronto, 1979, p.49.
82 Proudhon, *Selected Works*, p.60.
83 Ibid., p.45.
84 Proudhon, *Principle of Federation*, p.49.
85 John F.C. Turner, *Housing by People*, Marion Boyars, London, 1976, ch.8. 'Participation in Housing'.
86 Proudhon, *Selected Works*, p.49.
87 P. Kropotkin, *Mutal Aid – a Factor of Evolution*, Extending Horizons, Boston, undated, p.208.
88 Ibid., p.222.
89 Erich Fromm, *The Sane Society*, Routledge & Kegan Paul, London, 1956, ch.8.
90 Martin Buber, *Paths in Utopia*, Routledge & Kegan Paul, London, 1949, quoting Kropotkin, p.45.
91 Proudhon, *Selected Works*, p.50.
92 P. Kropotkin, *Fields, Factories and Workshops Tomorrow*, George Allen & Unwin, London, 1974.
93 Aldous Huxley develops some of Kropotkin's ideas in *Island*, Granada, Frogmore, 1976, and *After Many a Summer*, Triad/Panther, Frogmore, 1976.
94 Morton, op. cit., p.176.
95 Proudhon and Lenin both take the railway system as a paradigm for large-scale socialised industry, but with a different understanding of its elements.
96 Fromm, op. cit., p.284.
97 See A. Campbell, C. Keen, G. Norman and R. Oakeshott, *Worker-owners: The Mondragon Achievement*, Anglo-German Foundation, London, 1978, and Co-operatives Research Unit *Mondragon Co-operatives – Myth of Model?*, Milton Keynes, 1982.

CHAPTER 4: CO-OPERATIVE HOUSING IN BRITAIN: THE EARLY STAGES

1 The National Federation of Housing Co-ops lists 490 co-ops in its *Housing Co-ops Directory*, 1985. The estimate of co-ownership numbers is from Housing Corporation staff.

Notes to pages 88–94

2 These are 1980 figures, quoted by Kintrea and Monro, in Clapham et al. *Co-operative Housing in Norway and Sweden*. Discussion Paper, no. 4, University of Glasgow Centre for Housing Research, 1985. Cronberg gives slightly different figures, of 17 per cent of the total stock, 270,000 units. See Tarja Cronberg, 'Tenants' Involvement in the Management of Social Housing in the Nordic Countries', *Scandinavian Housing and Planning Research*, no. 3 p. 65–87, 1986.
3 See Clapham and Millar, 'Restructuring Public Housing – the Swedish Experience', in *Housing Review*, July/August 1985, and Clapham et al., op. cit.
4 Figures, now out of date, from Margaret Digby, *Co-operative Housing*, Plunkett Foundation, Oxford, 1978.
5 Figures from Wallace J. Campbell, *Co-operative Housing in the USA*. Report to the Seminar on Non-profit Housing Organisations, 1971.
6 Arnold Bonner, *British Co-operation*, Co-operative Union, Manchester, 1970 (revised ed.), p. 46.
7 John Greve, *Voluntary Housing in Scandinavia*, Occasional Paper no. 21, CURS, Birmingham, 1971.
8 John Greve, Andrew Gilmour and Colin Ward took the Scandinavian model as exemplary. The latest example of such importation of ideas is the Glasgow District Council's sponsoring of Clapham et al.'s visit to Norway and Sweden.
9 Greve, op. cit. Colin Ward uses a similar analogy in *Tenants Take Over*, Architectural Press, London, 1974, p. 50.
10 Colin Ward, *When We Build Again*, Pluto Press, London, 1985, p. 19.
11 See E. P. Thompson, *The Making of the English Working Class*, Penguin, Harmondsworth, 1963, and Enid Gauldie, *Cruel Habitations: A History of Working Class Housing*, George Allen & Unwin, London, 1974.
12 Thompson, op. cit., p. 460.
13 See Martin Boddy, *The Building Societies*, Macmillan, London, 1980. ch. 1.
14 Gauldie, op. cit.
15 Ibid.
16 Boddy, op. cit.
17 Gauldie, op. cit., p. 207.
18 From a book review in *Labour Co-partnership*, vol. 1, no. 7, Feb. 1895.
19 See A. L. Morton, *The Life and Ideas of Robert Owen*, Lawrence & Wishart, London, 1969, part 2, ch. 11.
20 Catherine Webb, *Industrial Co-operation*, Co-operative Union, Manchester 1904, p. 180.
21 See H. D. Lloyd, *Labor Co-partnership*, Hanger & Bros, London, 1898.
22 John E. Yerbury, *The Story of Co-operative Housing*, Tenant Co-operators Ltd, London, 1913, p. 1.

23 Ibid., p. 14.
24 See Catherine Webb's account of Tenant Co-operators Ltd, and the balance sheet at the back of Yerbury, op. cit., summarising 25 years of the Society.
25 Yerbury, op. cit.
26 Aneurin Williams, quoted in an unpublished paper by Malcolm Hornsby, entitled 'Housing Co-operation – an Outline History'.
27 Yerbury, op. cit., p. 58.
28 See Co-partnership Publishers Ltd, *The Pioneer Co-partnership Suburb*, London, 1912, and *Co-partnership in Housing*, London undated (1912?).
29 A point made by Malcolm Hornsby, op. cit.
30 Clapham and Millar, in Clapham et al., op. cit.
31 HSB National Federation, *Co-operative Housing*, undated.
32 Cronberg, op. cit.
33 See Lennart J. Lundquist, 'Housing Tenure Experiments in Sweden', in *Housing Review*, July–Aug 1983, pp. 120–2.
34 Cronberg, op. cit.
35 Kintrea and Munro, in Clapham, op. cit.
36 Housing Act 1964, pt1:1:1.
37 There were also some societies not registered with the Housing Corporation.
38 CCHS Minutes, AGM, 1979.
39 Reported in *Co-owner Magazine*.
40 Housing Corporation figures, 1983.
41 Dept of the Environment *Housing Associations*, HMSO, London, 1971, p. 54.
42 Housing Corporation, *Co-ownership Housing: Guidance Notes and Model Documents*, 1972.
43 Ibid., ch. 6.
44 Ibid., ch. 6:10.
45 Ibid., ch. 6:12.
46 Housing Corporation, *A Brief Introduction to Co-ownership Housing*, 1969.
47 CCHS Annual Report, 1979.
48 Dept of the Environment, *Report of the Working Party on Housing Co-ops*, HMSO, London, 1975, p. 58.
49 CCHS Discussion Paper, 1979.

CHAPTER 5: CO-OPERATIVE HOUSING IN BRITAIN: THE LATER STAGES

1 From Harold Campbell's introduction *A Roof Over Your Head, the Co-*

Notes to pages 110–131

    operative Way, Co-operative Party, London, 1977.
2. Co-operative Party, *Housing, a Co-operative Approach*, Co-operative Union, Manchester 1959.
3. Dept of the Environment, *Report of the Working party on Housing Co-ops*, op. cit.
4. See John Hands, *Housing Co-operatives*, Society for Co-operative Dwellings, London 1975.
5. Holloway Tenant Co-operative, *Five Years On*, London, 1977.
6. Hands, op. cit., p. 113.
7. Shelter's *Roof* magazine July/August 1986, p. 11.
8. Robert Cowan, *Roof* magazine Mar/April 1986, p. 7.
9. Simon Underwood, Steve Ross and Charlie Legg, *Who Lives in Housing Co-ops?*, National Federation of Housing Associations, London, 1986.
10. From an internal Housing Corporation paper by Brian Rose.
11. See National Federation of Housing Co-operatives, *Around the Houses* magazine, 15, Autumn, 1986, p. 9.
12. See especially DoE circular 8/76.
13. Housing Corporation, *Directory of Housing Co-operatives*, 1981.
14. National Federation of Housing Co-operatives, *Housing Co-ops Directory*, 1985.
15. Alexander F. Laidlaw, *Housing You Can Afford*, Green Tree, Toronto, 1977.
16. Co-operative Party, 1977, op. cit.
17. Charlotte Chambers, Stephanie Blythe and Liz Kennedy, *A Comparative Study of Secondary Housing Co-ops*, Housing Corporation, 1985.
18. Ibid., p. 17.
19. DoE 'Campbell Report', op. cit., p. 11.
20. Ibid., p. 19.
21. Quoted in Colin Ward, *Tenants Take Over*, Architectural Press, London, 1974, p. 177.
22. DoE Circular, 8/76 and Scottish Development Dept Circular 14/77.
23. See Secretary of State for the Environment, *Housing Policy, a Consultative Document*, HMSO, London, 1977, p. 103.
24. Department of the Environment *Management Co-operatives: Tenant Responsibility in Practice*, HMSO, London, 1982.
25. Martin Jelfs, *Mortgage Finance for Housing Co-operatives*, Empty Property Unit, London, 1984, provides some examples.
26. Peter Clarke, *Towards a United Co-operative Movement*, Co-operative Party, London, 1981, p. 40.
27. Advisory Committee on Co-operatives, *Co-operatives and Housing Policy* Co-operative Housing Agency, London, 1977, p. 10.
28. Solon Co-operative Housing Services, *Annual Report*, 1984–5.
29. See Jelfs, op. cit.

Notes to pages 132–167

30 *Guardian*, 19.9.86.
31 Housing Corporation discussion paper, *Fully Mutual Housing Societies*, 1985.
32 Andrew Harris, writing in *Housing Review*, Sept/Oct. 1986.
33 *Guardian*, 1.7.86.

CHAPTER 6: CO-OPERATION IN PRACTICE: SIX CASE HISTORIES

1 These case studies appear in more detail in Johnston Birchall, *'Housing Co-operatives: a Study in the Theory and Practice of User-control'*, DPhil Thesis, York University, 1985.
2 Jim Low, quoted in minutes of a public meeting, 3.4.77.
3 David Crease RIBA, *St Andrew's Street Beverley, A Feasibility Study*, York University Design Unit, York, 1977.
4 Co-op minutes, August, 1979.
5 This is the Housing Corporation's designation of house sizes. 4 person = 1 double and 2 single bedrooms, 5 person = 2 double and 1 single bedroom, etc.
6 From a Glasgow East Area Renewal Team leaflet.
7 These are secondary statistics, drawn from the original survey document.
8 Co-op minutes, September 1979.
9 Co-op minutes, March 1980.
10 Co-op minutes, July 1980.
11 Co-op minutes, March 1980.

CHAPTER 7: A FRAMEWORK FOR EVALUATION

1 P. A. Sorokin, *The Ways and Power of Love*, Beacon Press, Boston, 1954.
2 See Johnston Birchall, *'Housing co-operatives: a Study in the Theory and Practice of User-control'*, DPhil Thesis, York University 1985, ch. 5.
3 George C. Homans, *Social Behaviour, its Elementary Forms*, Harcourt Brace Jovanovich, New York, 1974, ch. 5.
4 See Johnston Birchall, *What Makes People Co-operate? A Strategy for Member Participation in Housing Co-ops*, Institute of Community Studies, London, 1987.
5 Gary Strudwick, in *Roof* magazine, July/August 1986, p. 22.
6 See Tarja Cronberg, 'Tenants' Involvement in the Management of Social Housing in the Nordic Countries', *Scandinavian Housing and Planning Research*, no. 3 pp. 65–87, 1986.
7 Alexander F. Laidlaw, *Housing You Can Afford*, Green Tree Publishing Co Ltd, Toronto, 1977, p. 142.

Notes to pages 167–182

8 John E. Yerbury, *The Story of Co-operative Housing*, Tenant Co-operators Ltd, London, 1913, p. 55.
9 See Chas Ambler, 'Management by General Meeting', in *Society for Co-operative Studies Journal*, 53, April 1985, pp. 58–61.
10 See Marva Rees, Derek Smith, Marion Stanton, *Short-life Housing Co-ops: a Members' Handbook*, National Federation of Housing Co-ops, London, undated, p. 15.
11 Nine per cent did not state which type they were.
12 See Johnston Birchall, 'Time, Habit and the Fraternal Impulse', in a forthcoming book on time sociology edited by Michael Young.
13 See Hans Skifter Andersen, 'Danish Low-rise Housing Co-ops' in *Scandinavian Housing and Planning Research* 2, 1985, p. 49.
14 Simon Underwood, Steve Ross and Charlie Legg, *Who Lives in Housing Co-ops?*, National Federation of Housing Associations, London, 1986, ch. 5 on 'Tenant Satisfaction'.
15 Paul Mugnaioni, *Community Ownership in Glasgow*, Glasgow District Council Housing Dept, Briefing Paper, 1985, p. 5.
16 See Department of the Environment, *Management Co-operatives: Tenant Responsibility in Practice*, HMSO, 1982.
17 E.g. National Federation of Housing Associations, *Checklists – to Help You Run Your Co-op*, London, 1985.
18 Homans, op. cit., calls this the 'satiation proposition', in his reward-based theory of motivations to participate. This theory has been applied in the study of housing co-ops (see Johnston Birchall, 'Housing Co-operatives'), but has not generally been found fruitful.
19 Underwood et al., op. cit., ch. 5.
20 See International Co-operative Alliance, *Report of the ICA Commission on Co-operative Principles*, ICA, London, 1967.
21 Ibid. All further introductory quotes are from the same source.
22 See for instance, National Federation of Housing Associations, *Housing Co-ops – Tackling Racism*, undated pamphlet.
23 Paul Lambert, *Studies in the Social Philosophy of Co-operation*, Co-operative Union, Manchester, 1963, ch. 2.
24 This is the principle which underlies a new socialist approach to housing. See Labour Housing Group, *Right to a Home*, Spokesman, Nottingham, 1984.
25 ICA, op. cit., p. 11.
26 Georges Fauquet, *The Co-operative Sector*, Co-operative Union, Manchester, 1951, p. 51.
27 See Alan McDonald, *The Weller Way*, Faber & Faber, London, 1986.
28 Robert Michels, *Political Parties*, Free Press, Glencoe, 1949, p. 156.
29 E.g. John Hands, *Housing Co-operatives*, Society for Co-operative Dwellings, London, 1975.

30 But see Johnston Birchall, 'Housing Co-operatives', where the issue is discussed in depth.
31 Arnold Bonner, *British Co-operation*, Co-operative Union, Manchester, 1970, p. 319.
32 ICA, op. cit., p. 16.
33 See Solon Co-operative Housing Services, *Annual Report 1985–6*, p. 21.

SELECT BIBLIOGRAPHY

GENERAL TEXTS RELEVANT TO CO-OPERATIVE PHILOSOPHY

BERGER, Peter, and R.J. NEUHAUS, *To Empower People*, Washington, 1977.
BEVERIDGE, William, *Voluntary Action*, George Allen & Unwin, London, 1948.
BIRCHALL, Johnston, 'Time, Habit and the Fraternal Impulse', in a forthcoming book on time sociology edited by Michael Young.
BUBER, Martin, *Paths in Utopia*, Routledge & Kegan Paul, 1949.
COLE, G.D.H., *Social Theory*, Methuen, London, 1920.
COLE, G.D.H. and MELLOR, *Self-government in Industry*, Hutchinson, London, 1972.
DAHL, Robert, *A Preface to Democratic Theory*, University of Chicago Press, Chicago, 1956.
DAHL, Robert A. and E.R. TUFTE, *Size and Democracy*, Stanford University Press, Stanford, California, 1973.
FROMM, Erich, *The Sane Society*, Routledge & Kegan Paul, London, 1956.
GLADSTONE, F.J. *Voluntary Action in a Changing World*, Bedford Square Press, London, 1979.
GORZ, André, *Farewell to the Working Class*, Pluto Press, London, 1982.
HADLEY, R. and S. HATCH, *Social Welfare and the Failure of the State*, Allen & Unwin, London, 1981.
HOMANS, George C. *Social Behaviour, its Elementary Forms*, Harcourt Brace Jovanovich, New York, 1974.
KROPOTKIN, Peter, *Mutual Aid – a Factor of Evolution*, Extending Horizons, Boston, undated.
KROPOTKIN, Peter, *Revolutionary Pamphlets*, Dover, New York, 1970.
KROPOTKIN, Peter, *Factories and Workshops Tomorrow*, George Allen & Unwin, London, 1974.
LOWE, Stuart, *Urban Social Movements*, Macmillan, London, 1985.
MACPHERSON, C.B., *The Life and Times of Liberal Democracy*, Oxford University Press, Oxford, 1977.

Select bibliography

MARX/ENGELS, *Selected Works*, Lawrence & Wishart, London, 1968, especially Engels, 'Socialism Utopian and Scientific', 'Letter to Bebel', 'Origins of the Family'.
MICHELS, Robert, *Political Parties*, Free Press, Chicago, 1949.
MILL, J. S. *Principles of Political Economy*, Penguin, Harmondsworth, 1970.
MONTAGU, M. F., Ashley, *The Direction of Human Development*, Watts, London, 1957.
MORTON, A. L., *The Life and Ideas of Robert Owen*, Lawrence & Wishart, London, 1969.
NISBET, Robert A., *The Quest for Community*, Oxford University Press, 1969.
PATEMAN, Carole, *Participation and Democratic Theory*, Cambridge University Press, London, 1970.
PROUDHON, P. J., *Selected Works*, (ed.) S. Edwards, Macmillan, London, 1970.
PROUDHON, P. J., *The Principle of Federation*, University of Toronto Press, Toronto, 1979.
SOROKIN, P. A., *The Ways and Power of Love*, Beacon Press, Boston, 1954.

GENERAL TEXTS ON HOUSING POLICY

ANDRUSZ, Gregory, *Housing in the USSR*, Macmillan, London.
CLAPHAM, David, and Muriel MILLAR, 'Restructuring Public Housing – the Swedish Experience', in *Housing Review*, July/August 1985.
COWLEY, John, *Housing for People or for Profit?*, Stage 1, London, 1979.
CRONBERG, Tarja, 'Tenants' Involvement in the Management of Social Housing in the Nordic Countries', *Scandinavian Housing and Planning Research*, no. 3 pp. 65–87, 1986.
DEPT OF THE ENVIRONMENT, *Housing Associations*, HMSO, London, 1971.
ENGELS, Friedrich, *The Housing Question*, Progress Publishers, Moscow, 1979.
GAULDIE, Enid, *Cruel Habitations: A History of Working Class Housing*, George Allen & Unwin, London, 1974.
HENNEY, Alex, *Trust the Tenant – Devolving Municipal Housing*, Centre For Policy Studies, London, 1985.
LABOUR HOUSING GROUP, *Right to a Home*, Spokesman, Nottingham, 1984.
Roof Magazine, published by Shelter, London.
TURNER, John F. C., *Housing by People*, Marion Boyars, London, 1976.

Select bibliography

TEXTS ON CO-OPERATION IN GENERAL

BONNER, Arnold, *British Co-operation*, Co-operative Union, Manchester, 1970.

CAMPBELL, A., C. KEEN, G. NORMAN and R. OAKESHOTT, *Worker-owners: The Mondragon Achievement*, Anglo-German Foundation, London, 1978.

CLARKE, Peter, *Towards a United Co-operative Movement*, Co-operative Party, London, 1981.

CO-OPERATIVES RESEARCH UNIT, *Mondragon Co-operatives – Myth or Model?*, Milton Keynes, 1982.

FAUQUET, Georges, *The Co-operative Sector*, Co-operative Union, Manchester, 1951.

INTERNATIONAL CO-OPERATIVE ALLIANCE, *Report of the ICA Commission on Co-operative Principles*, ICA, London, 1967.

LAMBERT, Paul, *Studies in the Social Philosophy of Co-operation*, Co-operative Union, Manchester, 1963.

LENIN, 'On Co-operation', in *Collected Works*, vol. 33, Lawrence & Wishart, London, 1966 pp. 467–75.

WEBB, Catherine, *Industrial Co-operation*, Co-operative Union, Manchester, 1904.

TEXTS ON HOUSING CO-OPERATIVES IN PARTICULAR

ADVISORY COMMITTEE ON CO-OPERATIVES, *Co-operatives and Housing Policy* Co-operative Housing Agency, London, 1977.

AMBLER, Chas, 'Management by General Meeting', in Society for Co-operative Studies Journal, 53, April 1985, pp. 58–61.

ANDERSEN, Hans Skifter, 'Danish Low-rise Housing Co-ops' in *Scandinavian Housing and Planning Research*, 2, 1985.

BIRCHALL, Johnston, *'Housing Co-operatives: A Study in the Theory and Practice of User-control'*, DPhil Thesis, York University, 1985.

BIRCHALL, Johnston, *What Makes People Co-operate? A Strategy for Member Participation in Housing Co-ops*, Institute of Community Studies, London, 1987.

BIRCHALL, Johnston, 'Housing Co-operatives: How successful are they?', in *Society for Co-operative Studies Journal* 53, April 1985, pp. 51–7.

CAMPBELL, Harold, *A Roof Over Your Head, the Co-operative Way*, Co-operative Party, London, 1977.

CAMPBELL, Harold, *Housing, a Co-operative Approach*, Co-operative Union, Manchester, 1959.

CAMPBELL, Wallace J., *Co-operative Housing in the USA*, Report to the Seminar on Non-profit Housing Organisations, 1971.

CHAMBERS, Charlotte, Stephanie BLYTHE and Liz KENNEDY, *A*

Select bibliography

Comparative Study of Secondary Housing Co-ops, Housing Corporation, 1985.

CLAPHAM David, Keith KINTREA, Muriel MILLAR and Moira MUNRO, *Co-operative Housing in Norway and Sweden*, Discussion Paper no. 4, University of Glasgow Centre for Housing Research, 1985.

CO-PARTNERSHIP PUBLISHERS Ltd, *The Pioneer Co-partnership Suburb*, London, 1912.

CO-PARTNERSHIP PUBLISHERS Ltd, *Co-partnership in Housing*, London, undated (1912?).

DEPT OF THE ENVIRONMENT, *Report of the Working Party on Housing Co-ops*, HMSO, London, 1975.

DEPT OF THE ENVIRONMENT, *Circular 8/76* and Scottish Development Dept Circular 14/77.

DEPT OF THE ENVIRONMENT, *Housing Policy, a Consultative Document*, HMSO, London, 1977.

DEPT OF THE ENVIRONMENT, *Management Co-operatives: Tenant Responsibility in Practice*, HMSO, 1982.

DIGBY, Margaret, *Co-operative Housing*, Plunkett Foundation, Oxford, 1978.

GREVE, John, *Voluntary Housing in Scandinavia*, Occasional Paper no. 21, Centre for Urban and Regional Studies, Birmingham 1971.

HANDS, John, *Housing Co-operatives*, Society for Co-operative Dwellings, London, 1975.

HOLLOWAY Tenant Co-operative, *Five Years On*, London, 1977.

HOUSING CORPORATION, *Co-ownership Housing: Guidance Notes and Model Documents*, 1972.

HOUSING CORPORATION, *A Brief Introduction to Co-ownership Housing*, 1969.

HOUSING CORPORATION, *Directory of Housing Co-operatives*, 1981.

HOUSING CORPORATION, Discussion paper, *Fully Mutual Housing Societies*, 1985.

HSB NATIONAL FEDERATION, *Co-operative Housing*, undated.

JELFS, Martin, *Mortgage Finance for Housing Co-operatives*, Empty Property Unit, London, 1984.

LAIDLAW, Alexander F., *Housing You Can Afford*, Green Tree Publishing Co Ltd, Toronto, 1977.

LUNDQUIST, Lennart J., 'Housing Tenure Experiments in Sweden', in *Housing Review*, July–Aug. 1983, pp. 120–2.

MACDONALD, Alan, *The Weller Way*, Faber & Faber, London, 1986.

MUGNAIONI, Paul, *Community Ownership in Glasgow*, Glasgow District Council Housing Dept, Briefing Paper, 1985.

NATIONAL FEDERATION OF HOUSING ASSOCIATIONS, *Checklists – to Help You Run Your Co-op*, London, 1985.

Select bibliography

NFHA, *Housing Co-ops – Tackling Racism*, undated pamphlet.
NATIONAL FEDERATION OF HOUSING CO-OPS *Housing Co-ops Directory* 1985.
NFHC, *Around the Houses* magazine.
REES, Marva, Derek SMITH, Marion STANTON, *Short-life Housing Co-ops: a Members' Handbook*, National Federation of Housing Co-ops, London, undated.
SOLON, Co-operative Housing Services, *Annual Report 1985–6*.
TUCKER, Vincent (ed.), *Co-operative Housing in Ireland*, Bank of Ireland Centre for Co-operative Studies, Cork, 1982.
UNDERWOOD, Simon, Steve ROSS, and Charlie LEGG, *Who Lives in Housing Co-ops?*, National Federation of Housing Associations, London, 1986.
WARD, Colin, *Tenants Take Over*, Architectural Press, London, 1974.
WARD, Colin, *When We Build Again*, Pluto Press, London, 1985.
YERBURY, John E., *The Story of Co-operative Housing*, Tenant Co-operators Ltd, London, 1913.

INDEX

Abbeyvale Co-ownership Housing Society, 150–6, 163–5, 169, 173, 184
acquisitive society, 51
adequacy of housing co-ops, 5, 169–72
Adys Lawn Association, 98
affluent society, 69
agency agreements in tenant management co-ops, 23, 112–3, 124, 149–50, 160, 182
agrarian society, 41
agricultural co-operatives, 53
alienation, 32–4, 38, 43, 45, 57, 66, 69, 79, 81, 170, 173, 193
allocations, 60, 113, 116–19, 127, 129, 141–2, 144–5, 148, 177, 192
American housing co-ops, *see* United States
anarchists, 71, 73
Anchor Boot and Shoe Society, Leicester, 94
Andersen, H.S., 169
antinomic method, 36, 50, 56, 67
architects, 2, 6, 16, 19, 24, 121, 152–5, 191
Around the Houses magazine, 127
Association of Local Councils, 123
Association of London Housing Estates, 123
assured tenancies, 5, 132

Bahro, R., 72
Battersea Tenants' Housing Co-operative, 166
Berger, P. and Neuhaus R.J., 43
Beveridge, W., 67, 69–70

Beverley Borough Council, 137
Blancists, 82
British housing co-operative movement, 2, 52, 88–9
Broadhurst, H, 94
Buber, M., 37, 52, 57–8, 72, 84–5
Buchez, P.H., 175
building club, 4, 91–2; at Colinburgh, 91; at Edinburgh, 92
building co-operative, 193
building society, 4, 53, 85, 91–2, 131, 133, 192
bulk-buy food co-ops, 79, 187
bureaucracy, 19, 33, 76, 118–19, 129, 168

Campbell, H., 110–11, 114
Campbell Report, 108–9, 111, 118, 122, 130;
Canada, house building co-ops, 24, 110; housing co-ops, 21, 54, 82, 110–12, 131, 171, 182
Canning Housing Co-op, Liverpool, 112
capitalism, 34, 36, 42, 46–50, 74, 84
Castells, M., 78
CDS Co-operative Housing, 114–15
CDS Liverpool, 132
Christian Socialists, 37
Circle 33 Housing Trust, 111
citizenship, 34, 39, 57, 64–6, 68–9, 82
city, medieval, 83
Clarke, P., 126
class struggle, 48, 55, 78, 87
Cloverhall Tenant Management Co-operative, 116, 118, 124, 167

Index

Cobbett, W., 85
Cockburn, C., 77, 79
Coin Street Community Builders, 116
Cole, G.D.H., 50, 52, 67
collectivist world view, 2-3, 31-4, 44-9, 70-81, 101
common ownership, 45, 77, 81; in housing co-ops, 4, 21, 99, 111, 113, 118-20, 128-9, 182, 189, 192-4
communes, 51-2, 58, 72-3, 84-5
communism, 32, 46-8, 50, 73, 82, 84
communitarian world-view, 2-3, 34-9, 49-58, 81-6
communities, experimental, 35, 64, 93
community, 1, 14, 16, 18, 36, 38, 43-5, 47, 49-50, 57-8, 69, 76-7, 79, 81, 83-4, 136-7, 157, 193; role of, 30; sense of, 3, 5, 18, 20, 39, 48, 68-9, 77, 109, 172-4, 187
community architecture, 2
community councils, 84
community health councils, 68
community housing associations, 10, 18-19, 26, 134
community leasehold housing co-ops, 114, 158-9
condominium, 23, 182, 191-2
consciousness: socialist, 78-9
Conservative government, 28-9, 40, 59, 61, 103, 105, 109, 123, 132-3, 160, 194
consumer choice, 61; control, 2, 33, 121; demand, 61; representation, 70
consumer co-operative, 4, 5, 30, 35, 42, 51, 53, 58, 68, 86, 89-91, 93, 97, 112, 176; in Sweden, 100; in Norway, 102
co-operation between co-ops principle, 5, 186-7
Co-operative Bank, 131
co-operative commonwealth, 5, 187
co-operative development, 89-90, 169; organisations, 99-100, 103; workers, 59
co-operative economy, 36, 53, 86
Co-operative Housing Agency, 118-20, 122, 127

Co-operative Management Project, 126
co-operative movement, 58, 80
Co-operative News, 94
Co-operative Party, 110
Co-operative Permanent Building Society, 93, 97
co-operative principles, 5, 51, 80, 92, 135, 142, 160, 175-87
Co-operative Union Ltd., 95
co-operative villages, 34, 54, 92
Co-operative Wholesale Society, 94
Co-owner Magazine, 105
co-ownership housing co-operatives, 20-1, 22, 28-9, 88, 94-5, 98, 103-9, 111-12, 118, 132, 178, 183-4, 192, 194
co-partnership housing societies (tenant co-partnership), 4, 22, 70, 96-8, 110-11, 193
cost-rent schemes, 103-4, 133-4, 178
council estates, 1, 45, 57, 77, 136, 173; their break-up, 47; conversion to tenant control/self-management, 2, 110-11, 194; sale of, 61, council housing, 4, 16, 34, 51, 53, 59, 62, 78, 80, 86, 97, 99, 101, 157, 192-3; housing companies, 62; housing departments, 26, 60, 64; management, 100-1; ownership, 46
Council of Co-ownership Housing Societies, 104-6
council tenants, 60-1, 82, 190, 194
Cowley, J., 78, 80
credit unions, 5, 53, 131, 187, 193
Cronberg, T., 100, 102
Czechoslovakian housing co-ops, 88

Dahl, R.A., and Tufte, E.R., 65-6
decentralisation, 32; of associations, 3; of estate management, 19, 101, 130, 171; of ownership, 74; of services, 79, 101; of society, 73, 84; of welfare services, 68-9
deferred payment mortgages, 132
democracy, 34, 39, 59, 64, 68, 71, 73; direct, 3, 4, 32, 59, 63-5, 73, 79, 81, 83-4, 179; in housing co-ops,

217

Index

99, 163, local, 51; national, 63, 84; participatory, 5, 65–6, 69, 77, 83, 129; pluralist, 67; polyarchal, 66; representative, 59, 65–6, 79, 81, 129

democratic principle, in housing co-ops, 5, 178–80

Denmark: housing associations, 70; housing co-ops, 169

Department of the Environment, 118, 122, 124, 127, 138–9, 181

Directory of Housing Co-operatives, 1981, 124

distribution of economic results principle, in housing co-ops, 5, 181–3

district valuer, 23, 139, 158–9

division of labour, 41, 49, 56, 81, 179

Doukhobors, 85

Dronfield Health and Housing Society, 98

duration, of housing co-ops, 163, 168–9

Durkheim, E., 56

dweller control, 5, 60, 180, 194

Ealing Tenants Ltd., 96–7

East Midlands Housing Association, 98

Economic and Philosophical Manuscripts, 32

education: co-operative; 30, 34, 52, 86, 95, 104, 107–8, 119–22, 130, 132, 142, 160, 169, 171, 186, 194; grants for, 122, 127; polytechnic, 36; principle of, 5, 183–6

Elthorne Tenant Management Co-operatives, 116, 123

equality, 2, 39–40, 42–4, 46, 49, 53–4, 59, 65, 73, 81

Engels, 31, 32–3, 44–5, 47–9, 70–3, 81, 83

environment, 5, 23, 35, 52; legal and financial for co-op promotion, 4, 89–91, 100, 109, 128, 195

environmental/public health, 17, 137, 152

equity, in housing co-ops, 20–1, 22

Equity Shoes, Leicester, 93

ethnic minorities, 61; in housing co-ops, 116, 177

Euro-communism, 71, 86

extensity, of housing co-ops, 167–8

Fairbridge Housing Management Co-operative, 142–6, 164–6, 173, 178, 184

fair rent, in co-ops, 21, 54, 63, 113–14, 117, 127, 131. 192

Family and Kinship in East London, 1

federation, 5, 52, 57, 81, 83, 85; in co-operatives, 96–7, 99, 104–6, 129, 185–6

Finsburg, G., M.P., 160

First World War, 4, 22, 93, 97–8, 182

fraternity, 2–3, 39–41, 43–4, 47, 49, 54–6, 59, 68–9, 73

freedom, *see* liberty

freehold landlords, 190–1

Freeson, R., Minister of Housing, 98, 111, 118

Friedman, M., 28, 61

friendly societies, 53, 68, 85, 91, 117, 159

Fromm, E., 33, 38, 84–5

Garden City Movement, 96, 101

Gauldie, E., 91–2

general meeting, 13, 113, 141, 144–6, 148, 155, 158, 163, 167, 177, 179, 185

Ginsburg, N., 76

Gladstone, F.J., 69–70

Glasgow City Council, 60, 123, 144, 147, 171, 189; community ownership housing co-operatives, 4, 123, 132–4; Co-op Promotions Unit, 149; East End Renewal Scheme, 143

Glenkerry Housing Co-operative, London, 22, 114, 156–61, 165, 173, 185, 193

Godin, M., 94

Goodman, P., 41

Gough, I., 76

218

Index

Granby Housing Co-op, Liverpool, 112
Greater London Council, 60, 116, 118, 123, 128, 158, 182
Greater London Enterprise Board, 186
Greater London Secondary Housing Association, 114, 123, 159–60
Greening, O., 94
Greenleaf Housing Co-op, Liverpool, 116
Greve, J., 89, 100
guild, medieval, 41, 57

Hadley, R. and Hatch, S., 69–70
Hampstead Co-partnership Societies: First, Second and Third, 168
Hands, J., 112
Hayek, F.A., 39–41, 59, 63
Hazell, W., 94
Henney, A., 61
Holloway Tenant Co-operative, London, 111
Homans, G., 163, 179
homelessness, 126
home-ownership, see owner-occupation
house-building co-ops, 24, 82, 193
house price inflation, 191–2
Housing Act 1957, 137
Housing Act 1961, 103
Housing Act 1964, 104, 107
Housing Act 1969, 112
Housing Act 1974, 18, 88, 111, 122, 181
Housing Act 1980, 88, 123, 128–9, 151
Housing and Planning Act 1986, 4, 130, 189, 194
housing, as a noun or verb, 15–19, 20
housing associations, 3, 11, 14, 18, 44, 60, 62, 64, 69–70, 82, 86–8, 111, 113–15, 117, 120, 122, 126, 131–2, 146, 152, 160, 181, 194
Housing Association Grant funding, 23, 105, 109, 113; mini-HAG, 114, 117, 122, 126, 131–3, 178
housing co-operative: arguments for, 3, 39, 83; definition of, 20–5; development of a federation, 126–7; evaluation of, 162–88; formation of, 11; future prospects for, 128–134; growth of, 4; history of, 89–134; knowledge of, 111; origins of, 115–17; revival in the fortunes of, 102; promotion of, 93, 110–12, 118–27, 130; significance of, 31; starting up process, 117–18; structure of co-operatives, 4, 89, 94, 112–15; types of, 2, 49, 101
Housing Corporation, 5, 8, 11, 54, 62, 104–8, 111, 113–14, 117–22, 128–9, 131–3, 137, 152–4, 159
Housing Finance Act, 1975, 89, 98, 111
housing management, 5, 17, 123, 133, 137, 160, 168, 170
housing managers, 2, 6, 19, 27, 59, 60; in housing co-op, 157–8, 160, 170
housing needs, 2, 89–90, 116, 125, 159, 166–7, 178
housing policy, 2, 42, 59, 70, 111, 195
housing revenue account, 133
Housing Support Grant, 133
HSB (Tenants' Savings Bank and Housing Association), Sweden, 99–101, 164, 184
human nature, 2–3, 27–39, 42, 59, 75
Hungarian housing co-ops, 88
Hunslet Housing Co-operative, 187
Hutterites, 85
Huyton Community Co-operative, 116

India, housing co-ops, 88
individualist world-view, 2, 27–29, 39–41, 59–63, 101, 107
Industrial Common Ownership Movement, 178
industrial and provident society acts, 91, 112
inner cities, 2, 18, 47–8
Institute of Community Studies, 1
Institute of Housing, 15
intensity, in housing co-ops, 5, 172–4
International Co-operative Alliance, 175, 183
Ireland, house-building co-ops, 24, 193
Iroquois people, 31, 54, 73

Index

Islington Community Housing Association, 117
Islington, London Borough of, 118, 182
Italy, housing co-ops, 88

Japanese Han groups, 187
Jones, B., 94, 110
Jones, Councillor T., 110

Kagan, A., 110
Kettering Boot and Shoe Society, 93
kibbutz, Israeli, 52, 85
kinship, 1, 52, 172–3
Kropotkin, P., 37–8, 49, 51–2, 54, 56–7, 83–5, 97

Labour Co-partnership Association, 96
Labour councils, 116
Labour government, 68, 104–5, 111, 123, 128
Labour party, 18, 110, 176; in Liverpool, 46, 129; in Norway, 102; *Green Paper* of 1977
Laidlaw, A., 20, 25, 110, 167, 171
Lambeth Federation of Housing Co-operatives, 126
Landauer, G., 38
Lassalleans, 48, 71
leasehold owners, 190
Lenin, V.I., 32, 45, 48, 73, 75, 189
Leytonstone Housing Co-operative, 117
Liberal party, 110
liberty, 2, 31, 39, 40, 42, 44, 49–50, 52, 55, 59–60, 73, 82–3
Liverpool, 47–8, 110, 112, 119, 124
Liverpool Gingerbread Housing Co-operative, 116
loan stock, 20, 21, 94, 97, 193
local authorities/councils/government, 65, 97, 114, 123, 126, 130, 193
local authority housing departments, *see* council housing
London Boroughs Grants Unit, 127
Lodge Lane East Housing Co-op, 168
London Trades Council, 94

loss-rent status in co-ownerships, 105–7, 156
Lowe, S., 78

MacPherson, C.B., 66
managing agents, 103, 106–8, 151, 153–5
management agreements, 106–8, 118, 129–30
management and maintenance, 5, 60, 78, 99, 124, 142–5, 150–1, 169; allowances for, 114, 148, 181–2, 194
management committees in housing co-ops, 103, 107, 113, 137, 141–2, 148, 153–6, 158, 160, 163, 180, 185
market: capitalist, 74, 193; socialist, 75
market economy, 41, 51
market exchange, 28, 41
market freedom, 40, 42, 61, 189
Marshall, T.H., 67
Marx, K., 32–3, 37, 44–8, 70–4, 81, 83–84
Michels, R., 179
Militant-controlled Liverpool Council, 47–8, 189
Mill, J.S., 29–30, 31, 42, 48, 63–7, 77, 83
missive of let, *see* tenancy agreements
Mondragon co-operatives, 85–6
Morris, W., 15
mortgage tax relief, 104, 131, 134, 159, 191, 194
mother-daughter structure in housing co-ops, 99, 101–2, 107
Mugnaioni, P., 170
municipal housing, *see* council housing
municipal housing companies, Sweden, 100
mutual aid, 1, 5, 37, 41, 45, 51, 57, 68–70, 76, 83, 85, 91–2; in housing co-ops, 125–6, 163, 172, 193
mutual co-operatives, 112–13, 129
mutual credit, 85–6
mutual housing society, 5, 131–3
mutual insurance societies, 131

220

Index

mutualism, 36, 81
mutual savings banks, 68, 131

National Federation of Housing Associations, 126–7
National Federation of Housing Co-operatives, 4, 126–7, 130–1, 186
National Federation of Norwegian Housing Co-ops, 102
National Health Service, 68
National House Building Council, 190
National Tenants' Union, Sweden, 99, 101
Nationwide Building Society, 155
Neale, H.V., and E.V., 94
neighbourhood, 57, 65, 67, 81, 96, 168
new-build type housing co-op, 24, 46, 141, 144
New Economic Policy, Soviet, 46
Newham Community Housing Federation, 168
Newham Short-life Housing Co-op, 168
New Harmony, 35
Newleaf Housing Co-operative, 168
New York housing co-ops, 54, 89, 110
Nisbet, R., 43–4
North Housing Association, 132, 141
North Islington Community Project, 111
Norway, housing co-ops, 4, 21, 22, 88, 98–9, 101–3, 164, 182, 184
Norwegian Union of Tenants, 102

OBOS, Norway, 101–2, 111
On Liberty, 29
open membership principle, 5, 34, 163, 177–8
Orbiston community, 93
Oslo housing co-operatives, 88, 101–2, 111
Owen, R., 34, 51, 54–5, 64, 84–5, 92, 183, 187
owner-occupation, 2, 22, 24, 28–9, 40, 43, 45, 53, 80, 93–4, 97, 99, 103, 109, 159, 173, 182, 190–2

Pakistan, housing co-ops, 88
Paris Commune, 37, 72–3
parish councils, 65
participation, 39, 49, 65–6, 69, 82, 87; by consumers, 69, 70, 78; by co-op members, 162–7; in design, 115, 163, 171, 190; by employees, 69; by members, 5, 64, 81; by tenants, 77, 101, 123, 130, 133
par-value housing co-operative, 21, 113
patronage refund, 5
Poland, housing co-ops, 88
political and religious neutrality principle, 175
premium payments in co-ownerships, 103–5, 107, 109, 183
Princes Park Housing Co-operative, 116
Principles of Political Economy, 30
Priority Estates Project, 101, 124, 170
private rented housing, 19, 40, 60, 93, 103, 110, 114, 131, 189, 194
private tenants, 82
privately-funded housing co-operatives, 4, 112, 125–7, 131–2, 189
producer co-operatives, 30, 34, 51, 93, 96
professionals, 68–9, 76, 79–80, 92, 129, 153, 156; in housing 1, 2, 59, 18–19, 107–8, 194; support to co-ops, 142, 149, 184–5
promoters, of co-operatives, 4, 89–90, 92, 96, 99, 107
property, 39, 44, 50–1, 53–4, 62, 81
proportional representation, 65–6
Proudhon, P.J., 35–7, 45, 49, 51–5, 58, 73, 81–5
psychological climate/climate of opinion, relating to co-ops, 4, 89–91, 93, 987–8, 100–1, 109, 122–3, 128, 130, 195
public housing, *see* council housing
Public Works Loan Board, 94
purity, of housing co-ops, 175–6

quantity surveyors, 24, 154
Queenwood community, 93

221

Index

Ralahine community, 93
rehabilitation-type housing co-op, 24, 113
rent pooling, 54-5, 78, 99, 192
Repo, M., 77
revenue deficit grant, 181
revolution, 36-8, 55, 71-3, 75, 79; Russian, 45
right to buy, in 1980 Housing Act, 113, 116, 128, 131, 189-90
right to occupy; 128; in Scandinavian housing co-ops, 104
right to sell, in co-ownerships, 151
Riksbyggen, Sweden, 100-1
Rochdale Pioneers, 89-90, 93, 101, 175, 177, 183
Rousseau, 35, 55, 59, 65
Royal Arsenal Co-operative Society's Well Hall Estate, 97
rules, of co-ops, 5, 169, 171, 191

Saint Andrew's Street Housing Co-operative, 115, 135-40, 163-4, 167, 173, 180, 185
satisfaction, among housing co-op members, 170
Scandinavia, housing co-ops, 1, 4, 24, 62, 82, 88-9, 98-103, 107, 126, 131, 165
Scandinavian Organisation of Housing Co-ops, 102
Scotland, housing co-ops, 125, 127
Scottish Federation of Housing co-operatives, 127
Scottish Office, 133-4
Scottish Special Housing Association, 143
Second World War, 22, 54, 68
secondary housing co-operatives, 4, 24, 26, 54, 120-2, 115, 117, 127-30, 159, 174, 177, 184-5, 194
security of tenure, 60
Seebohm Report, 68
Seghill Housing Co-operative, 115, 140-2, 163-6, 170, 173, 179-80, 182, 185-6
self-build housing co-operatives, 24, 41, 193

self-help, 4, 69, 76, 82
Seymour Housing Co-operative, 115
shared ownership housing co-operatives, 4, 22-3, 109, 114-15, 178, 192-3
share capital, in housing co-operatives, 21, 95
Shelter Neighbourhood Action Project, Liverpool, 112
short-life housing co-operatives, 4, 114, 118, 125-6, 131, 168
SKB (Stockholm Housing Co-operative Assocaition), 21, 55, 99
slum clearance, 17, 61, 94, 126
small scale, 54, 77, 83-4; in common ownerships, 32, 45, 50; in community organisations, 3, 18, 179; in co-operatives, 84, 172; democracy, 64-6
Smith Adam, 28, 40
social activities, in co-operatives, 5, 163, 166-7, 172
social contract, 55, 59, 81
social insurance, 68-9
social justice, 4, 35, 84
social order, 3, 36, 47, 54, 56-7, 59, 63, 75
social policy, 68
social security, 69; co-operatives, 86
social services, community-based, 68
socialism, 3; centralised state, 32, 36, 53, 73; co-operative, 32, 47; democratic, 78; prefigurative forms of, 80; transition to, 71
socialist society, 3, 32, 34, 46, 71; post-revolutionary, 3, 36-7, 44, 46-7
solidarity, 37, 39, 43-4, 49, 55-6
Solon Co-operative Housing Services, 177, 186
Sorokin, P.I., 5, 162, 167-8, 171
Soviet Union, 46, 48, 73
Speirs Tenant Management Co-operative, 116, 146-50, 163-4, 167, 170-1, 173, 179-80, 185
Spencer, H., 28, 41, 45, 61
squatting/squatters' movement, 76-7, 115, 117

222

Index

staircasing, in shared-ownership co-ops, 114, 131, 161
Stalin, J., 46
Standing Conference on Housing Co-operatives, 127
state aid/subsidy, 53, 71, 82, 100–2, 192; dual-source, 132–4, 195
state: authoritarian, 56; bureaucratic, 4, 63, 68–9, 78; capitalist, 3, 70–1, 86; local, 77; power of, 82–3; role of, 81–2
state ownership, 45, 102
Student Co-operative Dwellings, 111
Summerston Tenant Management Co-operative, 124, 144
surpluses made by co-ops, 5, 145, 165, 169, 171, 181–2, 185; returned as dividend or patronage refund, 93, 95, 181
Sweden, housing co-ops, 4, 21–2, 62, 88, 99–101, 164, 182, 184

Tawney, R.H., 51
tenancy agreements, 114, 125; called massive of let, 145, 150, 184
Tenant Co-operators Ltd, 4, 22, 94–6, 110–11
tenant co-partnerships, *see* co-partnership housing societies
Tenant Co-partnership Housing Council, 97
tenant management co-operatives/self-management, 4, 23, 42, 47, 62, 77, 94, 101, 110–11, 113–14, 116, 118, 122–5, 129–31, 164
Tenant Participation Advisory Service, 124
tenants' and residents' associations, 66, 76, 94, 115–16, 123, 138, 148, 164
tenants' charter, 123
Tenants' Take Over, 110
Thompson, E.P., 91
Tower Hamlets, 61, 159
town planning, 97
trade unions, 68, 76, 91, 124, 133, 184; Sweden, 100; Norway, 101–2, New York, 110
Treasury, 133–4, 195

tribal society, 32, 83
Tudor-Walters Report, 97
Turner, J., 82

unemployment, 86, 90–1, 100, 165
United States, housing co-ops, 21, 54, 62, 131; Section 213 co-ops, 112, 193
Unity Trust, 131
universal suffrage, 70–2
Unwin, R., 97
urban social movements, 78–9
use-value of housing, 5, 20, 52, 99, 191
user-control, 44, 82
Utopian Housing Association, 160

Vivian, H., 97, 110
voluntary associations, 3, 43–4, 46, 67, 69–70, 76, 81, 113, 146
voluntary membership principle, 5, 167
Von Humboldt, 29

Ward, C., 60, 90, 110, 123, 134
Welfare: human, 63, 85; mutual 69; social, 3–4, 42, 59, 67–8, 74–5, 84–5; state, 3, 63, 67, 69, 76
Weller Street Housing Co-operative, 115, 184
Williams, A., 96
Willmott, P., 1
Willow Park Housing Co-operative, Winnipeg, 111
worker co-operatives, 5, 33, 36–7, 50–1, 53, 56, 58, 67, 73, 83, 85–6, 178, 186–7
Workers' Housing Association, Sweden, 99
working class, 34, 65, 71, 74, 77, 91–2; culture, 91; government, 73; housing, 90; movement, 3; mutualist associations, 4, 91; origins, 17, people, 95, 129

Yerbury, J.E., 94–6, 167
York Housing Association, 137
Young, M., 1

223